THE · MACDONALD · ENCYCLOPEDIA · OF

Mushrooms
and Toadstools

THE · MACDONALD · ENCYCLOPEDIA · OF

Mushrooms
and Toadstools

Giovanni Pacioni

Macdonald

A **Macdonald** Book

© 1981 Arnoldo Mondadori Editore S.p.A., Milan
© 1985 in the English translation
   Arnoldo Mondadori Editore S.p.A., Milan

Translated by Simon Pleasance

First published in Great Britain in 1985
by Macdonald & Co (Publishers) Ltd
London & Sydney

A member of BPCC plc

British Library Cataloguing in Publication Data

Pacioni, Giovanni
   The Macdonald encyclopedia of mushrooms and
   toadstools
   1. Mushrooms
   I. Title
   589.2′22   QK617

   ISBN 0-356-07913-9

Printed and bound in Italy
by Officine Grafiche A. Mondadori Editore, Verona

Macdonald & Co (Publishers) Ltd
Maxwell House
74 Worship Street
London EC2A 2EN

CONTENTS

ABOUT THIS BOOK

The illustrated section of this book has been divided into five parts: (1) mushrooms with stems and gills, which are grouped primarily according to the colour of the spore deposit (**1–238**); (2) mushrooms with pores or spines on underside of cap (**239–288**); (3) bracket or crust mushrooms (**289–324**); (4) coral, bush or club mushrooms (**325–352**); (5) spheres, stars, pears and cup-shaped mushrooms (**353–420**). The fungi are thus arranged, regardless of the systematic group to which they belong, on the basis of their morphological appearance and follow the order proposed in the keys (see pages 57–69). The names of the species follow current nomenclature, although for the sake of simplicity reference is made in the keys to a few large genera which have now been considerably divided up, for example *Polyporus*. The term 'fungi' is used throughout the book in its broad sense, to include both edible and poisonous mushrooms as well as bracket fungi, mildews and moulds.

Entries for each species explain the meaning of the Latin or Greek name, provide a full description, indicate whether or not the species is edible and give data on habitat, season and frequency. Many entries conclude with comments designed to prevent confusion with similar fungi. In addition there are symbolized data for each species on the left-hand side of the page covering colour of spores, edibility and whether it occurs symbiotically, parasitically or saprophytically. The remarks about edibility should always be taken to mean 'after being correctly cooked'.

When using this book one should note that although the measurements given for each species cover the usual expected range of variation, abnormally large or small specimens may be found from time to time. Likewise, the season quoted is that in which the fungus is usually encountered, but it is possible for odd specimens of almost any fungus to occur out of season. Frequency refers generally to the British Isles, but certain uncommon species may be usually abundant either locally or nationally following freak weather conditions in certain years. In general the same frequency ratings can be taken to apply to continental Europe except where otherwise indicated, but considering such a large land mass showing great variation in altitude and climate from north to south as well as diversity of forest communities, such ratings are at best approximate.

Readers of this book are strongly advised against eating any species with which they are not personally familiar. There is no safe way of distinguishing between edible and poisonous fungi other than by thorough examination of both macroscopic and microscopic features, many of the latter not quoted in this text. Before eating any unfamiliar mushroom one should always have it checked and verified by an expert.

KEY TO SYMBOLS

SPORE COLOUR

Spore colour white, whitish, yellow

pinkish to salmon

yellow-brown to rust brown

dark purple-brown, violet, and black

EDIBILITY

READ WITH CARE

deadly

poisonous

inedible

good

excellent

TYPE OF FUNGUS IN RELATION TO SURROUNDING PLANT ENVIRONMENT

symbiotic

parasitic

saprophytic

INTRODUCTION

FUNGI AND THE ENVIRONMENT

What are fungi? Fungi form an isolated group within the plant kingdom and indeed are regarded by many as forming a separate kingdom of their own. They differ from all other plants by their lack of the green pigment chlorophyll, in the construction of thread-like units known as *hyphae* and their method of reproduction.

Reproduction Reproduction occurs by spores either of sexual or asexual origin. The spore germinates, sending out a germ-tube that elongates to produce a thread-like, usually septate, filament that then branches out repeatedly. By continued ramification these threads or hyphae (singular *hypha*) form a cobweb- or felt-like sheet known as a *mycelium*. In most instances fusion between two hyphae, usually from different *mycelia*, must occur before a fruit-body can be produced. Even then this process will only take place given the correct climatic factors and a sufficient food supply.

Nutrition Fungi differ from the higher plant forms by the absence of the green pigment chlorphyll, which enables plants to photosynthesize. By this process green plants are able to obtain their carbohydrates; the chlorophyll in their leaves fixes atmospheric carbon dioxide in the presence of sunlight and water to manufacture sugar for their nutrition. As fungi are unable to do this they have to obtain their carbohydrates from decomposed animal or plant tissues. Hence they are found in habitats rich in rotting vegetation such as woodland, grassland, compost heaps, sawdust piles, on dung or manure heaps and on burnt ground colonized by moss. Fungi obtaining their food from these sources are known as *saprophytes*; others obtaining their food materials directly from living plants or animals are known as *parasites*. Examples of parasitic fungi on trees and herbaceous plants are the woody bracket fungi and mildews respectively; diseases of man such as athlete's foot, ringworm and farmer's lung are also caused by parasitic fungi.

Mycorrhizae or mycorrhizal symbiosis Some fungi enter into a special symbiotic relationship with the roots of certain green plants whereby both partners benefit. This condition is described as a mycorrhizal association (literally meaning fungus root). In the case of many forest trees the fungus partner, often a gill-bearing mushroom or *bolete*, forms a sheath of threads around the tree's ultimate rootlets, some of the threads running out into the soil and others penetrating between the cells of the root. In this way

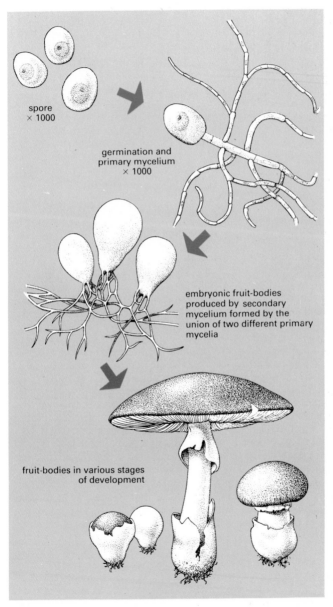

The development cycle of a fungus. A spore germinates, producing a primary mycelium which comes into contact with the mycelium produced by another spore. Their union gives rise to the secondary mycelium that will form what is technically known as the carpophore (fruit- or fruiting body).

spore
× 1000

germination and
primary mycelium
× 1000

embryonic fruit-bodies
produced by secondary
mycelium formed by the
union of two different primary
mycelia

fruit-bodies in various stages
of development

Ozonium stage of Coprinus radians *(230).*

substances absorbed from the soil by the fungus, after the breakdown of rotting tree or plant material, are diffused through the fungal mycelium and ultimately into the tree root. In effect the sheath of fungal hyphae surrounding the tree roots greatly increases the area of absorption of food materials in the soil available to the tree and confers on it a great benefit, especially when growing in poor soils where competition for available food supplies is intense. The fungus partner in turn receives its carbohydrates and a constant supply of water from the tree via the roots.

This relationship, in which the fungal threads are mostly outside the plant root, is referred to as an *ectotrophic mycorrhiza*. If the threads of the fungal partner are inside the host cells the condition is described as an *endotrophic mycorrhiza*. Such mycorrhizae are found in most orchids and indeed many orchid seeds are unable to germinate, or germination is unable to progress very far, unless there is infection with the correct endotrophic fungus partner. The fungal threads are being destroyed constantly by the plant, which obtains from the fungus a growth factor it otherwise lacks. These types of mycorrhizal association are considered controlled parasitism.

The ectotrophic mycorrhizal association is often very specific, involving a single species of fungus with a single species of host tree. Sometimes the range of hosts may be wider, involving other species of the same genus or even species of different families. Likewise, a single specimen tree may have a root system comprising a mosaic of different mycorrhizae involving associations between its roots and many different fungal partners.

It follows that many gill-bearing fungi are found in certain types of woodland beneath specific trees because they can form the necessary mycorrhizal relationship only with that tree species. Thus *Suillus grevillei* (**251**) is found only under larch trees, while *Amanita muscaria* (**2**) usually is found associated with birch trees and only rarely with other host trees.

Parasitic fungi Many plant diseases are caused by fungi; such diseases may seriously affect crops and harvests and can be a major contributive factor to the shortage of food in the world. Downy and powdery mildews, rusts, smuts, etc. (diseases with which farmers are all too familiar) make up a significant proportion of the fungus kingdom and cause a great deal of damage, but they are on the whole inconspicuous, and of absolutely no interest at all to the mushroom gatherer. Some fungi do cause reactions in plant tissues and form strange and clearly visible structures called *galls*. Suffice it to mention the effect of *Taphrina deformans* on the leaves of peach trees and the distorted shapes of maize caused by the smut *Ustilago maydis* (**420**).

Fungi attack other organisms too, including other fungi and every sort of animal, ranging from man to the tiniest vertebrate, from molluscs to insects, and worms to protozoans. Parasitic fungi are very specific, attacking only specific hosts. In some cases this specialization is extreme: the parasite of a species of beetle, for example, is capable of growing only on its elytra (wing covers) or legs. Conspicuous fruit-bodies are formed, however, by fungi that are parasitic on trees and, in some rare cases, by fungi that are parasitic on other fungi and insects.

Fungi that are parasitic on insects There are numerous associations between insects and fungi. Of particular importance among them, because of their possible practical implications, are those that are established with the *entomophagus* fungi, i.e. fungi that are parasitic on insects: these fungi could well offer mankind an alternative weapon in the war against pests.

When out picking mushrooms you may well stumble upon entomophagus fungi. In temperate climates members of the genus *Cordyceps* are relatively common; these usually have thread- or club-shaped carpophores, often brightly coloured. The commonest species, *Cordyceps militaris* (**347**) forms orange-red clubs on larvae of Lepidoptera and Coleoptera. *Cordyceps sinensis*, parasitic on Lepidoptera, has been used in China for medicinal purposes since earliest times.

Fungi that grow on other fungi Some fungi grow on the carpophores of other fungi, whether still living or in the process of decomposition. In addition to the numerous moulds that are parasitic on fungi, we find actual higher fungi, with carpophores, that grow on the carpophores of other fungi.

Two members of the Ascomycetes, both club-shaped, grow out of the ground but are, in effect, parasitic on two subterranean fungi: *Cordyceps ophioglossoides* (**350**) and *C. capitata* (**349**), which attack the false truffles *Elaphomyces granulatus (387)* and *E. muricatus.*

Boletus parasiticus (**243**), a small yellow-brown bolete, grows on *Scleroderma citrinum* (**376**), a member of the Gasteromycetes. The strange *Collybia racemosa* (**47**), together with *C. cirrhata* (**42**) and *C. tuberosa*, grows on decomposing remains of other fungi. The decomposing carpophores of particular species of *Russula* and *Lactarius* frequently host small fungi with gills, *Asterophora lycoperdoides* (**50**) and *A. parasitica. Volvariella surrecta* grows on the malodorous *Clitocybe nebularis* (**83**).

Some fairly common lower fungi should also be mentioned: *Sepedonium chrysospermum* is the name of a mould that attacks some boletes. The fungus produces coloured spores that cause the carpophore to be covered by a powdery yellowish mass. *Mycogone rosea* grows on the *Amanita* group, particularly *A. caesarea* (**1**) and *A. rubescens* (**11**), which turn pink. *Hypomyces lactiflorum* causes the deformation of some white species of *Lactarius* and *Russula*, and actually improves the quality of the attacked mushroom as food. (Of course, this is by no means the case with other parasitized mushrooms.)

Saprophytic fungi There is no organic matter that is not attacked and destroyed by fungi and bacteria. Everything that forms organic substances comes from nature and re-enters the natural 'economic' cycle because of the action of micro-organisms. The breakdown of organic substances is achieved by fungi in the mycelial stage.

In natural conditions the breakdown of given types of matter is carried out exclusively by specific species of saprophytic fungi. For this reason we shall now take a look at certain substrates and environments that promote the production of fungi.

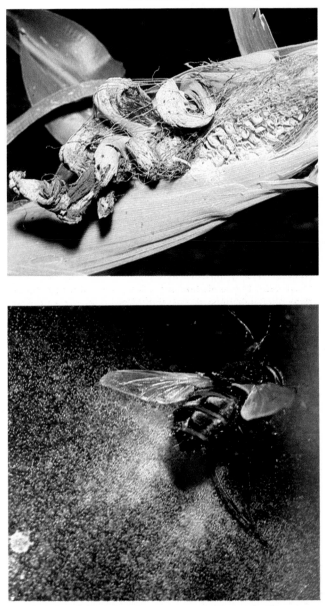

Top: Ustilago maydis *(420) growth on a corncob. Below: A cloud of spores around a fly that has been killed by* Entomophthora muscae.

The fruit-body of Asterophora lycoperdoides (50) growing on the cap of a Russula.

Substrate specificity Some saprophytic fungi have as their exclusive habitat no more than fragments of certain plant species. These are for the most part higher fungi of small dimension, such as *Marasmius epiphylloides*, which grows on ivy leaves, *M. buxi*, found on box leaves, *M. hudsonii*, found on the leaves of holly, *M. epidryas*, which grows on the roots of mountain avens, *Strobilurus* species, found on conifer cones, *Mycena seynii* on pine cones, etc. The total list would be a very lengthy one, and longer still if we started to look at the *Collybia*, *Marasmius*, *Mycena* and *Clitocybe* groups, and the various other fungi that grow on the leaves and ligneous fragments of coniferous and broadleaved trees in general.

Even more curious and unusual organic matter plays host to the strange species of the genus *Onygena*, which grow on horses' hooves or the horns of animals (*O. equina*), on feathers (*O. corvina*) and on the skin or fur of rodents (*O. pilifera*).

LOOKING FOR MUSHROOMS
Equipment Looking for mushrooms usually entails wandering over large wooded areas and grassland, and in most cases there is no guarantee that hours of walking will be rewarded by a rich crop. Clothing should be as practical as possible. The terrain in which mushrooms are found is often somewhat treacherous: it

may be strewn with rocks and have dense undergrowth, and it may also be slippery and muddy. A pair of sturdy walking shoes or hiking boots is the best footwear.

Some kind of stick will be useful for probing the leaves covering the ground and will also offer support in rugged terrain. You should also carry a knife so that you can pick the carpophore complete with the stipe (stalk) – important for an accurate identification of the mushroom in question – and a basket in which you can arrange your mushrooms by type. The basket should be well ventilated and strong enough to protect your crop from being bruised or damaged. The use of plastic bags, desirable for keeping green vegetables fresh, will only hasten the deterioration of mushrooms and should *not* be used. Instead, mushrooms should be wrapped carefully in wax paper or placed in separate open containers in the collecting basket. If too many mushrooms are placed on top of one another, those underneath will deteriorate quickly; nor should different kinds be placed together. Especially in hot weather or warm rooms, mushrooms kept enclosed can rapidly start to rot and thus become dangerous when eaten.

What to pick Avoid picking mushrooms that are too old, or specimens that are invaded by insect larvae or *worms*; any such mushrooms would be of poor quality for eating and if left alone they will still shed spores and reproduce their kind. If you are picking mushrooms for eating, pick only those species with which you are well acquainted and do not experiment with unfamiliar species except under expert guidance. When you come upon a large group of mushrooms that you do not know, all you need do is pick one or two specimens to show to an expert. It is definitely more responsible to go back to pick the rest – at the risk of finding them picked by some other eager hands – than to have to throw away a basketful of inedible mushrooms that can no longer play their part in the environment.

For those who have different interests and look for mushrooms in order to study them, it is important to know in advance the sorts of species that probably will occur in a particular environment. The various *epigeal fungi*, i.e. those growing above ground, especially if they are fairly large, are easy to find, being at worst hidden by leaves or moss.

It is worth looking particularly closely in hollow tree stumps, among mosses and on rotting tree trunks. Many smaller fungi grow in the litter beneath trees, on moss and on the droppings of herbivorous animals. All these habitats may harbour species of no concern to the gourmet but of great interest to the student. As a rule little attention is paid to species with small fruit-bodies, which are rarely included in popular books about fungi. But where these very small fungi are concerned, with the help of a hand-lens (10x magnification), a microscope and access to the technical literature, you can often make an identification that at first seemed impossible. You may be lucky enough to come across certain roundish fungi under dead leaves on this type of detailed search. These deserve special mention because they are part of a very specific and extremely varied category: the *hypogeal* fungi, which grow below the ground.

Looking for hypogeal fungi When looking for and gathering fungi that grow below the ground it is necessary to disturb the litter, comb the layer of humus with a knife or even lightly rake the ground. Any slight bulge in the ground can give away the pressure of hypogeal fungi.

A sparse covering, or absence of grass, in an area beneath a broadleaved tree (oak or some other species) indicates the possible presence of the mycelium of certain hypogeal fungi. Many truffles, and first and foremost the highly prized French or Perigord truffle, *Tuber melanosporum* (**389**), in fact produce substances that impede the growth of grass.

A handsome basketful of field mushrooms
(Agaricus arvensis, **204**).

The use of specially trained dogs, or pigs in some European countries, makes it possible to find many species of subterranean fungi and thus avoids indiscriminate digging that damages both the root apparatus of plants and any mycelium present.

Growing sites or habitats The most favourable places for the emergence of mushrooms are in the woods. The various types of woodland all have their own, sometimes unique, mycological flora made up of epigeal, hypogeal and mycorrhizal fungi, fungi that are saprophytic on leaves and pieces of wood and parasitic fungi (even though it is not always possible to paint a decisive picture of the particular relationship between the fungus and a specific type of tree). The range of preferences may vary and often the data that have been gathered are subsequently modified by the discovery of an hitherto unsuspected fungus-plant relationship. In this respect, and in relation to a certain habitat, the fungi can be divided into three groups: exclusive, preferential and indifferent.

Within the various woodland formations we also find lesser environments or habitats where it is possible to find fungi that do not occur in the thickest parts of the wood or forest, but in the so-called open habitats – near tracks and paths, in sunny glades and clearings and in areas covered with bushes and other undergrowth. Deforested areas constitute a specific type of open habitat. As well as being better 'ventilated', these areas are exposed to more accentuated thermal variations and fluctuations than actual woodland and in this respect they resemble another important environmental category – fields, meadows and grassland.

The term grassland describes open grassy spaces, with a fairly wide range of soils and differing levels of moisture in the ground; they also differ in terms of altitude and the species of plants present in them. The presence in grassland areas of grazing animals introduces a very special and fairly specific habitat: dung. A large number of species, known as *coprophilous* or *fimicolous*, usually small in size and shortlived, grow on dung. Here we find coprophilous species which are specialized to grow on the dung of particular animal species: *Agaricus bisporus* (**206**) grows best in horse dung, whereas *Psilocybe cubensis* occurs on cow dung.

Some selective substrates are formed by decomposing sawdust, oakbark or spent tan, the sediment of apples used in cider-making, coffee dregs and other waste matter from human activities. Burnt ground and the remains of charcoal kilns or bonfires play host to a rich *anthracophilous* flora, including the much-prized morels that, though not actually anthracophilous, are often found growing in burnt ground. This is one reason why peasants in various parts of Europe burn weeds and brambles along embankments.

Sand, be it in sand dunes, or by rivers or lakes, or along the seashore where there can be fairly high mixtures of humus (a compound of organic substances mainly of vegetable origin) or any sort of chemical composition or mineralogical structure, also plays host to an *arenicolous* or *psammophilous* (sand-loving) mycological flora and to other adapted species. A much more selective habitat is the upland peat bog and lowland bog or marsh that play host to species adapted to the high level of humidity and acidity in the substrate. In mountainous regions around the snow line, in ground that is not affected by thaws with the accompanying water, many members of the Discomycetes group, Ascomycetes (cup fungi), and other small fungi manage to survive.

The colonizing capacities of the fungi are such that they can spread beneath the surface of the ground. Lime-rich ground greatly encourages the growth of hypogeal fungi, especially the truffles, but sandy and flinty ground also plays host to interesting species.

Of various other habitats, the oddest of all is undoubtedly the monumental termites' nest found in Africa. The carpophores form inside these huge constructions where the mycelium of fungi belonging to the genus *Termitomyces* grows extensively. The stipe, surmounted by a very hard pointed cap, lengthens and once it has reached the outside world the tip of the cap unfolds and the cap itself, which can reach up to 60 cm (23.5 in) in diameter, looks like a parasol placed above the sun-baked termites' nest. The termites feed on the fungus and help to distribute new mycelia inside the nest's tunnels and galleries. The environmental conditions are so favourable to the growth of the fungus that the mycelium often tends to block the passages inside the termites' nest; the termites are then forced to eject the mycelial masses that have formed. These masses, once outside, produce small carpophores, whch differ somewhat from those that force their way up through the inside of the nest.

Carried around by wind and water, suspended in the atmosphere, the light spores of fungi are ready to germinate as soon as they come into contact with a suitable substrate, if the nutritional and climatic circumstances permit. So the fungi manage to live and thrive all over the world, from the surface of the land (cultivated or otherwise) and sand dunes along the seashore to the edge of the snowline, from human habitations to dense forests.

The nature of the ground The ground or terrain is the result of the physical, chemical and biological alteration of the original rock.

In general the distribution of fungi is much less dependent on the pH of the soil (the measure of hydrogen ion concentration) than on the pH influencing the distribution of the host tree in the case of parasitic species, or the mycorrhizal host partner. There is no very striking calcicole or calcifuge fungal flora as with the flowering plants, although such species as *Amanita echinocephala* (**13**) and *A. solitaria* (**12**) seem to be restricted to lime-rich soils whereas *Cystoderma amianthinum* (**18**) prefers acid heaths.

As far as pH is concerned, ground can be neutral, basic or acidic. Correspondingly, the various species of fungi may be considered either acidophilous or basophilous even if, in reality, the optimum pH of many fungi is close to a neutral level. In some cases trees can modify the pH of the ground in which they are growing. This applies, for example, to the chestnut tree, a typically acidophilous species: if planted in calcareous ground it tends to acidify the surface soil. In fact, plants can generate particular environmental factors such as the accumulation of humus and they can produce *rhizospherical* phenomena, i.e. phenomena

connected with the volume of earth modified and affected by the root apparatus. These can create actual islands in the midst of the surrounding environment. Many fungi become adapted to such changes; others do not. The French or Perigord truffle *Tuber melanosporum* (**389**) grows in markedly basic, calcareous soils, whereas the white truffle *Tuber magnatum* (**391**) prefers clayey, marly, acid soil. On their respective preferential grounds these two truffles can become associated with numerous species of trees, some of which are symbiotic with both the French and the white truffle. But the symbiosis with one or the other type is established by the type of soil. Moreover, in truffle-growing areas the French truffle does not extend into the denser areas of the wooded formations made up of its symbionts because the accumulation of dead leaves, which creates humus, acidifies the upper strata of the soil.

In addition to humidity and temperature we should also briefly mention light and wind. There are many species of fungi that can form fruit-bodies in the complete darkness of mines and caves. For most species, however, a minimal ration of light is needed both to form carpophores and for the normal development of the fruit-bodies. In fact some of the species grown in the dark do not always grow properly. Other species fail to form fruit-bodies if they do not have adequate light. For some species strong bright

The life cycle of a tree, from seed to plant (left) is like that of a fungus, from spore to fruit-body (right). The various species of fungi establish mycorrhizal symbiotic relationships with green plants by attaching themselves to their root apparatus; or parasitic relationships, where they actually penetrate the plant through cracks etc.; or saprophytic relationships, where they transform wood and dead leaves into mineral substances.

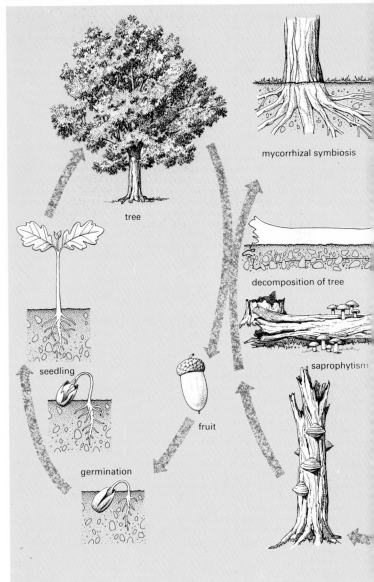

tree

mycorrhizal symbiosis

decomposition of tree

saprophytism

seedling

fruit

germination

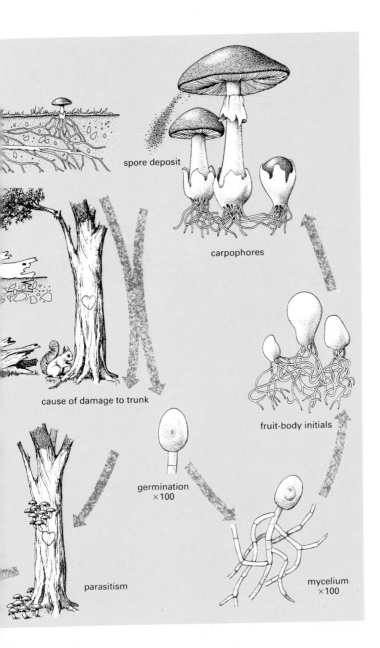

spore deposit

carpophores

cause of damage to trunk

fruit-body initials

germination
×100

parasitism

mycelium
×100

An unusual crowd of field mushrooms (in the foreground,
Coprinus comatus, **224**).

light can be harmful, whereas high-altitude and desert fungi
thrive on it.

The influence of the wind is well known to all mushroom
gatherers. In fact a windy spell – even if it lasts only for one day –
can irreparably harm the fruiting capacities of fungi. The ventila-
tion causes the water present in the ground to evaporate quickly
and the mycelium dries out, as do the developing carpophores.
The cuticle of already developed fungi wrinkles and splits.

WHEN TO LOOK FOR MUSHROOMS

It is well known that periods of dry weather or intense cold are not
favourable for the development of the fruit-bodies of fungi. But
this does not mean that the fungi have ceased to reproduce. Many
sorts of hypogeal fungi, truffles and other types continue to grow
and ripen during winter and summer, and many species living in
very humid environments find the conditions suitable for their
development during the hottest and driest periods of the year.
The best conditions for the occurrence of a massive production of
carpophores have to do with the presence of humidity in the
nutritional substrate and in the air, and with a mild temperature.

It is difficult to put precise values to those conditions, not least
because there exist, for each species, an optimum temperature
and an optimum humidity, just as there exist upper and lower

Not even furniture is safe from invasion by lignicolous fungi such as Serpula lacrimans.

temperature and humidity limits outside of which the fungus cannot form fruit (sometimes cannot even survive). The climatic pattern of the world's regions thus affects the period when fungi appear as well as their geographical distribution. On the whole, in temperate climates, the highest production of carpophores occurs in late summer and early autumn, when the atmospheric precipitation lowers the August temperature and raises the humidity level of the ground. These conditions usually occur in successive stages, moving from cooler to warmer areas.

In Mediterranean regions there are two periods of production that are sometimes very similar as far as fungus composition is concerned: one occurs in the spring, the other in the autumn. In the autumn rain helps to lower the summer heat; in the spring the sun heats up the cold, wet ground. And sometimes, if the spring temperature and humidity levels are optimal, autumnal species will emerge along with the typical species found in the spring. In desert areas or in sand dunes by the sea, on the other hand, we find species whose appearance is associated with the presence of minimal amounts of water. Here, too much water in the ground may impede the germination capacities of the spores or the potential fruit-forming capacities of the fungus. Thus in excessively rainy seasons many of the species normally present will not form fruit.

During very dry seasons the most abundant species belong to the group of saprophytic fungi, especially those saprophytic on wood, since this substrate retains the necessary moisture for a longer period than ground leaves and other surface substrates.

A dry period coming after a particularly wet one will encourage the fructification of those mycelia that have been able to develop properly. There is plenty of information and evidence to confirm this. Also, it has been maintained that in hot or warm regions in particular, the fruit-forming capacities of fungi are due not only to rain but also to the dry period preceding the rainy one. The morphogenetic action of dry weather has led to the formulation of what is known as the 'theory of fructification by endurance'. This theory finds supporting evidence in the ways in which the champignon and other cultivated mushrooms are grown.

For most fungi the temperature of the substrate is more important than the air temperature. Thus sunshine and the sun's heat play an important part in the fructification of fungi, and here too the requirements of the various species are fairly diverse. Alongside species that prefer sunny open spaces, we find others that seem to shy away from the direct rays and heat of the sun. But almost all the fungi disappear as the cold season approaches. Apart from the hypogeal species, which find protection below the ground, only a few other fungi continue to grow during the cold winter months; these include a few *lignicolous* species (growing on wood), among them the well-known oyster fungus, *Pleurotus ostreatus* (**113**), and *Flammulina velutipes* (**46**), various Gasteromycetes such as the *Tulostoma* and *Cyathus* groups, and certain minute species that grow in mosses.

The life span of fairy-rings is quite long. The mycelium is killed off only by environmental changes, such as in a valley invaded by the overflow from a hydroelectric dam, or on a hillside or mountain undergoing reafforestation. In some areas where man's interference has been very limited hitherto, enormous fairy-rings have been found; the age of some of them has been calculated in hundreds of years. The species that most often give rise to these formations being the genera *Agaricus*, *Amanita* and *Lepiota*, and the best-known fairy-ring mushroom is *Marasmius oreades* (**31**). Fairy-rings can also form in woods, with other genera responsible for them, but since there is no grass they are only visible when the carpophores appear.

THE LIFE OF FUNGI AND THE FAIRY-RING

In the case of the short-lived species, such as the coprophilous fungi, the life cycle is somewhat speeded up and in some cases the carpophore itself survives no more than a single day. From the moment when the spores of saprophytic species make contact with the substrate and germinate, the life span of that species is closely correlated to the nature of the substrate. The *xylophagous* (feeding on wood) species live until the cellulose of the host structures has completely decomposed and has been removed by other rival organisms. Among the species that grow on wood, those with the longest life span belong to the family *Polyporaceae*, which start to attack trees that are still living. The sometimes exclusive presence of a *polypore* causes the wood to rot slowly, eventually killing the tree; when the tree dies, there follows the fairly swift demise of the parasite as well, it being increasingly restricted in its nutritional needs by other new xylophagous species. The mycorrhizal species seem to have an even longer life span and they are also more prudent, as it were, from a survivalist point of view. The symbiotic relationship with plants, though subject to constant competition and an almost 'dialectical' pattern, can mean a life span of several decades for some fungi.

Sometimes you will come upon long strips of ground or circular areas where the grass is greener and more lush. In these areas, at the right time, numerous carpophores will grow, also arranged in a line or circle: the 'fairy-ring'. These fairy-rings are caused by a natural phenomenon that, sadly, has nothing to do with magic. They originate where two spores of the correct strain germinate in close proximity to give rise, after fusion, to a mycelium that grows out equally in all directions from a central point. At its periphery the fungal hyphae secrete enzymes that break down the available humus and plant debris resulting in a flush of food material; some is used by the fungus and the remainder is available to the grass. The latter reacts as if fertilizer had been added by producing lush green growth on the outermost edge of the ring. Immediately inside this there is often an almost bare zone in which the fungal fruit-bodies will form and where there is almost no grass. Some authorities believe that the grass is killed by the fungus directly or by substances resulting from the decomposition of the old, effete fungal hyphae; others think it is a result of the air spaces in the soil being clogged by fungal hyphae that prevent the grass roots from functioning. On the inner side of the ring there may be another zone of lush green grass resulting from the growth cycle of the fungal hyphae: growing through the soil and exhausting the food supply, then dying off and breaking down by the action of bacteria. This releases another flush of food substances that again have a stimulatory effect on the grass. Not all fairy-rings show these three zones; the zonation varies depending on the fungus involved.

FUNGI AND MAN

The first hints of our mycological knowledge relating to plant diseases are recorded as far back as 1200 BC in the ancient Vedas of India; the effects of poisonous fungi were dealt with in an epigram written by Euripides in about 450 BC. The larger types of fungi (macrofungi) have been of interest to mankind from very earliest times; the use of their prodigious metabolic capacities began when people developed a taste for wine and leavened bread. Even today few people realize how their lives are closely bound up with the presence or activities of these organisms; and few people realize how not a day passes when each one of us is not helped or harmed, directly or indirectly, by these 'citizens' of the microcosm surrounding us.

Fungi play an extremely important part in the slow but continual changes taking place in both nature and society. They are the agents responsible for the breaking down of much of the organic matter (saprophytism), and as such they cause huge amounts of damage by destroying foodstuff, hides and skins, fabrics, wood and other consumer goods, as well as books and works of art. In addition, fungi are the cause of the majority of known plant diseases, as well as many diseases that affect animals and man (parasitism). On a positive note, fungi are at the root of many industrial processes, which include some of man's most ancient activities: the production of wine, beer and bread, and the distillation of alcohol. And their use has been gradually extended to the commercial production of antibiotics, vitamins, organic acids, enzymes and other alimentary and pharmaceutical products.

In our agricultural activities, too, fungi are both a help and a hindrance. Though they are responsible for considerable damage to crops and harvests because of the plant diseases they cause, they also make agricultural land more fertile by means of the degrading action they have on organic substances. This action is also called 'mineralizing', and because of it nutritional elements are formed that can be reused by certain green plants.

The cultivation of mushrooms The observation that certain edible mushrooms grow naturally on certain decomposing organic matter combined with the desire to produce a tasty source of food has led to the development of various techniques for the cultivation of mushrooms and in some cases they have been

fairly profitable. But the cultivated species have never been the most prized by gourmets. Their favourite types are still the boletes, specific species of *Amanita* and truffles; all these are mycorrhizal fungi and their carpophores cannot be developed without the right symbiotic plant.

To date the only successes have been with the saprophytic species, i.e. those that feed on dead organic matter. Among these the best known is undoubtedly the mushroom *Agaricus bisporus* (**206**), which has given rise to a thriving agricultural industry. Each year millions of pounds of these mushrooms are produced for direct consumption, for the canning industry and for the preparation of soups and sauces. This activity dates back to the seventeenth century in Paris, during the reign of Louis XIV: to begin with the mushrooms were cultivated in outdoor gardens; subsequently, with the use of underground tunnels and stone cellars, this activity turned into a fully fledged industry. In the nineteenth century, in fact, 1500 miles (2414 kilometres) of tunnels and underground chambers were used for the cultivation of mushrooms. The soil used was made up of horse dung, a cheap and convenient substrate on which this mushroom grows naturally.

In recent decades, following the development of the micro-biological industry, the process has been enormously improved

A typical example of a fairy-ring, a completely natural phenomenon that used to be a source of much superstition.

and the production of mushrooms in a controlled environment has become an expression of highly advanced technology. Today horse dung still constitutes the basis of the culture soil. With a given quantity of straw and droppings, the dung initially undergoes a process of natural, though controlled, fermentation, first out of doors and then in an enclosed area where it is enriched with nitrogenous sugar substances and vitamins required for the development of the mushroom. After variable periods of time, depending on the composition of the substrate, now called 'compost', sowing takes place, using cereal seeds covered with *Agaricus bisporus* (**206**) mould. Today two main varieties of mushrooms are used: white and brown. The first is preferred in Britain, while the second, with its hazel-coloured cap and small brown scales, is more widely used in continental Europe for direct consumption.

The spores are mixed with the compost and left in very humid chambers at a temperature of 24–25°C (75–77°F). After a couple of weeks, when the mycelium has spread throughout the compost, the soil – arranged variously in long mounds, on platforms, or in boxes piled on top of one another – is covered with a few inches of a mixture of crushed stone and peat and sterilized with a solution of formalin. The temperature is lowered by about 8–10°C (16°F) and after ten days or so the first fruit-bodies are produced;

these will reform each week, producing 'flushes'. After five or six flushes the culture is renewed.

The cultivation of the oyster mushroom, *Pleurotus ostreatus* (**113**), and closely related species is also highly developed, especially in the Orient, and they are found in Western markets in various varieties. *Volvariella volvacea* (padi-straw, **159**) and *Lentinula edodes* (shii-take), common in Oriental cuisine, can also now be obtained in some delicatessens. For other species, such as the morels, production techniques still have to be improved, while, with the constant demand that currently exists, production is being developed in various parts of the world for *Stropharia ferrii* (**210**) and *Agrocybe cylindracea* (**195**).

Many saprophytic species, especially those growing on wood, can easily be cultivated even though in many instances they do not command a large market because of their meagre amount of flesh. The species that lend themselves best of all to this practice are *Armillara mellea* (**85**), *Flammulina velutipes* (**46**), and *Pleurotus ostreatus* (**113**).

The cultivation of mycorrhizal fungi, which need to live with a host plant in order to produce their fruit-bodies, is a demanding undertaking. This is known as 'indirect cultivation'. The only mycorrhizal symbiotic type that is cultivated quite extensively in France – and now in Italy – is the legendary French or Perigord truffle, the high quality and price of which amply justify the cost of installing artificial truffle beds and the long years of waiting before the carpophores can be picked.

In centres of modern truffle cultivation, production is followed extremely closely and nothing is left to chance. The acorns are sterilized on the outside in a chemical bath or dip and are then put in direct contact exclusively with truffle spores. The seedlings that develop in small bags filled with sterilized earth will have the truffle as the only symbiotic organism with which to associate. Once planted in soil with the right characteristics, and with due care, they will produce their first truffles after about ten years.

FUNGI AND ANIMALS

The cultivation of fungi is not an activity exclusive to man; in fact, various insects need fungi for their survival and have thus become exceptionally efficient mushroom farmers.

A good example of the relationship between fungi and animals is given by certain ants in tropical America of the genus *Atta*. These ants take green leaves inside their nest. In special rooms the leaves are finely shredded and neatly stacked. Mycelium then develops on the organic substratum and makes up the food of the

ants. It is also probable that African termites (see p. 00) have a very similar relationship with fungi of the genus *Termitomyces* that grow in termites' nests. In addition, one constantly comes upon fungi that have been to some extent eaten by animals and, despite what is commonly believed, not all of these fungi are edible by man. Slugs, for example, casually devour the fearsome death cap, *Amanita phalloides* (**4**); in fact their tolerance to the *Amanita* toxins is about 1000 times higher than man's. In the animal kingdom the most impressive consumers of fungi are the insects, many of which spend their larval stage as worms inside fungi. How many times is one reluctantly forced to leave plump boletes, snow-white field mushrooms and priceless truffles to the voracious appetite of larvae!

As well as slugs and insects, some mammals also seek out and feed on fungi. Pigs and wild boar are particularly fond of fungi, as well as a large number of other herbivorous animals, both wild and domestic, who vary their diet by eating them.

THE TOXICITY OF FUNGI

There are a number of popular misconceptions about the toxicity of fungi: that a poisonous one will cause silver to tarnish and

garlic to blacken; that if a cap has been eaten by a slug or animal it can safely be eaten by a human; that any dried fungus is safe because toxins lose their strength as the carpophore dries; that no lignicolous (i.e. growing on wood) fungus is deadly; and that symptoms of poisoning will appear immediately upon ingestion. The facts are otherwise. Although many fungi will cause a stomach upset within thirty to sixty minutes, the deadly *Amanita phalloides* (**4**), *A. verna* (**7**) and *A. virosa* (**8**) do not produce noticeable symptoms until eight to twelve hours after ingestion. *Galerina autumnalis* (see **Note** at **196**), which contains the same toxins as the deadly species of *Amanita* (amatoxins), is common on wood. Although certain fungi do lose their toxicity upon drying, other fungi, especially those containing amatoxins, are poisonous no matter how they are processed. No reliable conclusions about the edibility of a fungus can be drawn from seeing that it has been eaten by a slug, insect or any animal. And old wives' tales regarding the nature of poisonous fungi are nonsense.

The toxicity of fungi is a genetic characteristic of the species and the only way of establishing the edibility of a species is to have a thorough knowledge of its morphological features.

In addition, the dispersal of large amounts of highly toxic substances like pesticides (fungicides and insecticides) can make any fungus that may come into contact with them dangerous. Similarly, fungi that grow in areas where there is heavy traffic or a high incidence of industrial pollution may also become poisonous, even though they are normally excellent to eat. Here the fungus acts like a sponge and concentrates in its carpophore certain highly dangerous metals such as lead and mercury. These pollutants accumulate in the soil and are absorbed and concentrated by the mycelium of the fungi.

Cases of poisoning by fungi are mainly due to substances produced by and contained in the fruit-body; these substances may act immediately at the gastro-intestinal level, causing a violent stomach upset that in turn causes the intestine to evacuate its contents, thus preventing a complete absorption of the poison; or they may enter the bloodstream as toxins and affect various organs, in some cases fatally, or irremediably. In the first instance the outcome is almost always positive, as long as there are no complications, but in the latter, irreparable damage to vital organs (liver and kidneys) can occur and there is some possibility of death. In all cases requiring hospitalization, whatever specific remedies are used, fluids, sugars and salts must be replaced and maintained.

Many of the organic compounds responsible for the toxicity of fungi are known to us because they have been isolated and identified chemically; and for some we have satisfactory knowledge about the way they act. These studies have made it possible to elaborate remedial methods that have shown themselves to be fairly effective in cases of mushroom poisoning; there have even been successes in cases of poisoning by the deadly death cap, *Amanita phalloides* (**4**), and other similar species. Good hospital care and fluid maintenance have also helped to reduce the fatality rate caused by this kind of poisoning.

THE EDIBILITY OF FUNGI

Many of the fungi in this book are among the most common species but except for a few distinctive kinds fungi are difficult to identify. Because a few common species are deadly and many are known or believed to cause various degrees of poisoning, it is necessary to exercise the utmost caution in determining the identity of a collection.

Until the commoner (and particularly the poisonous) species can be identified with certainty, ask an experienced collector to accompany you on field trips.

Lignicolous fungi are easy to cultivate. This photograph shows the fructification of Agrocybe cylindraceus (*195*) in a laboratory.

Be sure to collect the whole fungus: do not leave a portion of the stipe in the ground because one of the identifying characteristics of a deadly *Amanita* is the cup sheathing the base of the stipe.

Keep all species in separate containers to avoid contamination.

Make a spore print before attempting to identify gilled fungi: often the colour of the gills gives no indication of the colour of the spores.

Keep fungi refrigerated until eaten and eat only those fungi you know to be edible and that are in prime condition.

Never eat wild fungi raw.

Always observe moderation in eating fungi. Eat a very small amount the first few times you try a new species to be certain you are not allergic to an otherwise edible fungus and preferably get it checked by an expert first.

The gilled fungi, while very common during wet periods throughout the season, are the most difficult to identify safely for eating. After having been introduced to them by an expert, the beginner should be content to attempt their identification, but should reserve for the dining-table those more easily identified non-gilled fungi. These include boletes (**239–258**) except for those with red pore mouths and those that are bitter; the chanterelle (**154**) and horn of plenty (**156**); the cauliflower fungus (**329**); morels (**282–288**); fleshy polypores (**325–327**); puffballs (**368–373**); and tooth fungi, especially *Hericium erinaceus* (**314**).

Once one has taken proper advice and acquired sufficient experience of mushroom collecting, one may want to try some of the choice gilled fungi. Some of the more easily identifiable of these include the almond- or anise-scented species of *Agaricus* (**202, 204**); the honey fungus (**85**); *Lactarius volemus* (**127**); two *Pleurotus* species (**113, 114**); the parasol (**20**); and the shaggy ink cap (**224**).

HOW TO STUDY FUNGI

Attempts to identify a fungus by looking for a picture of it in a book are not usually successful. This is first and foremost because no book exists that can boast that it includes or illustrates every fungus; it is also because not all the fungi have been illustrated yet, especially in colour, let alone photographed. This situation is sometimes aggravated by the inaccuracy of some illustrations and reproductions, by the fact that the specimens photographed were not in a perfect state or because the printing process has altered some of the colours. In addition, one should bear in mind that while certain mushrooms are relatively easy to identify, most are not; and there are a great number of look-alikes. In order to

Top: The cultivation, on straw, of Pleurotus ostreatus *(oyster fungus, **113**) out of doors. Below: Harvesting cultivated mushrooms* (Agaricus bisporus, ***206***) *in a modern, enclosed environment.*

Fungi that are eaten by insects, slugs and other animals may nevertheless be poisonous to humans.

avoid any unpleasant experiences and in order to begin a valid identification method, you must inspect your fungi with a critical eye. In particular, the structures that form the carpophore must be closely examined. Comparison of the specimen with a coloured illustration can help to substantiate a tentative identification but only microscopic examination can confirm it.

It is also important to take note of the environment in which the fungus is picked. As well as trying to fit the fungus into the systematic mycological classification, it must also be fitted into its natural surroundings; in other words one must understand its ecological role. For this reason it is important to know whether the fungus grows directly out of the ground, whether it has grown on a pinecone or on a decomposing branch, or on a tree trunk or on the remains of another fungus. In addition one must not overlook the fact that the fungus may have been picked in a wood or in grassland, and note must be taken of which trees, grasses or mosses were present in the area of the find. It is also worth noting the type of ground in or on which the fungus was growing. There are many factors to be taken into account and in some cases they can be of fundamental importance for a correct identification of the species of fungus that has produced the carpophore.

The identification of a fungus, i.e. the species to which it belongs, will follow this sort of logical sequence:

1) Observation of the morphological features of the carpophore (shape, possible remains of veils, form of the hymenium, colour, cuticle, consistency of the flesh and the possible production of latex at the point where it has been broken off, and habitat). This first series of observations should indicate the genus to which the fungus belongs or, at the very least, certain similar genera that will be able to be ascertained only on the basis of their microscopic features.

2) Colour of the carpophore, presence of typical veil remains, shape of cap and stipe, colour of flesh, any possible colour change, colour of latex (where applicable), smell, taste and habitat form the second level of observation. Once these data are known the systematic position of the fungus can be more precisely ascertained and in many cases it will be possible to identify on this basis.

3) With macro- and microchemical reactions and observation of microcharacters, you will have virtually all the data needed to name the precise fungus in question. In some works colour terms may be unfamiliar and reference to a colour chart may be necessary.

The ordinary individual, unfortunately, does not always have the right technical means at his or her disposal for microscopic and chemical examination of the carpophore, nor the right bibliographic references (which are scattered through dozens of scientific journals or incompletely compiled in books and publications often written in foreign languages, usually impossible to find in bookshops, and very expensive).

THE CLASSIFICATION OF FUNGI

Fungi are considered members of the plant kingdom. But there are many mycological systematists who put the fungi in a completely separate kingdom with the same status as the plant and animal kingdoms. A fairly wide variety of organisms are considered members of the fungus family.

This book deals only with fungi that form fruit-bodies visible to the naked eye, the *macromycetes* (large fungi). Without going into too much detail we can say that the larger fungi that produce carpophores fall into two major groups: the Ascomycetes and the Basidiomycetes. In the first class the spores are produced inside microscopic cylindrical organs called *asci*; in the second the spores are formed on the outside of a microscopic club-shaped reproductive organ, the *basidium*.

The number of species It is hard to say how many types of fungi there are. In the past mycologists working in isolation have

THE TOXICITY OF FUNGI

Syndrome	Species	Incubation
Gastro-intestinal	*Agaricus xanthodermus* (**203**) *Boletus satanus* (**246**) *Entoloma sinuatum* (**163**) *Hebeloma crustuliniforme* (**187**) *Lactarius torminosus* (**131**) *Hypholoma fasciculare* (**214**) *Omphalotus olearius* (**86**) *Pholiota squarrosa* (**191**) *Ramaria formosa* (**330**) *Scleroderma citrinum* (**376**) *Tricholoma pardinum* (**65**)	30 minutes–2 hours (up to 3 to 6 hours)
Botulinic	Altered carpophores	1–4 hours
Amanitin poisoning	*Amanita phalloides* (**4**) *Amanita verna* (**7**) *Amanita virosa* (**8**) *Galerina autumnalis* (see **196**)	8–24 hours (up to 48 hours)
Amanitin-like poisoning	*Lepiota helveola* (see **25**) and related small species	5–15 hours
Orellanine	*Cortinarius orellanus* (**186**) *Cortinarius speciosissimus* (**178**)	3–14 days
Gyromitra (false morel poisoning)	*Gyromitra esculenta* (**279**) and possibly related species	6–12 hours, sometimes after 2 hours
Psilocybin (psychoactive)	*Gymnopilus junonius* (**198**) *Psilocybe* species some species of *Panaeolus* and *Conocybe*	30–60 minutes
Muscarine poisoning	*Clitocybe dealbata* (see **31**) *Clitocybe phyllophila* (**78**) most species of *Inocybe* (**168–171**)	15 minutes–4 hours
Muscimol (fly-agaric poisoning)	*Amanita muscaria* (**2, 3**) *Amanita pantherina* (**10**)	30 minutes–2 hours
Coprine	*Clitocybe clavipes* (**81**) *Coprinus atramentarius* (**223**)	30 minutes after drinking alcohol, up to 2 days after eating mushrooms
Immune Injury	*Paxillus involutus* (**236**)	gradually acquired hypersensitivity

Principal Effects	Duration
affects the gastro-intestinal apparatus (vomiting, diarrhoea, colic pains, cramps)	6 hours to 2 days, cases of poisoning by *Entoloma sinuatum*, *Omphalotus olearius* and *Tricholoma pardinum* may be more severe and may require hospitalization
affects the gastro-intestinal apparatus and nervous system	3–5 days, sometimes fatal
severe vomiting, diarrhoea and cramps for 12–24 hours, followed by a brief remission and the onset of kidney and/or liver dysfunction or failure	10–20 days; when fatal, death coming usually 4 to 7 days after first symptoms
intestinal symptoms, muscular cramps, sweating, congestion of internal organs	not properly known
damage to liver, kidneys, spinal cord, with intestinal upset, fever, chill, headache, muscular pain	1–5 months, often fatal
bloating, abdominal pains, vomiting, jaundice, bloody diarrhoea	5–10 days, death can occur after 2 days; dose related
mood change; pleasant or apprehensive sensations, unmotivated laughter, hallucinations	4–6 hours, sometimes longer
dizziness, blurred vision, shivering, profuse sweating, salivating, nausea, circulatory disorders	12–24 hours, sometimes 2–4 days; may require hospitalization; death rare
dizziness, hyperactivity, deep sleep, delirium, sometimes sweating	1–2 days
flushing on upper body, tingling in extremities, hypersensitivity, nausea	2–4 hours, rarely serious
diarrhoea, vomiting, cardio-vascular upsets, allergic reactions (anaphylactic shock), massive haemolysis	2–4 days, rarely fatal

occasionally described new species unnecessarily or misinterpreted species described from other parts of the world; this has meant that the same fungus sometimes has several names and that different fungi sometimes have the same name. Despite the impossibility of giving a precise figure, there can be no doubt that the number of fungus species runs into tens of thousands.

The aim of this book is to give some idea of the great complexity of just a small area of mycology, the area occupied by the macrofungi (large fungi), and the vast variety of forms which can be found among the members of this group. For these fungi the essential criterion for their classification lies in the fruit-body, an ephemeral and fairly changeable structure. The large fungi found in any country with a temperate climate total many thousands of species. Becoming an expert on the macrofungi in your particular area will be a challenging and rewarding lifetime pursuit.

The geographical distribution of fungi Fungi are now known to be less widely distributed around the world than earlier research indicated. It is true that some species do have a wide distribution (see for example *Schizophyllum commune* (**291**) and *Trametes versicolor* (**300**)), but even species that appear to the eye to be virtually identical in North America and Europe have been shown to be genetically isolated and intersterile. Fungi are not easily dipersed between continents because the spores, especially if small and thin-walled, while being blown for long distances, do not remain viable for long. Further, in order for a fungus to establish itself on a new continent two viable spores have to land within a millimetre or so of each other to ensure fusion between the resulting mycelia. In many instances the chance of this happening is greatly reduced owing to the fact that the spores have to be of the correct mating type. Assuming fusion does occur the local soil and climatic factors must be such as to encourage fruit-body formation.

Dispersal of fungi from one continent to another does occur but it is usually the result of the activity of man either transporting mycelial fragments on soil on his boots, or on soil adhering to roots of imported plants. Indeed, many countries have legislation to prevent accidental import of pathogenic species in soil or on infected plants.

The colour of the flesh The colour of the flesh is an important feature. It is examined by cutting the carpophore in two, from top to bottom. The inside of the carpophore, the 'flesh', can be of

The structure of a fungus with cap and stipe.

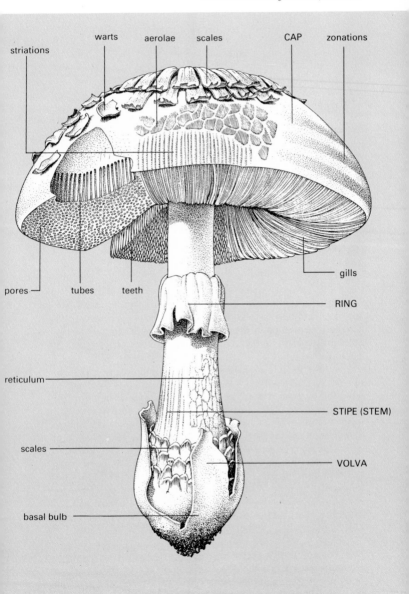

striations

warts

aerolae

scales

CAP

zonations

gills

pores

tubes

teeth

RING

reticulum

STIPE (STEM)

scales

VOLVA

basal bulb

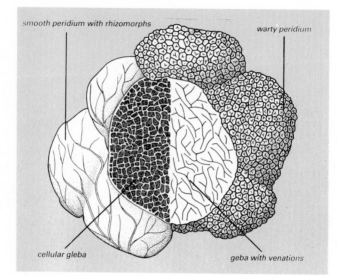

Model ot a spheroidal fungus.

smooth peridium with rhizomorphs

warty peridium

cellular gleba

geba with venations

various colours and in some instances will change colour as the fungus matures, as in the puffballs, which begin as white and apparently undifferentiated but which colour dramatically as they mature.

As a rule the colour of the flesh is important for the identification of cap-and-stipe fungi (Agaricaceae, Boletaceae, Hydnaceae) and slightly less so for the Polyporaceae and Thelephoraceae. Most fungi have a fairly white flesh that stays white when cut, in other words it is unchanging, or does not react. But special attention should be paid to specific parts, especially beneath the cuticle and on the sides of the stipe and at the base, which may have typical, though often only slight colorations. In many cases, however, the colour of the flesh changes when the fungus is touched or broken. The colour change often also affects the hymenium. There are also many fungi that have a flesh which is often the same colour as the whole fungus, such as all-yellow *Cantharellus cibarius* (**154**).

The colour of the latex or milk Some fungi produce large amounts of juice, called *latex* or *milk*, when even lightly scratched or damaged. This is a major characteristic of an important genus of fungi called *Lactarius*. But it also occurs in a few species of the

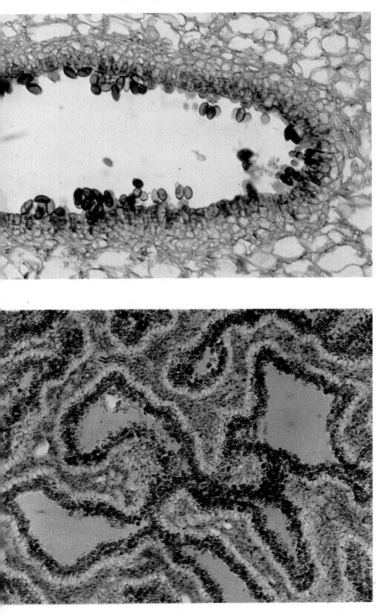

Top: Cross section of a gill fungus seen through a microscope; the darker elliptical structures are the spores. Below: Cross section of the gleba of a puffball under the microscope; the spores are the small spheres which form the darker stratum.

A Coprinus *basidium with two mature spores (on left), seen under the microscope.*

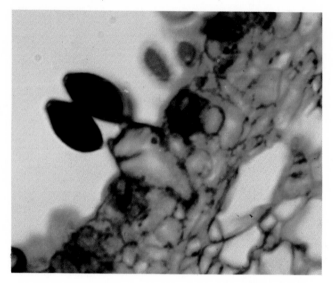

genus *Mycena*, a large group but one of little interest to the mushroom gatherer because most of the members are so small. In the *Lactarius* group the milk may be a constant white or strikingly coloured from the start or it may slowly change colour.

Consistency Most gill-bearing fungi have fruit-bodies of a relatively thick fleshy consistency, but in others, notably the smaller species, the flesh may be very thin indeed. In contrast, the fruit-bodies of *Pleurotus*, *Panus* and *Leutinus* are often tough and leathery. The flesh of the bracket fungi may be soft and watery, rubbery (suberose), or hard and woody. And some of the jelly fungi such as *Tremella* and *Auricularia* have a gelatinous texture, drying to a horny consistency and then rehydrating during wet conditions.

Taste and smell Taste and smell can be helpful in identification of various fungi. Normally when commencing a study of the fungi one should avoid tasting any species. However, when one is able to recognize the genera *Russula* and *Lactarius* (and this is not difficult, especially since species of the latter genus all produce a white or coloured milk when the gills are broken) it will soon be apparent that one has to taste the fruit-body before it can be

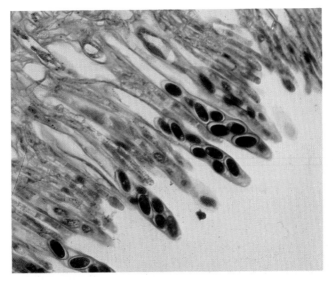

identified. This is perfectly safe, the only trouble being that many species of both genera have a burningly acrid taste whereas others have an innocuous, mild taste. In species of *Lactarius* it is more common to taste the milk with the same result and only the smallest drop on the tip of the tongue is sufficient. Other fungi belonging to a wide range of genera may have a bitter taste or mealy flavour. However, in all instances it is advisable to spit out the chewed portion and avoid swallowing it.

Smell is also an important aid to identification but the range of smells found in fungi is almost infinite. Pink-spored gill-bearing fungi often have a strong smell of meal when crushed, exemplified by *Clitopilus prunulus* (**162**). Some *Mycena* have an alkaline nitrous smell, some species of *Russula* smell of apple, whereas *R. xerampelina* (**149**) smells of crab. In some instances smells may be weak and if so it helps to keep the fruit-bodies in a closed tin overnight. In other instances the smell may be overpoweringly strong as in the stinkhorn *Phallus impudicus* (**358**), which smells like rotting carrion. *Clitocybe odora* (**84**) is remarkable for having a delicious smell of anise. In some fungi smell is intensified by drying and some species of *Lactarius* and *Phellodon* develop a strong smell of bedbugs or fenugreek when dried. It is therefore always advisable to smell fungi as soon as they are collected and

*Cross sections of carpophores. Left: a puffball (Vascellum pratense, **374**), showing the fertile part (the gleba) and the sterile part (the subgleba). Right: a morel (Morchella conica, **285**).*

to note any peculiarities of the intact and bruised or crushed specimens.

Spores The spores are the fungi's means of propagation and survival. The quantity of spores produced by each carpophore is incredibly large. A typical field mushroom, for example, produces about 16 billion spores, released at a rate of about 100 million an hour. A large puffball with a diameter of 30.5 cm (12 in) can produce up to 700 billion spores. The minute spores of the puffballs are scattered by the wind and, given their infinitesimally small weight, it is possible for a spore to be carried long distances on air currents. Spores are an important factor in the study of fungi and the systematics of fungi and their classifications are based in large portion on spore characteristics.

In order to study the method of formation, the size, the morphology and the chemical reactions of spores you will need a microscope and considerable experience, two things out of reach of most. Apprentice mycologists will find in the spores, or more correctly in the spore-print, a fairly important element on which to base their verdicts; the spore-print will help them find their way among the thousands of species of fungi with caps. The spore-print is a deposit of spores in mass. It is obtained by placing a cap with the hymenium facing down on a sheet of white paper or a piece of glass. After a few hours (sometimes not until the following day) a layer of spores will be deposited. This way you can determine the real colour of the spores, which will fall into four or five broad types: white, pink, brown and blackish-violet; often this last group is divided into two groups, purple and black. In the large corresponding groups – the leucospores (with white to pale yellow spores), the rhodospores (with pinkish spores), the ochrospores (with ochre to brown or rust brown spores) and the iantino- or melanospores (with violet or black spores) – there are very few exceptions. The most notable exception is the poisonous green-spored *Chlorophyllum molybdites*, which does not occur in Britain.

The colour of the spores can be somewhat roughly detected by looking at the colour of the gills of a mature specimen, but sometimes the colour of the gills may in fact mask that of the spores. A violet fungus such as *Lepista nuda* (**74**), for example, has pale pinkish buff spores that do not show up against the surface of the bright lilac-violet gills.

It should be noted that the colour, size, shape and ornament, along with the chemical reactions of the spores, are constant and diagnostic for every species of fungus.

MACROCHEMICAL REAGENTS

Various chemical substances produce specific colour reactions on contact with the various structures of the carpophore.

The use of reagents, which are *not* used to distinguish between edible and poisonous fungi, has opened up a new frontier in mycological systematics. The discovery and formulation of new reagents is a very slow process and they are not infrequently stumbled upon by chance.

The mycologist who wishes to use chemical reagents should be extremely careful. In most cases the reagents are **corrosive** and often **highly toxic**. Avoid all contact with them and never eat the specimen on which the test has been carried out.

If these substances act in a visible and evident way that does not require the use of a microscope, they are called *macro-chemical* reagents. We shall now deal briefly with the reagents most commonly used and most easily found; these will be of some help in the identification of fungus species:

Strong bases. Fairly concentrated solutions with 10 per cent sodium hydroxide (NaOH) and potassium hydroxide (KOH); particularly useful for the *Cortinarius* group, these are widely used in the practical systematics of fungi, as is ammonia (NH_4OH), both in solution and in vapour form.

Iron salts. Ferrous sulphate ($FeSO_4$) in crystals or in water solution (10 per cent) is commonly used for the *Russula* group, while ferrous chloride (Fe_2Cl_6) is useful for the *Cortinarius* group.

T1.4 (Henry's) reagent. This reagent is used essentially for the *Cortinarius* group but also gives interesting reactions with other fungi. In preparing it great care must be taken because of the dangerous nature of the ingredients; if possible, have it prepared by specialized staff. The thallium oxide (1 g) is dissolved in nitric acid (4 cc). Using great care, 1 g of sodium bicarbonate is then added bit by bit to the solution.

Phenol or carbolic acid. In 2 per cent water solution it reacts in time with the flesh of almost all fungi, but a speedy reaction (about one minute) is a typical and specific characteristic of certain fungi.

Aniline. Oil of aniline passed over the cuticle makes it possible to divide the field mushrooms (*Agaricus*) into two major groups, depending on whether they turn yellow. The trace of aniline crossed with concentrated nitric acid can produce a major reaction, coloured orange-yellow, known as 'Schaeffer's cross reaction'. By stirring a few drops of oil of aniline in water one obtains water of aniline, an important reagent for the *Russula* group.

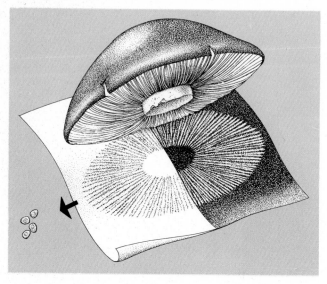

Phenolaniline. Used for the *Cortinarius* group, it is prepared by putting three drops of oil of aniline into five drops of concentrated sulphuric acid and mixing these two with 10 cc of phenol at 2 per cent.

Lygol. An iodized water solution (1 g iodine, 2 g potassium iodide dissolved in 150–220 cc distilled water), this is sometimes used instead of the dangerous T1.4 reagent, but is used mainly for identifying fungi with amyloid flesh or hyphal elements, i.e. flesh that reacts blue-violet with amide.

Phenoloxidase reagents. Not always specific, these give coloured reactions with the flesh of fungi. The most widely used are: guaiacol (guaiacum resin in water) which reacts red; guaiacum tincture (guaiacum resin in alcohol, 60–70 per cent), blue; pyramidon (solution in water), violet; naphthol (solution in alcohol), 30 per cent grey-violet; and tyrosinem, reddish, then black.

MICROCHEMICAL REAGENTS

Microchemical reagents often enable one to examine and identify mushrooms that otherwise are too difficult to name, mostly because of the large number of look-alikes in some groups. The most important regents are:

Melzer's reagent. This is a yellowish compound that when applies to mushroom tissue, spores in particular, may produce a

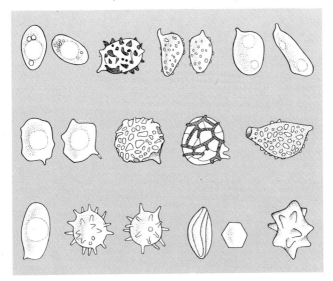

blue-black (amyloid) or red-brown (dextrinoid) reaction, or none at all. This is useful in studying agarics, especially species of *Amanita* (some of which have amyloid spores) and *Lepiota* (most of which have dextrinoid spores). All species of *Lactarius* and *Russula* have amyloid ornamented spores, as do some other gill mushrooms. Some cup fungi have asci that are amyloid, especially around the tip, and this characteristic is used in differentiating some look-alike genera. Formula: mix 20 g chloral hydrate, 0.5 g iodine, 1.5 g potassium iodide and 20 cc water; warm this solution and stir.

Bases. A weak solution (3–5 per cent) of ammonium hydroxide (NH_4OH) or potassium hydroxide (KOH) is used to inflate mushroom tissues when preparing microscopic mounts of dried material. Both are used to show staining of internal organs, such as cystidia (sterile cells) in *Hypholoma* and *Stropharia*, which become golden yellow in part.

Congo red. A 1 per cent solution is used to stain the walls of hyphae.

Cotton blue. This stain is used to test the spore wall of agarics; those that become blue or darken appreciably are said to be cyanophilic. To prepare this stain, combine 50 cc of 1 per cent solution of cotton blue in lactic acid (100 g), phenol (100 g), glycerine (150 cc) and 50 cc water.

THE KEYS

HOW TO USE THEM

Keys used in botany and zoology are groups based on the most conspicuous characteristics of the organism in question, the aim being to make it as quick and easy as possible to identify the genus or species. The procedure in mycology is as follows:

Let us imagine that we have picked a mushroom that we do not know. Let us have a look at it: it is a fungus with a cap and a stipe; beneath the cap are pores. Now let us look at the corresponding key. The first question we must ask is: 'Can the tubes that run into the pores be detached from the cap or not?'

Let us try with a fingernail. Yes, they can. Across from 'detachable tubes' is the number 2. Number 2 is therefore the next question we must answer: 'Is the stipe central and does the fungus grow on the ground?' or 'Is the stipe lateral, is the fungus red and does it grow on wood?' In this case the stipe is central and it has been picked on the ground: a bolete.

This method of classifying fungi is not strictly 'scientific', but it enables us to find our way quite efficiently in the world of fungi. The characteristics of the carpophores examined progressively and alternately enable us to draw up the appropriate keys, which are a vital factor for anyone wishing to delve deeper into the study of fungi.

The keys on the following pages have been considerably simplified and do not take microscopic characteristics into account. But despite the gaps inherent in them they will enable the most common genera to be identified.

Carpophore forms

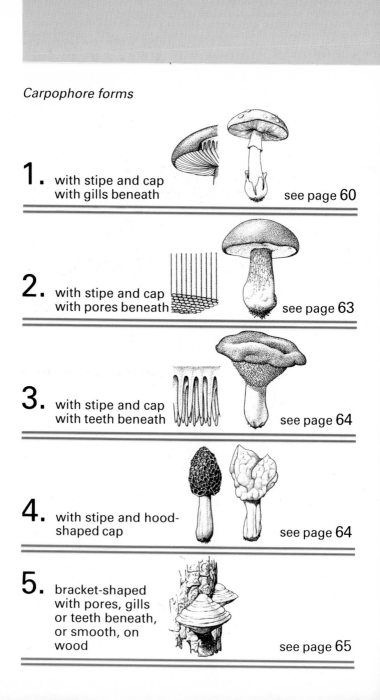

1. with stipe and cap
with gills beneath

see page 60

2. with stipe and cap
with pores beneath

see page 63

3. with stipe and cap
with teeth beneath

see page 64

4. with stipe and hood-
shaped cap

see page 64

5. bracket-shaped
with pores, gills
or teeth beneath,
or smooth, on
wood

see page 65

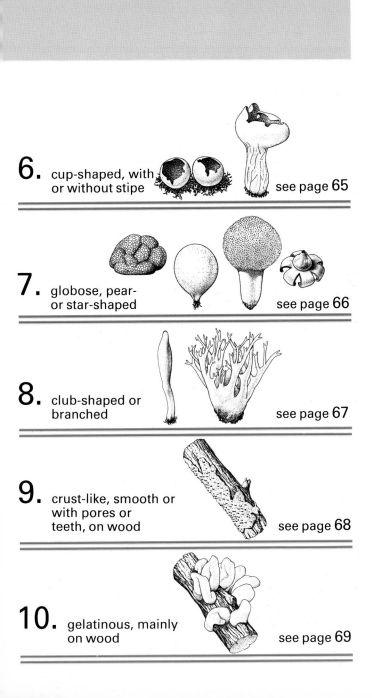

6. cup-shaped, with or without stipe — see page 65

7. globose, pear- or star-shaped — see page 66

8. club-shaped or branched — see page 67

9. crust-like, smooth or with pores or teeth, on wood — see page 68

10. gelatinous, mainly on wood — see page 69

1 FUNGI WITH STIPE AND CAP AND GILLS BENEATH

a) spores white, cream or yellowish

1a	lignicolous (on wood)	2
b	terricolous (terrestrial)	12
2a	with eccentric to lateral stipe or none	3
b	with central stipe	8
3a	gill-edge entire	4
b	gill-edge serrated or split lengthwise	6
4a	cap fan-shaped, stipe short and thin, spores amyloid	*Panellus*
b	stipe large, often with several caps	5
5a	brown, leathery, dry	*Panus*
b	grey, bluish, brown, whitish, fleshy	*Pleurotus*
6a	edge of gill split, cap greyish, tomentose (downy)	*Schizophyllum*
b	gills serrate	7
7a	stipe eccentric, cap coarsely squamose, spores non-amyloid	*Lentinus*
b	stipe lateral to absent, cap smooth to hairy, spores amyloid	*Lentinellus*
8a	entirely white, slimy, with ring	*Oudemansiella mucida*
b	otherwise	9
9a	tufted, caps yellowish brown, with fibrils, gills adnate to decurrent, with ring	*Armillaria*
b	tufted, caps orange, without fibrils, gills decurrent, without ring	*Omphalotus*
c	otherwise	10
10a	gills notched	*Tricholomopsis*
b	otherwise	11
11a	fruit-body small, stipe often horsehair-like, long, slender, cap convex, spores non-amyloid	*Marasmius* (in part)
b	stipe thin, fragile, cap conical to bell-shaped, spores mostly amyloid	*Mycena* (in part)
12a	gills adnate to decurrent	13
b	otherwise	17
13a	flesh brittle	14

b	flesh of stipe fibrous	15
14a	with latex (milk)	*Lactarius*
b	without latex	*Russula*
15a	gills crowded, thin-edged cap often funnel-shaped	*Clitocybe*
b	otherwise	16
16a	gills distant, wedge-shaped, thin-edged, waxy	*Hygrophorus*
b	gills often distant, thick-edged, forked or vein-like	*Cantharellus*
17a	with distinct volva in young stage, often with ring, cap varied, gills typically free	*Amanita*
b	without volva, gills free or attached	18
18a	with ring or stipe or veil remains	19
b	without remains of partial veil	24
19a	cap viscous or glutinous in damp weather	*Limacella*
b	cap coarsely squamose, granular, dry	20
20a	cap finely granular	21
b	cap coarsely squamose, fibrillose or smooth	22
21a	fruit-bodies tan or whitish, gills attached	*Cystoderma*
b	otherwise	*Lepiota* (in part)
22a	gills free	*Lepiota* (in part)
b	gills attached	23
23a	stipe with marginate bulb	*Leucocortinarius bulbiger*
b	stipe cylindrical, gills notched at stem	*Tricholoma* (in part)
24a	spores smooth, non-amyloid, fruit-bodies large, fleshy, gills sinuate (notched) at stem	*Tricholoma* (in part)
b	spores smooth, non-amyloid, fruit-bodies often less robust with tall stems, gills not sinuate	25
c	spores warty, amyloid	*Melanoleuca*
25a	stipe thin and rubbery, often tufted, revives in water, cap surface of globular cells	*Marasmius* (in part)
b	stipe cartilaginous, non-reviviscent, cap surface of repent hyphae	*Collybia*

| c | stipe fragile, hollow, non-reviviscent, cap bell-shaped | *Mycena* (in part) |

b) **spores pink to salmon-coloured**

1a	stipe lateral or absent	2
b	stipe central to eccentric	3
2a	fruit-bodies large, spores pinkish	*Phyllotopsis*
b	fruit-bodies small, spores brownish	*Crepidotus*
3a	with volva	*Volvariella*
b	without volva	4
4a	gills free, typically on wood	*Pluteus*
b	gills attached, typically on ground	5
5a	gills adnexed to notched	6
b	gills long, decurrent, spores with longitudinal ridges	*Clitopilus*
6a	spores angular, pinkish-salmon	*Entoloma*
b	spores smooth to minutely roughened, pinkish-buff	*Lepista*

c) **spores ochreous or brown**

1a	stipe lateral, fruit-body fan-shaped, on wood	*Crepidotus*
b	otherwise	2
2a	with veil or membranous ring	3
b	without veil or ring	7
3a	large terrestrial fungus with granular cuticle, tawny-yellow	*Phaeolepiota aurea*
b	cap smooth, white or brown, stipe smooth, not scaly	*Agrocybe*
c	cap typically scaly	*Pholiota*
d	fruit-bodies bell-shaped, thin, in moss	*Galerina*
e	otherwise	4
4a	on wood, large, orange-yellow with ring	*Gymnopilus junonius*
b	otherwise	5
5a	quite variable in colour and shape, rust-brown spores, veil cobweb-like	*Cortinarius*
b	cap dry, fibrillose to coarsely squamose, spermatic or other odour	*Inocybe*

c	cap viscid, stipe rooting, odour of bitter almonds	*Hebeloma radicosa*
d	otherwise	6
6a	cap fleshy, yellow or reddish	*Gymnopilus* (in part)
b	small species, brownish, reviviscent	*Phaeomarasmius*
7a	gills decurrent, margin involute	*Paxillus*
b	otherwise	8
8a	radishy odour, gills adnate, cap slimy, sometimes with veil when young	*Hebeloma*
b	otherwise	9
9a	cap shiny yellow, fragile	*Bolbitius*
b	otherwise	10
10a	cap pointed and viscid, with stipe rooting	*Phaeocollybia*
b	cap small, conical, stipe slender, brittle	*Conocybe*

d) spores purplish-brown or blackish

1a	gills self-digesting, i.e. dissolving into a sort of ink	*Coprinus*
b	gills not self-digesting	2
2a	gills decurrent, with glutinous veil	*Gomphidius*
b	otherwise	3
3a	cap dry, gills free or attached	4
b	cap glutinous-viscid or tacky, gills attached	5
4a	cap white or brown, sometimes coarsely squamose, with ring, gills free	*Agaricus*
b	tall, fragile species, stems white, brittle, caps conical, gills attached	*Psathyrella*
5a	often yellowish with cobweb-like veil, typically tufted	*Hypholoma*
b	otherwise	7
6a	ring or remains visible	*Stropharia*
b	without ring and/or bruising blue	*Psilocybe*

2 FUNGI WITH STIPE AND CAP WITH PORES BENEATH

1a	tubes detachable	2
b	tubes not detachable	3

2a	stipe central, typically terrestrial	*Boletus*
b	stipe lateral, liver-red, on wood	*Fistulina*
3a	on wood, often forming rosettes	4
b	terrestrial	*Grifola, Meripilus*
4a	stipe central, often black at base	*Polyporus* (in part)
b	stipe lateral	5
5a	surface crusty, shiny	*Ganoderma*
b	without crust, flesh brown	6
c	without crust, flesh white	*Polyporus* (in part)
6a	spores white	*Phaeolus*
b	spores yellowish	*Coltricia*

3 FUNGI WITH STIPE AND CAP WITH TEETH BENEATH

1a	stipe central	2
b	stipe lateral	4
2a	flesh pale, spores cream-coloured	*Hydnum*
b	flesh brightly coloured, often zonate	3
3a	consistency fleshy, tough, often bitter taste	*Sarcodon, Hydnellum*
b	consistency tough or leathery	*Phellodon*
4a	gelatinous, grey	*Pseudohydnum*
b	otherwise	5
5a	on pinecones, surface velvety, stipe present	*Auriscalpium*
b	otherwise	6
6a	white, cushion-shaped, with long dependent teeth, on wood	*Hericium* (in part)
b	white, coralloid, with dependent teeth, on wood	*Hericium* (in part)

4 FUNGI WITH STIPE AND HOOD-SHAPED CAP

1a	honeycomb-like cap	*Morchella*
b	smooth or folded	2
2a	cap smooth or folded, bell-shaped	*Verpa*
b	cap with contorted folds, brain-shaped	*Gyromitra*
c	otherwise	3
3a	cap saddle- or cup-shaped	*Helvella* (in part)
b	cap knob-like, irregular	4
4a	cap gelantinous, with smooth base	*Leotia*

	b	cap dry, with tomentose base	*Cudonia*

5 BRACKET-SHAPED FUNGI

1a	with gills	*Lenzites*
b	with teeth or ridges	2
c	with pores	3
2a	with completely free teeth	*Irpex*
b	with plate-like ridges	*Sistotrema*
3a	tubes not forming distinct layer	4
b	hymenial layer distinct from flesh	6
4a	with maze-like hymenium	*Daedalea*
b	otherwise	5
5a	pores very large, hexagonal, surface crust-like	*Hexagona*
b	pores average to small, roundish, surface hairy	*Trametes*
6a	flesh basically tender, also fragile when hardened	7
b	flesh hard to ligneous	8
7a	cap spongy, bristly	*Spongipellis*
b	surface smooth	*Tyromyces*
8a	surface crust-like	9
b	surface velvety, not crust-like when young, flesh yellow-brown	11
9a	typically applanate, flesh brown	*Ganoderma*
b	otherwise	10
10a	applanate to hoof-shaped, flesh and pores whitish	*Fomitopsis*
b	hoof-shaped, flesh and pores brownish	*Fomes*
c	hoof-shaped, flesh and pores yellow-brown to orange-brown	*Phellinus*
11a	large with short thick stalk, whitish spores	*Phaeolus*
b	small with slender stalk, yellowish spores	*Coltricia*

6 CUP- OR SAUCER-SHAPED FUNGI

1a	bright red, yellow-green or violet	2
b	brown or blackish	8
2a	terrestrial	3
b	on wood	4

3a	red with smooth edge, or ochre-yellow	*Peziza* (in part)
b	red with hairy edge	*Scutellinia*
4a	red with pubescent outer surface	*Sarcoscypha*
b	otherwise	5
5a	green, on green wood	*Chlorosplenium*
b	otherwise	6
6a	violet	*Ascocoryne*
b	yellow	7
7a	yellow, smooth	*Bisporella*
b	yellow or whitish, hairy	*Dasyscyphus*
8a	brown, on wood, fir cones, chestnut husks, etc.	*Rutstroemia*
b	otherwise	9
9a	brown with hypogeal sclerotia	*Sclerotinia*
b	otherwise	10
10a	cup with grooved stipe	11
b	otherwise	12
11a	stipe slender	*Helvella* (in part)
b	stipe thick	*Paxina*
12a	reddish-brown, flattened, with rhizoids from lower surface	*Rhizina*
b	without rhizoids	*Peziza* (in part)

7 GLOBOSE, PEAR- OR STAR-SHAPED FUNGI

1a	on earth or wood (epigeal)	2
b	subterranean (hypogeal)	11
2a	gleba (spore mass) powdery at maturity	3
b	gleba not powdery	8
3a	fruit-body opens in form of a star, with globose centre, with or without ostiole	*Geastrum*
b	as above but fruit-body almost woody, opening and closing depending on moisture	*Astreus*
c	as above, central part with many ostioles	*Myriostoma*
d	fruit-body not opening star-like	4
4a	globose part with peduncle normally sunk in the ground	*Tulostoma*
b	stipe short or absent	5
5a	outer layer yellowish, thick, mature gleba blackish	*Scleroderma*

b	outer layer smooth, with scales or warts, slender, white, grey or brown	6
6a	with stipe, gleba with blackish-blue spherules, in sandy ground	*Pisolithus*
b	otherwise	7
7a	peridium smooth, consisting of two layers, the outer one dropping off at maturity, the inner turning grey or blackish, with no sterile part	*Bovista*
b	peridium smooth, just one layer, no sterile part	*Langermannia* (*Calvatia gigantea*)
c	external peridium with spines, sterile tissue at base	*Lycoperdon*
8a	on wood	9
b	terrestrial	10
9a	blackish, concentrically zoned internally	*Daldinia*
b	reddish-brown, blackish, small	*Hypoxylon*
c	vermilion-red, minute	*Nectria*
10a	white, with a gelatinous layer inside and red or green gleba	*Phallus, Clathrus, Anthurus,* etc.
b	with no inner gelatinous layer	11
11a	yellowish or reddening peridium, gleba with distinct cells	*Rhizopogon*
b	otherwise	12
12a	finely warty peridium, yellowish-brown, gleba first slightly venose, then powdery	*Elaphomyces*
b	peridium finely warty or smooth, gleba venose	*Tuber* (in part)
c	peridium black, markedly warty	*Tuber* (in part)

8 CLUB-SHAPED OR BRANCHED (BUSH-LIKE) FUNGI

1a	club-shaped or slightly branched	2
b	plentifully branched	6
2a	on wood	3
b	on other matter	4
3a	black, woody	*Xylaria*

b	yellow, elastic, slightly viscous	*Calocera*
4a	finely speckled or with warts, on insects or hypogeal fungi	*Cordyceps*
b	terrestrial	5
5a	yellow, smooth, spores in asci	*Spathularia*
b	black or greenish, spores in asci	*Geoglossum*
c	yellow, yellowish, white, spores in basidia	*Clavaria*
6a	dark brown, leathery with slightly flattened ramifications, terrestrial	*Thelephora*
b	otherwise	7
7a	on wood, yellow, tough to horny	*Calocera*
b	on wood, black, leathery	*Xylaria*
c	otherwise	8
8a	markedly ramified with flattened branches	9
b	markedly ramified with cylindrical branches	10
9a	cauliflower-like	*Sparassis*
b	with poroid hymenium	*Grifola*
10a	thick branches	*Ramaria*
b	slender, thread-like branches	*Pterula*

9 CRUST-LIKE FUNGI ON WOOD

1a	crust-like with free margins	2
b	completely crust-like	6
2a	with pores or gills	3
b	reticulate or with teeth	4
3a	with gill-like plates and brown flesh	*Gloeophyllum*
b	round or rhomboid pores	various polypores
4a	with teeth	various hydroid fungi
b	reticulate	5
5a	gelatinous, orange, radiating folds, white spores	*Merulius*
b	yellow-brown radiating folds, brown spores	*Serpula*
6a	blackish	7
b	otherwise	8
7a	unevenly crust-like	*Ustulina*
b	disc-like	*Diatrype*
8a	orange	*Phlebia*
b	white, greyish or brown	9

9a	with small warts, olive-brown with white margin	*Coniophora*
b	smooth, brownish or yellow	*Stereum*

10 GELATINOUS FUNGI

1a	with toothed hymenium and stipe	*Pseudohydnum*
b	otherwise	2
2a	brown, yellow, conspicuously lobed or discoid	3
b	cup-shaped	4
3a	yellow, on living juniper	*Gymnosporangium*
b	yellow or brown, foliose, on dead wood	*Tremella*
c	blackish or white, discoid	*Exidia*
4a	cushion-shaped, yellowish, on dead wood	*Dacrymyces*
b	other colours	5
5a	ear-shaped, with violet-brown hymenium	*Auricularia*
b	otherwise	see cup- or saucer-shaped fungi

1 AMANITA CAESAREA

Etymology From Latin, 'of Caesar' or 'regal', because it was a favourite of the early Roman Emperors.

Description Cap 8–20 cm, hemispherical to flat, orange-red washing out to yellow, cuticle separable, sometimes with evident membranous remains of white veil, margin striate. Gills free, crowded, yellow. Stipe 8–15 × 2–3 cm, narrowing at top, hollow when mature, with yellow falling ring, slightly swollen at base, with large white membranous volva. Flesh whitish, yellowish beneath cuticle. Without evident odour. Spores white, elliptical, smooth, 8–14 × 5–8.5 microns.

Edibility Excellent cooked.

Habitat In open parts of dry oak woods, in slightly acid ground and with pines.

Season Spring to autumn. In Europe, especially in warmer areas. Not known in Britain.

Note In North America there is a common form that may be a distinct species and that has a somewhat umbonate cap, a thinner (1–2 cm) yellow stipe and occurs from eastern Canada to Florida and west to the central United States; the same or a similar form occurs in the southwest and Mexico.

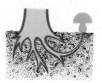

---

2 AMANITA MUSCARIA MUSCARIA

Common name Fly agaric.

Etymology From Latin, 'of flies', because of the northern European folk custom of using the cap, soaked in milk, to kill or stupefy flies.

Description Cap 8–25 cm, hemispherical to slightly concave, cuticle detachable, red, covered with white pyramidal warts that may be removed by rain, margin striate. Gills white, crowded, free. Stipe 12–25 × 1.5–2.5 cm, basal bulb with volva of several concentric warty rings, ring white, membranous. Flesh soft and white, orange-red beneath cuticle. Not very conspicuous odour. Spores white, ovoid, smooth, 9–11 × 6–8 microns.

Edibility Fairly poisonous, depending on the season.

Habitat Under birch, less commonly with conifers.

Season Autumn. Common.

Note Reported from Siberia as producing hallucinations. The red-capped North American variety found in northern forests and higher altitudes in the south causes delirium, manic behaviour and deep sleep, sometimes accompanied by profuse sweating.

3 AMANITA MUSCARIA (American Form)

Common name   American fly agaric.
Etymology   From Latin, 'of flies'; see previous entry.
Description   This variety has a yellowish to orange coloration, or has a tinge of red at the centre. All the velar remains (ring, volva and warts) are white and the description of *A. muscaria* (**2**) applies to this variety in all other respects.
Edibility   Toxicity appears to vary widely from place to place and seems to lie for the most part in the cap cuticle.
Habitat   This variant is very common in North America, but becomes rarer, more slender and tinged with a salmon-like coloration in the southern states. In western North America we also find the typical red-capped *A. muscaria* (**2**).
Season   Summer and autumn.

Note   Although the toxins in both the species and this variant are reportedly concentrated in the coloured skin of the cap, peeling the mushroom does not render it harmless and poisonings do occur. The hallucinations for which the red-capped Siberian variety is notorious do not seem to occur with either American variety; rather, the experience is often one of delirium and deep sleep, sometimes accompanied by profuse sweating.

4 AMANITA PHALLOIDES

Common name   Death cap.
Etymology   From Latin, 'phallus-like' because of the shape of the carpophore in the early stages of growth.
Description   Cap 5–20 cm, subspherical to flat, rarely with membranous velar remains; fairly deep olive green to olive brown but paler towards margin, usually with dark innate radial fibrils. Gills white or slightly yellowish, quite crowded, free. Stipe 8–20 × 1–2 cm, tapering towards top, hollow when mature, white speckled with greenish-grey stripes, white, membranous ring, striate at top, base bulbous with large, white membranous volva. Flesh white, but greenish-yellow just beneath cuticle. Odour first neutral, then nauseous. Spores white, ovoid to nearly round, smooth, 8–11 × 7–9 microns, amyloid.
Edibility   **Deadly poisonous.**
Habitat   With a preference for broadleaved trees, particularly oak.
Season   Autumn. Widespread in southern England.

Note   When cut, the outline of the carpophore is white, faintly green in the cuticle area. As little as one cap can prove fatal to an adult. Symptoms do not occur for about 10–12 hours (or longer).

5 AMANITA CITRINA

Etymology From Latin, 'lemon-like', because of the colour of the cap.

Description Cap 6–12 cm, hemispherical to flat, cuticle various shades of yellow, covered with flat, irregular warts, whitish turning to brown, margin smooth. Gills crowded, whitish, free, sometimes semi-free. Stipe 6–12 × 0.5–1.5 cm, whitish cap coloured with membranous ring, bulbous base, whitish turning to brown, with a large, punky, marginate volva. Flesh white, faintly yellow beneath cuticle. Odour of radish or potato. Spores white, subglobose, smooth, 7–10 × 6–7 microns, amyloid.

Edibility Slightly poisonous when raw, rather mediocre cooked.

Habitat Preferably beneath broadleaved trees.

Season Autumn.

Note The presence of an irritant substance like that secreted by the skin glands of toads makes this mushroom slightly poisonous when eaten raw.

Caution A. citrina should not be eaten either raw or cooked because its cap colour is often difficult to distinguish from that of the deadly A. phalloides (**4**).

6 AMANITA GEMMATA

Etymology From Latin, 'bejewelled', because of the warts on the cap.

Description Cap 4–8 cm, hemispherical to flat, cuticle slightly sticky, straw or orange-yellow, sometimes with floccose volva fragments, easily detachable, margin finely striate. Gills free, semi-free, or slightly adnate, white. Stipe 6–10 × 1–2 cm, narrowing towards top, full when mature, whitish, with fragile, short-lived ring, volva close to basal bulb, which may split into one or two rings or collars. Flesh tender, white, slightly lemon yellow beneath cuticle. No odour. Spores white, elliptical, smooth, 10–12 × 7–8 microns.

Edibility Edible, although it has apparently caused cases of poisoning.

Habitat Beneath broadleaved and coniferous trees, with a preference for acid soil. In Britain it is uncommon, usually found with conifers.

Season Autumn.

7   AMANITA VERNA

Common names Fool's mushroom; spring destroying angel.

Etymology From Latin, 'spring', which is when it appears.

Description Cap 3–10 cm, hemispherical to flat, cuticle white, silken, sometimes with shades of ochre at centre, normally without universal velar remains, margin thin and smooth. Gills white, crowded and free. Stipe 7–13 × 1–1.5 cm, narrowing at top, hollow when mature, white with ring and membranous sac-like volva, both fairly close, base sometimes slightly enlarged. Flesh white. No odour in young specimens, pungent in mature ones. Spores white, subspherical, smooth, 8–10 × 7–9 microns, amyloid.

Edibility Deadly poisonous.

Habitat Preference for broadleaved trees in fine, sandy, acidic soil.

Season Spring and summer, also found in autumn. Rare in Britain.

Note Unlike many poisonous plants, which are bitter or otherwise unpalatable, some poisonous mushrooms, and especially the deadly *Amanitas*, taste good. It takes 8–12 hours or more before the appearance of any symptoms.

8   AMANITA VIROSA

Common name Destroying angel.

Etymology From Latin, 'fetid', because of its smell.

Description Cap 4–10 cm, conical to convex, never completely opened, white. Cuticle detachable, margin smooth. Gills white, crowded, free with pruinose aspect. Stipe 8–15 × 1–1.5 cm, narrowing at top, hollow when mature, with woolly-fibrillose surface, ring incomplete and fragile, volva membranous, sac-like and close to stipe. Flesh white, soft. Usually an unpleasant, yeast-like odour. Spores white, round, smooth, 9–12 microns, amyloid.

Edibility Deadly poisonous.

Habitat Preference for broadleaved trees. Rare in southern England, more frequent in Scotland.

Season Autumn.

Note The cuticle of this species gives a golden yellow reaction with KOH, a reaction lacking in *A. verna* (**7**).

9 AMANITA SPISSA

Etymology From Latin, 'massive' or 'huge', because of its appearance.

Description Cap 7–15 cm, hemispherical to flat, grey-brown with greyish-white mealy patches, margin smooth. Gills white, crowded, free. Stipe 8–12 × 1–2.5 cm, narrowing towards the top, full, with a white, membranous ring, striate like the upper part of the stipe, small, close, brown scales beneath, basal bulb (or napiform base), volva reduced to a zone of small scales. Flesh white, constant, firm. Slightly radish-like odour. Spores white, ovoid, smooth, 8–10 × 6–8 microns, amyloid.

Edibility Good, but caution is required. See **Note** below.

Habitat In broadleaved and coniferous woods.

Season Summer and autumn. Common.

Note This species should not be eaten unless the identity is first checked by an expert, since it can be readily confused with allied poisonous species.

Caution See **Note**

---

10 AMANITA PANTHERINA

Common name Panther cap.

Etymology From Latin, 'panther', because of the spotted appearance of the cap.

Description Cap 6–12 cm, hemispherical then flat, cuticle brown covered with small pyramidal warts, short-lived margin clearly striate. Gills white, crowded, free. Stipe 6–12 × 0.5–2 cm, tapering towards the top, with membranous white ring with striate surface towards the gills and basal bulb with a marginate volva often split into two or three rings. Flesh white, not very firm. Odour at first neutral, then acrid and nauseous, flavour quite sweet. Spores white, ovoid, smooth, 10–12 × 7–8 microns.

Edibility Poisonous, symptoms similar to those produced by A. muscaria (**2**), but more serious.

Habitat Beneath broadleaved and coniferous trees.

Season Autumn. Occasional.

Note The cap colour varies from dark brown to yellowish or cream to nearly white and its best identifying characteristics are its collar-like volva, striate cap margin and typically unchanging white flesh. Another striking feature, especially evident in the more commonly found dark forms, is the contrast between cap colour and the snow-white scales.

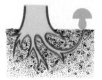

11 AMANITA RUBESCENS

Common name Blusher.

Etymology From Latin, 'reddening', because of the discoloration of the flesh on bruising or ageing.

Description Cap 5–20 cm, semi-globose to flat, cuticle reddish-brown to whitish, with wine red markings, covered with greyish pink warts, easily washed off by rain, margin smooth. Gills free, crowded, white, with wine red markings particularly after being picked. Stipe 7–20 × 1–3 cm, fairly sturdy at first, tapering towards top, hollow when mature, tawny to brown, with coppery shades, large membranous ring, white often speckled with reddish-brown markings especially at edge, basal bulb with scattered wart-like universal velar remains. Flesh white, slowly turning to red when exposed to air, especially stipe. Odourless. Spores white, ovid, smooth, 8–10 × 6–7 microns, amyloid.

Edibility Excellent cooked or fried, **toxic raw**.

Habitat In broadleaved and coniferous woods.

Season Late summer to autumn. Very common.

Note If for eating take care not to collect *A. pantherina* (**10**), which differs in snow-white warts on cap, a very distinct collar-like volva and flesh that does not redden on exposure.

Caution Toxic when raw. See **Note**.

---

12 AMANITA SOLITARIA

Etymology From Latin, 'solitary', because generally isolated specimens are found.

Description Cap 5–20 cm, hemispherical to flat, cuticle moist and whitish, with large flat-topped, greyish warts, margin smooth, large velar remains. Gills white, crowded, free or slightly adnate. Stipe 6–25 × 1.5–3.5 cm, white, sturdy, always solid, cottony, with short-lived ring, mealy velar remains. Flesh white, soft. Odour insignificant. Spores white, elliptical, smooth, 10–13 × 7–9 microns, amyloid.

Edibility Good, better when earthy-tasting cuticle is removed.

Habitat In sunny areas in broadleaved woods, especially with birch, in southern England.

Season Summer to early autumn. Occasional.

Note Similar to *A. solitaria* is *A. echinocephala* (**13**), which occurs in similar habitats, sometimes even growing with it, but differing in having prominent pointed warts on the caps and gills of a creamy or greenish tint, especially in old fruit-bodies.

13 AMANITA ECHINOCEPHALA

Etymology From Greek, 'spiny-headed'.
Description Cap 7–20 cm, subglobose, hemispherical, convex, flat or slightly depressed, whitish tending to become ochre-coloured, covered with large pyramidal warts (usually pointed), on the whole adherent then falling off from the edge inwards, margin with cottony remains of partial veil, cuticle completely removable. Gills whitish, free or slightly adnate, with creamy, cottony quality, crowded, with cream-yellow or pale green shading when mature. Stipe sturdy, 8–20 × 1.5–2.5 cm, often with bulb, tapering towards top and pointed at base, whitish, covered at base with scales of the same colour. Ring large, membranous, striate lengthwise, floccose at the margin. Flesh off-white, soft, especially in the stipe, tending to pale yellow when drying. Slightly earthy odour, no significant flavour. Spores white, with green or yellow shades of colour, elliptical, smooth, 9–12 × 8–11 microns, amyloid.
Edibility Non-toxic, but poor in flavour.
Habitat Under broadleaved trees, especially birch in southern England, in calcareous soil, in dry sunny places.
Season Summer, autumn. Occasional.

---

14 AMANITA INAURATA

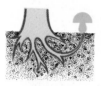

Etymology From Latin, 'gilded', from the cap colour.
Description Cap 8–12 cm, campanulate to convex, with slight umbo if flat or depressed, varying from greyish-brown to olive-ochre-yellow to yellowish-brown and other shades. Darker at the disc, with paler marginal area, markedly striate, with charcoal grey velar patches. Gills free, whitish, turning grey or cream-coloured when mature. Stipe 12–20 × 1.5–3 cm, slightly narrower at top, no ring, with grey or brownish stripes, hollow, with white volva turning greyish, reduced to ring fragments at base that is only slightly enlarged. Flesh white. No odour. Spores white, spheroid, smooth, 12 × 14 microns.
Edibility Adequate.
Habitat Usually in deciduous woodland.
Season Autumn. Rare.
Note The group of ringless *Amanita* species has many members with distinctive features that overlap in the intermediate forms and are thus not easily identifiable. Because of the difficulty encountered in identification, mushrooms so identified should not be eaten.

15 AMANITA FULVA

Synonym *Amanita vaginata* v. *fulva*.

Common name Tawny grisette.

Etymology From Latin, 'reddish' or 'tawny', after the colour.

Description Cap 4–10 cm, conical to flat, reddish-yellow, glabrous, markedly striate margin. Gills white, free, long, crowded. Stipe 8–12 × 0.5–1.5 cm, narrowing at top, whitish or uniformly pale orange, ringless, volva whitish, membranous, sheath-like. Flesh fragile and white. Odour neutral. Spores white, spherical, smooth, 8–12 microns.

Edibility Mediocre.

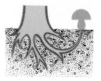

Habitat In acid ground, under broadleaved trees.

Season Summer and autumn. Very common.

Note A stipe with orange scales and the orange interior of the volva are the distinguishing features of *A. crocea*, a similar though less common species mainly found in broadleaved woods.

---

16 AMANITA UMBRINOLUTEA

Etymology From Latin, 'yellowish-brown', after the colour of the cap.

Description Cap 4–10 cm, conical then flattened with a central umbo, colour varying from brown to ochre-grey, margin markedly striate, with darker zonation at start of striations. Gills crowded, long, free and white. Stipe 8–17 × 0.5–2 cm, narrowing at top, tapered, hollow when mature, white with orange-brown stripes, ringless, volva membranous, tall, sheath-like, whitish. Flesh fragile, subtle, white. Odourless and without specific flavour. Spores white, elliptical, ovoid, smooth, 11–16 × 9.5–13 microns.

Edibility Good.

Habitat Preference for beech and fir woods, often in open places.

Season Summer to autumn. It is uncertain whether this species occurs in Britain. However, it is found in Europe.

Note In the very large group of species that resemble *A. vaginata*, this one is easily recognizable because of the darker circular area before the cap striations and because of the spores, which are not round.

17 LIMACELLA GUTTATA

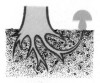

Synonyms *Limacella lenticularis; Lepiota lenticularis.*
Etymology From Latin, 'with droplets'.
Description Cap 4–12 cm, subglobose to convex-campanulate, pinkish-cream-coloured, deeper at disc, paler at margin, which is slightly glutinous in damp weather, otherwise smooth and glabrous. Gills whitish, sometimes with olive green shading, free, crowded, ventricose, often forked. Stipe 8–10 × 1–2 cm, white or cream-coloured, cylindrical or slightly enlarged at the base, solid, the upper part covered with droplets of moisture in very damp or wet weather. Ring membranous, pendent, whitish, marked like the stipe. Flesh white, faintly reddish near base, yellowish at base. Strong odour of flour, flavour sweetish. Spores white, elliptical, smooth, 7–8 × 4–5 microns.
Edibility Good.
Habitat In damp, coniferous woodland.
Season Autumn. Rare.
Note A relatively rare genus, *Limacella*, like *Amanita*, contains white-spored mushrooms (with free or nearly free gills) that develop within an egg-like universal veil, but in *Limacella* this veil is slimy.

---

18 CYSTODERMA AMIANTHINUM

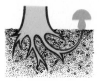

Etymology From Greek, 'uncontaminated' or 'pure'.
Description Cap 3–5 cm, ochre-yellow tending to orange, quite fleshy, convex then flat with slight umbo at centre, furfuraceous and granulose, often rugose. Gills cream-coloured, adnate, crowded. Stipe 3–6 × 0.4–0.6 cm, whitish above ring, covered below it, with ochre-coloured granules, cylindrical. Ring ochreous, inferior, granulose like stipe. Flesh yellow, darker towards base. Loamy odour and sweetish flavour. Spores white, elliptical, smooth, typically 4.5–7.5 × 3–3.5 microns, amyloid.
Edibility Medicore.
Habitat In coniferous woods and on healthland and moors.
Season Autumn. Occasional.
Note *Cystoderma* is a genus of white-spored mushrooms that are generally orange in colour and have a granular cap and stipe, with attached gills and usually a ring. Most are difficult to identify without a microscope and chemicals. *C. amianthinum rugosoreticulatum* has a distinctly wrinkled cap, a strong green-corn odour and is usually found in moss.

19 CYSTODERMA CARCHARIAS

Etymology From Greek, 'with a rough surface'.
Description Cap 2–5 cm, sometimes white but usually shaded with pinkish- or, more rarely, pale lilac, convex, flat, often umbonate, covered with minute granules, with appendiculate margin or cap edge. Gills white, crowded, adnate. Stipe 3–6 × 0.4–0.8 cm, cap-coloured below ring and covered with small pointed warts, white higher up, slightly enlarged at base and slightly narrower at top. Ring of the same colour, smooth on interior, like the lower part of the stipe externally. Flesh whitish or ochreous. String fetid smell and unpleasant flavour. Spores white, elliptical, smooth, 4–5 × 3–4 microns, amyloid.
Edibility Can be eaten though quality poor.
Habitat Conifers. Rare in southern England, less so in Scotland.
Season Autumn.
Note It is not clear whether *Cystoderma* is symbiotic or saprophytic. *C. ambrosii* is an entirely white species with the cap initially covered with small conical warts, becoming fairly smooth, as does the stipe. *C. ponderosum*, with the cap up to 11 cm, is ochreous or yellowish-brown, scaly, with a whitish stipe and inconspicuous ring. Although occurring in Europe, neither species is known in Britain.

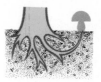

---

20 MACROLEPIOTA PROCERA

Synonym *Lepiota procera*.
Common name Parasol mushroom.
Etymology From Latin, 'tall', after its height.
Description Cap 10–25 cm or more, whitish with a thick brown cuticle that breaks up into large scales, short-lived and detachable from the edge inwards, remaining whole on the wide raised umbo. Mainly oval, then broadly campanulate turning to flat, with fibrillose, frayed edge. Gills whitish, turning darker, free, crowded, ventricose, wide, soft. Stipe 15–30 × 1.5–2 cm or larger, with brown snake-like marking prominent, base with large flat bulb. Ring movable. Flesh soft in cap, fibrous in stipe, whitish. Pleasant odour and hazelnut-like flavour. Spores white, elliptical, smooth, 15–20 × 10–13 microns, dextrinoid.
Edibility Cap excellent.
Habitat Occasionally in meadows and edges of woods.
Season Autumn.
Note This mushroom is delicious, so keep in mind its salient features: long, slender, scaly stipe, scaly cap with an often prominent umbo, free gills and ring that can be loosened and freely moved up and down the stipe.

21 MACROLEPIOTA RHACODES

Synonym *Lepiota rhacodes.*
Common names Shaggy parasol; wood parasol.
Etymology From Greek, 'frayed' or 'ragged'.
Description Cap 7.5–20 cm, globose then convex to flat,
cuticle brownish, smooth, soon breaking into concentrically
arranged polygonal scales, cap margin usually frayed. Gills
whitish, bruising yellowish to brown, free, crowded. Stipe
10–20 × 1.5–2.5 cm, club-shaped, often with large basal
bulb; double ring, frayed, movable, white, aging brownish.
Inconspicuous odour and flavour. Spores 8–15 × 6–8 microns, white, elliptical, smooth, dextrinoid.
Edibility The caps are very good but see **Note** below.
Habitat Beneath trees in parks and shrubberies, and in
woods. Common.
Season Autumn.
Note A salient feature of this species is that the flesh
reddens or becomes saffron-orange especially in the resulting socket when cap and stem are separated.

---

22 MACROLEPIOTA PUELLARIS

Synonym *Lepiota puellaris.*
Etymology From Latin, 'child-like', because of its pure
white colour.
Description Cap 4–8 cm, campanulate then convex, white,
slightly raised at the ochre-coloured disc, turning brown,
with the surface breaking up into small floccose, raised
scales, tending to be darker at the tip. Gills white, free, fairly
crowded. Stipe 9–13 × 1–2 cm, enlarged at the base, almost
bulbous, narrowing toward the top, hollow, slightly farinose
above the ring, white. Ring white, movable. Flesh white,
pinkish at edges of stipe, where it is also fibrous. Odourless
and with no specific flavour. Spores white, elliptical,
smooth, 12–18 × 7–8 microns, dextrinoid.
Edibility Good.
Habitat In meadows or in sunny woods, prefers conifers,
often in groups. Rare in Britain.
Season Autumn.
Note The slight colour change of the flesh may cause
confusion with *M. rhacodes* (**21**), of which it has long been
considered a variety.

23 LEUCOAGARICUS PUDICUS

Etymology From Latin, 'chaste', from its pure colour.
Description Cap 5–10 cm, white or whitish, with slight shades of pink or yellow, globose then spreading, with a hint of an umbo, cuticle thin giving the cap, when it breaks up, a granular or pubescent appearance, but never squamose. Gills white, free, ventricose, crowded, soft. Stipe 4–8 × 1–1.5 cm, white, narrowing towards the top, hollow when mature, fibrous, slightly enlarged at the base, with a white ring, ascending, with frayed margin, short-lived (dropping off) in old specimens. Flesh white, thick in the cap, soft. Odourless and without specific flavour. Spores white, slightly pinkish, ovoid, smooth, 7–9 × 4.5–6 microns, dextrinoid.
Edibility Young caps very good, but see **Caution**.
Habitat In meadows, gardens and open woodland. Common.
Season Autumn.
Note It resembles the field mushroom, *Agaricus campestris* but has white spores.
Caution This ubiquitous mushroom may cause digestive upsets; grey-capped or iodine-smelling forms should not be eaten.

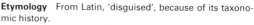

24 CYSTOLEPIOTA ADULTERINA

Etymology From Latin, 'disguised', because of its taxonomic history.
Description Cap 2–5 cm, semi-globose-campanulate, then spreading, mainly whitish, then greyish-brown, rather rust-coloured in old damp specimens, covered in thick farinose granulation. Gills whitish, tending to turn greyish. Stipe 4–6 × 0.3–0.6 cm, tapered, mealy like the cap, whitish then with rust-coloured marking, veil with mealy consistency only visible in young specimens. Flesh whitish, tending to turn red in stipe towards bottom. No particular odour or flavour. Spores white, elliptical, smooth, 5–6 × 2–2.5 microns.
Edibility Not known.
Habitat Broadleaved woods, usually under beech. Rare.
Season Summer and autumn.
Note The veils that envelop the embryonic carpophores consist of spheroid-shaped cells. Their remains on the cap and stipe have a mealy texture for this reason.

25 LEPIOTA CRISTATA

Etymology From Latin, 'crested', because of the ornamentation of the cap.

Description Cap 3–4 cm, campanulate then spreading, often with a large obtuse umbo, whitish, fibrillose, with adpressed reddish-brown scales and entire similarly-coloured disc. Gills white, free, crowded. Stipe 4–6 × 0.3–0.7 cm, white, fibrillose, tending to turn yellow or pale reddish-brown, cylindrical fragile, almost smooth, with a small membranous ring, often reddish, short-lived. Flesh white, reddish, fine. Strong, unpleasant, acidic flavour. Spores white, wedge-shaped, smooth, 6–8 × 3–4 microns, dextrinoid.

Edibility Poisonous.

Habitat In humus-rich ground, in shady woodland or in gardens. Common.

Season Autumn.

Note Various small species, with the cap covered in scales or brownish warts, are very poisonous. One such is *L. helveola*; the cap is initially ochre-coloured, turning reddish when picked; ring often conspicuous.

26 LEPIOTA CLYPEOLARIA

Etymology From Latin, 'shield-shaped'.

Description Cap 3–8 cm, campanulate then spreading with large obtuse umbo, cuticle brown, breaking up outside disc into large numbers of small scales or granules, margin with festooned velar remains. Gills white or cream-coloured, free, soft and wide. Stipe 6–8 × 0.4–1 cm, covered with cottony down below ring, which is also floccose and not always conspicuous. Flesh white, soft. Slightly fruity odour and sweetish flavour. Spores white, fusiform, smooth, typically 12.5–14 × 4.5–5 microns, dextrinoid.

Edibility Not recommended (see **Caution**).

Habitat Woodland.

Season Autumn. Rare.

Note This species is recognized by the cottony material on the stipe and confirmed by an examination of its distinctive, elongated, spindle-shaped spores.

Caution Although edible, this species is one of several small *Lepiotas* about which little is known except that some are poisonous. For this reason, and because of difficulty of identifying it with any certainty in the field, it should *not* be eaten.

27 LEPIOTA ACUTESQUAMOSA

Synonym *Lepiota friesii.*
Etymology From Latin, 'sharp-scaled'.
Description Cap 8–10 cm, hemispherical then convex, flattened latterly, dark brown covered with downy, pointed, reddish-brown warts. Gills white, free, straight, often forked. Stipe 8–11 × 1.5–2 cm, same colour as cap, cylindrical or enlarged and squamose at base, with white, descending ring that is pendant. Flesh white tending to turn yellow. Strong, somewhat acid odour and fairly unpleasant flavour. Spores white, elliptical, smooth, 7 × 3–4 microns, detrinoid.
Edibility Not recommended becasue of the disagreeable flavour.
Habitat In bare ground in gardens, near trees or in woods of broadleaved trees, in particular oak and beech.
Season Autumn. Occasional.
Note There are several similar species with raised, pointed cap scales; none is known well enough to recommend as edible.

28 MARASMIUS ANDROSACEUS

Common name Horsehair fungus.
Etymology From a Greek word for an unknown marine plant.
Description Cap 0.4–1 cm, fairly umbilicate, radially striate, whitish or washing to (or entirely) pinkish-brown or cocoa brown. Gills fairly distant, cap-coloured. Stipe 3–6 × 0.1 cm, filiform, strong, black, glabrous, straight, twisted and striate when dry, directly inserted in substrate with black rhizomorphs present about base. Flesh virtually non-existent. No distinctive odour or flavour. Spores white, elliptical, smooth, 6.5–9.5 × 3–4 microns.
Edibility Of no value because of size.
Habitat Grows in large numbers on fallen conifer needles.
Season Autumn. Common.
Note A similar but foul-smelling species is *M. perforans* (**32**). Another similar species is *M. splachnoides*, which has a whitish cap with the disc fairly pinkish-yellow and the stipe very villose in the upper part; it grows on dead oak and chestnut leaves. The fruit-bodies of *M. hudsonii* grow on holly leaves and are entirely covered with long hairs; *M. buxi* is found on box leaves with short hairs on just the stipe.

29 MICROMPHALE FOETIDUM

Synonym *Marasmius foetidum.*
Etymology From Latin, 'foul-smelling'.
Description Cap 1.5–4 cm, fairly dark brown, membranous, sometimes almost diaphanous, convex becoming flat then depressed, radially striate and plicate. Gills reddish, adnate or slightly decurrent, distant and connected by venations. Stipe 1–4 × 0.1–0.2 cm, brown quickly becoming blackish, narrowing abruptly towards base, velvety, in rare cases with mycelial formation, roundish at base. Flesh fine, yellowish in cap, blackish-brown in stipe. An odour and flavour of putrid water, also slightly garlicky. Spores white, elliptical or pear-shaped, smooth 8–12 × 4–6 microns.
Edibility Non-toxic, but terrible flavour.
Habitat On rotting branches and twigs in broadleaved woods.
Season Autumn. Occasional.
Note *M. inodorus* is very similar, with whitish gills, but has no odour. The nasty odour does, however, occur in some other species: *M. brassicolens*, in small groups on detritus and leaves of beech trees; *M. perforans* (**33**); and *M. acicola*, which forms dense groups of fruit-bodies on needles of conifers.

---

30 MARASMIUS RAMEALIS

Synonym *Marasmiellus ramealis.*
Etymology From Latin, 'of branches', from its habitat.
Description Cap 0.6–1.5 cm, white, reddish at disc, convex then flat and eventually also depressed, slightly rough. Gills white or pinkish, cream-coloured, not very crowded. Stipe 6–10 × 0.1–0.2 cm, whitish, reddish at base, often curved, mealy and squamulose in upper half. Flesh whitish, reddish-brown at base. No odour or flavour. Spores white, elliptical, smooth, 8.5–10.5 × 3.4 microns.
Edibility Of no value because of size.
Habitat In groups on dead wood and sticks, in woods.
Season Autumn. Common.
Note *M. amadelphus* grows on conifer wood, with a pale ochre cap, whitish at edge, slightly pruinose beneath the microscope, striate; stipe is usually cap-coloured. *M. tricolor* and *M. omphaliformis* have a fairly deeply depressed cap and fairly decurrent gills. The former, growing on grass debris, has a white cap, cream-coloured gills and the stipe turning from whitish to brown-grey or blackish. The latter species, which is not British, has a brownish-yellow diaphanous cap, distant white gills and a yellowish stipe.

31 MARASMIUS OREADES

Common name Fairy-ring champignon.
Etymology From Greek, 'of the mountains'.
Description Cap 2–6 cm, convex becoming eventually flat, sometimes slightly depressed with a slight umbo the colour of yellow leather, ochreous, more brightly coloured in young specimens, tending to turn pale when drying with striate margin when wet. Gills whitish, free, wide alternating with lamellae. Stipe 4–10 × 0.2–0.4 cm, pale ochre, cylindrical, very sturdy, elastic, solid with mycelium at base. Flesh fine, pale ochre, leathery in stipe. Pleasant cyanic odour, and a tasty flavour. Spores white, elliptical, smooth, 8–10 × 5–6 microns.

Edibility Caps very good, ideal for drying.
Habitat Meadows, grassland and roadsides, in lines or rings.
Season May to October. Common.
Note Tiny amounts of highly toxic hydrocyanic or prussic acid are sometimes produced when the basidia mature, causing a faint almond odour but not affecting edibility.
Caution Do not confuse with toxic *Clitocybe dealbata* (attached to slightly decurrent gills), nor with whitish species of *Inocybe* (producing a brown spore-print).

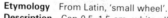

32 MARASMIUS ROTULA

Etymology From Latin, 'small wheel'.
Description Cap 0.5–1.5 cm, white all over or with central umbilicate part shaded with yellow or grey, membranous, never flat, plicate or with margin regularly crenate. Gills white, adnate, typically attached to a collar that may or may not be attached to stipe. Stipe 2–5 × 0.1 cm, filiform, blackish, horny, striate when dry. Flesh almost non-existent. No odour or flavour. Spores white, piriform, smooth, 7–10 × 3.5–5 microns.

Edibility Of no value because of size.
Habitat In groups on wood or dead roots, in woods.
Season Late summer to autumn. Common.
Note Almost identical *M. bulliardii* grows on leaves; the centre of the small depression is a black or brown point. Two species with the cap umbilicate, grooved and plicate, and identical gills grow on grass debris: *M. limosus* and *M. graminum*. The former may also grow on debris of sedges, with a brownish-ochre cap, uniform and pale, with 6–10 gills; the latter has a red, orange-red, or reddish-brown cap, often with a brown or blackish papilla.

33 MICROMPHALE PERFORANS

Synonym *Marasmius perforans.*
Etymology From Latin, 'making a hole'.
Description Cap 0.8–1.2 cm, whitish turning reddish, convex becoming flat and slightly umbonate with striations. Gills whitish, adnate, fairly crowded, connected by venations. Stipe 2–3 × 0.1 cm, brown turning blackish, pinkish at the top, tough and velvety. Flesh virtually non-existent. Strong odour and flavour of putrid water, with a hint of garlic. Spores white, lanceolate, smooth, 5.5–6 × 3 microns.
Edibility Of no value because of size and flavour.
Habitat On conifer needles, one or two fruit-bodies per needle. Occasional.
Season Autumn.
Note *Marasmius*, *Marasmiellus*, and *Micromphale* are three very similar genera that differ microscopically and chemically.

34 COLLYBIA DRYOPHILA

Synonym *Marasmius dryophilus.*
Etymology From Greek, 'living among oaks'.
Description Cap 2–5 cm, colour varying from whitish, ochreous, reddish to brown, often paler towards the edge, diaphanous in wet weather, smooth. Gills quite crowded, white, adnate. Stipe 4–7 × 0.2–0.4 cm, whitish or yellowish or orange-brown, glabrous at the base as well, which often has small mycelial threads, fistulose, tough. Flesh white, ochreous when wet or damp. No special odour or flavour. Spores white, elliptical, smooth, 4.5–6 × 3–4 microns.
Edibility Mediocre.
Habitat In small groups in broadleaved and coniferous woods.
Season Autumn. Common.
Note *C. butyracea* (**43**) is very similar but the cap has a buttery feel and the spore-print has a pinkish tinge. In late summer and autumn *C. dryophila* may be found parasitized by what looks like a translucent jelly fungus, but is actually deformed inflated *C. dryophila* tissue covered by a very thin layer of a fungus called *Christiansenia mycetophila.*

35 MARASMIUS ALLIACEUS

Etymology From Latin, 'garlicky'.

Description Cap 1–4 cm, campanulate, then flattened and mildly umbonate, eventually striate and grooved radially, turning from whitish to grey-brown with age. Gills whitish, sometimes apparently free, usually adnexed, ventricose, with edge curled when dry. Stipe 4–20 × 0.2–0.4 cm, blackish, tough, rigid, almost cylindrical, pruinose and velvety, extending into rhizomorphs or covered with hairs at base. Flesh white, blackish in stipe. Strong odour and flavour of garlic. Spores white, almond-shaped, smooth, 8–11 × 6–7 microns.

Edibility Caps good for flavouring or seasoning.

Habitat Beechwoods on chalk, wood or dead leaves, rarely found beneath other broadleaved trees.

Season Autumn. Occasional in the south of Britain. Widespread in Europe.

Note The odour is strong and persistent. Other species also have a marked garlicky odour: *M. prasiosmus* with a light brown cap, ochre or brownish stipe narrowing towards top, markedly tomentose, base woolly with mycelium that clings to and embraces the litter, especially with oaks; *M. porreus*, yellowish with striate cap edge, stipe reddish, pubescent, hairy at base, gills yellowish, flesh red and juicy; and *M. scorodonius* (**36**).

---

36 MARASMIUS SCORODONIUS

Etymology From Greek, 'garlicky'.

Description Cap 1–3 cm, orange-ochre with rapid tendency to lose its colour, becoming whitish from the edge, membranous, soon flat, with wavy margin. Gills whitish, adnate, connected by veins, fairly crowded and slender. Stipe 2–5 × 1–0.2 cm, dark red-brown towards base, smooth, glabrous, almost shiny, tough and hard, cylindrical or more often enlarged towards the top. Flesh meagre. Strong smell and flavour of garlic. Spores white, lanceolate, smooth, 5–9 × 3.5–5 microns.

Edibility Caps can be used for flavouring.

Habitat On sticks, roots, bits of wood, leaves or needles, in acid soil.

Season Autumn. Occasional.

Note The caps of the larger species of the *Marasmius* group that smell of garlic are usable, fresh or dried, as flavouring. Some foul-smelling species may have a slight garlicky smell but are inedible, such as *M. perforans* (**33**), *M. foetidum* (**29**) and to a lesser extent *M. impudicus*, which is brown with pinkish shading, more conspicuous on the gills, and has a stipe covered with fine whitish down becoming floccose at the base.

37 COLLYBIA PERONATA

Synonym *Marasmius peronatus.*
Common name Wood woolly foot.
Etymology From Latin, 'booted', from the shape of the base.
Description Cap 3–7.5 cm, yellowish or pale brick red, eventually light ochre-brown, convex then flat, depressed and umbonate, rough, with a striate cap edge.Gills cream-coloured then ochreous-brown or cap-coloured, adnexed then detached, free, crowded. Stipe 5–9 × 0.2–0.6 cm, cap-coloured, narrowing towards top, slightly curved, base covered with evident white or yellowish hairs, solid. Flesh pale yellow, rather leathery. Insignificant odour, but spicy flavour. Spores white, elliptical, smooth, 6–8 × 3–4 microns.
Edibility Used as flavouring because of sharp taste.
Habitat In litter and wood detritus, especially broadleaved.
Season Autumn. Common.
Note The litter of broadleaved woods plays host to groups of *Marasmius wynner*, with a campanulate cap, initially white with faint pink or violet shading, stipe leathery, white, supple and brownish at base. It is pleasant to eat, with the same odour as *M. oreades* (**31**).

38 OUDEMANSIELLA RADICATA

Synonym *Collybia radicata.*
Common name Long root.
Etymology From Latin, 'with roots'.
Description Cap 3–15 cm, olive brown, brownish-grey or whitish, campanulate then expanded, umbonate, often irregular, humped, radially rough, very slimy in wet weather, smooth when dry. Gills bright white, with cream-coloured or brownish areas at the edge in old specimens, almost free, ventricose, quite distant. Stipe 10–20 cm or more with a diameter of 0.5–1 cm, whitish or pale brown-ochre, narrowing towards top, with an enlarged base extending into the ground with a long rooting appendage, fusiform, smooth at the end, lengthwise striations, cartilaginous. Flesh white, soft in cap, fibrous in stipe. No particular odour or flavour. Spores white, broadly elliptical, smooth, 14–15 × 8–9 microns.
Edibility Mediocre because of cap's slimness.
Habitat Very common in beechwoods, buried wood or rotting wood or tree stumps.
Season Late summer to autumn.
Note *O. longipes* is dry and has a velvety stipe and pruinose, sooty grey-brown cap.

39 OUDEMANSIELLA MUCIDA

Synonyms *Mucidula mucida; Armillaria mucida.*
Etymology From Latin, 'viscid' or 'slimy'.
Description Cap 3–8 cm, pure white or shaded with grey or olive green at centre, thin, almost diaphanous, hemispherical then convex, obtuse, fairly rough radially, with cap edge tending to becoming striate as it becomes thinner. Gills white turning to cream, adnate-decurrent, distant, wide, thin, soft. Stipe 4–7.5 × 0.4–1.5 cm, white with base enlarged and covered with small blackish-brown scales, tough, elastic, curved, striate above ring. Ring white, then turning darker when drying, pendent, often grooved. Flesh white, mucilaginous. No particular odour or flavour. Spores white, globose, smooth, 15–17 microns.
Edibility Non-toxic but indifferent flavour.
Habitat Isolated or in small clusters on beech trunks, very rarely on oak and birch.
Season Autumn. Common.

40 STROBILURUS TENACELLUS

Synonym *Collybia tenacella.*
Etymology From Latin, 'quite tough', because of the consistency of the stipe.
Description Cap 1–3 cm, greyish-brown turning paler, very rarely whitish, convex or broadly conical-campanulate, then flat, sometimes slightly raised at centre, moist. Gills greyish then white, with frequent tendency to turn yellow, adnexed, crowded. Stipe 2–6 × 0.2–0.3 cm, white, soon turning ochre-brown, white at top, cylindrical, with rooting base extending into a dark brown fibrillose mycelial thread. Flesh leathery and tough in stipe, softer in cap, white. Slightly mealy odour, somewhat bitter flavour. Spores white, elliptical, smooth, 4–5 × 2.5–3 microns.
Edibility Mediocre.
Habitat On buried or moss-covered pinecones or on spruce cones.
Season Autumn to early spring. Common.

41   COLLYBIA CONFLUENS

Synonym   *Marasmius confluens.*
Etymology   From Latin, 'confluent', because of the tufted stipes.
Description   Cap 2–4 cm, campanulate, convex then flat, slightly raised at centre, yellowish-white, with reddish or pinkish shades, slightly hygrophanous, silken when dry, cuticle not detachable, cap edge often wavy when old. Gills very crowded, small, white turning to cream, pale nut brown. Stipe 6–12 × 0.2–0.3 cm, cylindrical, often slightly curved, same colour as cap, downy from top to bottom, hollow, compressed, flared and pruinose at top, leathery. Flesh whitish, thin. Odour initially cyanic. Spores white, elliptical, smooth, 7–12 × 3–6 microns.
Edibility   Only the caps are good.
Habitat   In clusters in broadleaved woods.
Season   Autumn. Common.
Note   *C. hariolorum*, if a distinct species, forms tufted fruit-bodies on the leaf litter, especially beneath beech. The stipe is finely velvety, downy at base, whitish or cream-coloured, often spotted with red. Gills crowded but longer than those of *C. confluens*. The odour is like Camembert cheese.

42   COLLYBIA CIRRHATA

Etymology   From Latin, 'fringed' or 'frayed', because of the base of the stipe.
Description   Cap 0.5–1 cm, white, reddish-brown at centre, or ochreous, initially convex then flat, slightly depressed, often with a very small central protuberance, cuticle slightly silken, often broken up concentrically when mature, slightly grooved, Gills white, crowded, unequal, adnexed, separate from stipe when mature. Stipe 2.5–5 × 0.1 cm, whitish, rather filiform, supple with powdery surface that extends to the base in a tuft of interwoven fibrils. Flesh white, very meagre. Spores white, elliptical, smooth, 4–5 × 2 microns.
Edibility   Of no value because of size.
Habitat   On the remains of old mushrooms, in woods among dead leaves.
Season   Autumn. Common.
Note   *C. cookei* and *C. tuberosa* are very similar and found in the same habitat; the former originates from a roundish, yellowish-orange sclerotium, the latter from an appleseed-shaped, brownish sclerotium.

43 COLLYBIA BUTYRACEA

Common name   Buttery collybia.

Etymology   From Latin, 'of butter' or 'buttery'.

Description   Cap 5–8 cm, reddish-brown, purplish-grey, tending to turn yellow when dry, convex then expanding, fairly umbonate, smooth, greasy to the touch, Gills white, slightly adnexed, sometimes free, thin, crowded, with a crenate edge. Stipe 5–8 × 0.5–1 cm, ochreous or greyish, conical and narrowing towards top, white and downy at the base, with a rigid cuticle, cartilaginous, striate, smooth, rarely downy. Flesh pinkish or very light brown, then white, soft and watery. Rancid odour, sweetish flavour. Spores whitish, creamy pink in mass, arched, smooth, 6.5–8 × 3–3.5 microns.

Edibility   Mediocre.

Habitat   In woods.

Season   Autumn. Common.

Note   *C. dryophila* (**34**) is very similar but lacks a buttery feel to the cap and its pores are white in mass.

44   COLLYBIA FUSIPES

Common name   Spindle shank.

Etymology   From Latin, 'spindle-footed'.

Description   Cap 4–10 cm, reddish-brown tending to fade or darken, convex then flat, centre slightly raised, smooth, dry, edge often incised. Gills whitish, becoming cap-coloured with dark brown spots, adnexed then separate and almost free, distant, connected by veins. Stipe 7–15 × 1 cm, cap-coloured, cartilaginous, enlarged, ventricose at centre, narrowing at top and bottom, pointed at base, compressed, often curved, striate-grooved lengthwise, almost blackish at base. Flesh cap-coloured, fading with age, firm. Faintly rancid odour, sweet flavour. Spores whitish, creamy pink in mass, elliptical, smooth, 5–6 × 3–4 microns.

Edibility   Mediocre, see **Note** below.

Habitat   Tufted at base of oaks, chestnuts or old tree stumps.

Season   Late summer and autumn. Common.

Note   The stipes of the carpophore grow from the remains of the fruit-bodies of previous years, which form a sort of hypogeal sclerotium. This species can sometimes cause stomach upsets, not least because the fruit-bodies that are dead remain for long periods virtually unaltered on the ground.

45 COLLYBIA MACULATA

Common name Foxy spot.
Etymology From Latin, 'spotted'.
Description Cap 7–12 cm, white then with reddish spots, sometimes becoming reddish all over, fleshy, compact, flat-convex, obtuse, smooth, with slender cap edge, initially involute. Gills cream-coloured, often with reddish spots, semi-free, straight, very crowded, denticulate. Stipe 7–12 × 1–2 cm, with reddish spots, sometimes ventricose, narrowing towards the base, compact, extremely fibrous, striate, cartilaginous, solid. Flesh firm and white. Flavour somewhat bitter or unpleasant. Spores whitish, creamy pink in mass, subglobose, smooth, 5–6 microns.

Edibility Mediocre, must be boiled.
Habitat In woodland, usually with conifers, gregarious, sometimes in rings.
Season Autumn. Common.

---

46 FLAMMULINA VELUTIPES

Synonym *Collybia velutipes.*
Common name Velvet shank.
Etymology From Latin, 'velvet-footed'.
Description Cap 2–10 cm, orange-red, yellower at edges and dark at centre, convex then flat, often eccentric, irregular, lobate, cuticle smooth, viscid, with slightly striate margin. Gills pale yellow tending to light nut brown, slightly adnexed, unequal. Stipe 5–10 × 0.4–0.8 cm, cylindrical and slightly tapered towards base, curved or twisted, yellow, velvety all over, soon becoming blackish-brown or black starting from the base, cartilaginous, tough. Flesh pale yellow, fine, watery and soft in the cap, leathery and fibrous in the stipe. Odour and flavour insignificant. Spores white, elliptical, smooth, 7–10 × 3–5 microns.

Edibility Caps quite tasty.
Habitat On dead wood, mainly stumps and roots or in wounds of living trees, often tufted.
Season Late autumn to early spring. Common.
Note One of the few gill-bearing fungi found in winter in temperate regions. Easy to cultivate and is sold in oriental food stores.

47 COLLYBIA RACEMOSA

Etymology From Latin, 'branched'.

Description Cap 0.5–1.5 cm, greyish, thin, convex then flat, often imperfectly formed, with a papilla at the disc, downy, striate. Gills greyish, adnate, small and quite crowded. Stipe 3–5 × 0.1 cm, grey with numerous single ramifications, almost perpendicular to the main axis, terminating in a capitate spheroid formation, transparent, slightly glutinous, producing asexual spores. The spite grows from a black sclerotium buried in the substratum. Flesh greyish. Odour insignificant. Spores white, elliptical, smooth, 5 × 2.5–3 microns.

Edibility Of no value because of size.

Habitat Grows on old mushrooms, especially large species of *Russula* and *Lactarius*.

Season Late summer and autumn.

Note This is a small, rather rare fungus with features that make it easy to identify. It may also live like a simple saprophyte with host carpophores.

---

48 MELANOLEUCA STRICTIPES

Synonyms *Tricholoma cnista; Melanoleuca cnista; Melanoleuca evenosa.*

Etymology From Latin, 'very straight-stemmed'.

Description Cap 6–15 cm, whitish-grey then cream white and darker at centre, convex then flat around umbo, fleshy, cuticle easily detachable, shiny when dry, tough, with fairly concentric crack lines. Gills whitish-cream, crowded, unequal, separable, uncinate, not venose. Stipe 6–10 × 0.6–1.5 cm, colour of gills, pruinose at top, solid, hard, quite slender, subbulbous at base, fibrillose. Flesh white turning to brownish when exposed to air, tender, fibrous in stipe, thick at centre. Odour of anise, flavour first sweet then bitter. Spores white, elliptical-ovoid, verrucose, 8–10 × 4–4.5 microns, amyloid.

Edibility Good but not to everyone's taste.

Habitat Gregarious, in rings or lines, in wet riverside meadows and in mountain pastures.

Season An early species, spring to autumn. Occasional.

Note In meadows large carpophores of *M. grammopodia* grow, with a brownish rounded cap and fibrillose striate stripe. *M. subbreviges* is possibly a variety of it, but has a cap up to 30 cm in diameter, with a short fragile stipe of 5–7 × 1.–1.3 cm. Although edible, their strong odour puts some people off.

49 MELANOLEUCA MELALEUCA

Synonym *Tricholoma melaleucum.*

Etymology From Greek, 'black and white', because of the contrast between gills and cap.

Description Cap 4–10 cm, grey-brown or soot-coloured, brighter in wet or damp weather, convex then flattened, with fairly conspicuous central umbo, fleshy. Gills snowy white, crowded, ventricose, worn at edges. Stipe 5–10 × 0.5–1.2 cm, cap-coloured, covered with brownish fibrils, base darker and slightly bulbous, covered with whitish fluff, solid, elastic. Flesh whitish in dry weather, pale ash grey when wet, yellowish in stipe, turning brownish and rather leathery with age. No particular odour or flavour. Spores white, elliptical, spotted, 7–10 × 5–6 microns, amyloid.

Edibility Fair.

Habitat Grows in clearings and meadows and in both broadleaved and coniferous woods.

Season Autumn. Common.

50 ASTEROPHORA LYCOPERDOIDES

Synonym *Nyctalis asterophora.*

Etymology From Greek, 'like a puffball'.

Description Cap 1–2 cm, first white or whitish then quickly turning brownish-ochre, becoming cottony and powdery after the formation of asexual spores (clamydospores). Gills white, then brown, adnate, distant, thick, sometimes forked or absent. Stipe 1–3 × 0.3–0.8 cm, white then greyish-brown, pruinose, solid. Flesh dark grey. Odour and flavour insignificant. Sexual spores white, ovoid, smooth, 5–6 × 3.5–4 microns. Asexual spores brown, spiny, winged, round-ish, 12–18 microns.

Edibility Of no value becaue of size.

Habitat Isolated or in groups, with a preference for the large carpophores of blackening *Russulas* (in the *Russula nigricans* group).

Season Autumn. Occasional.

Note A similar fungus is *A. parasitica*, which also grows on *Russulas* of the *R. delica* (**141**) group, or on white *Lactarius* species. It is more tapered and has a grey silken cap with radial fibrils; and never becomes powdery. It also produces clamydospores that are fusiform and smooth in the gills among the basidia.

51 CYPTOTRAMA CHRYSOPEPLUM

Synonym *Collybia lacunosa.*
Etymology From Greek, 'richly gilded'.
Description Cap 1.5–3 cm, fairly fleshy, subglobose, convex then expanded, margin slightly striate, dry, orange-yellow, covered with spines that initially form pyramidal warts joined at the apex, then separate to form a hairy layer of the same colour. Gills whitish then pale yellow, quite distant, adnate-decurrent. Stipe 2.5–5 × 0.2–0.4 cm, sometimes a bit eccentric, golden or sulphur-yellow, almost cylindrical, solid, surface squamulose, then furfuraceous. Flesh yellowish-white, orangish at base and beneath cuticle. No distinctive odour or flavour. Spores white, elliptical, smooth, 10–12 × 3.5–4.5 microns.
Edibility Uncertain.
Habitat Isolated or in small groups on rotting wood in tropical forests throughout the world, and therefore not in Britain or Europe.
Season In rainy periods.
Note The early stages of the carpophores resemble those of the small and conspicuously aculeate species of *Lycoperdon* (puffballs). Quite common and easily recognizable in its habitat, this fungus has been included in many different genera and has had many names.

---

52 CATATHELASMA IMPERIALE

Synonyms *Biannularia imperialis; Armillaria imperialis.*
Etymology From Latin, 'imperial', from its size.
Description Cap 5–20 cm, hemispherical to flat, often with a wavy cap edge, cuticle dry, brown, at first having cottony velar remains, tending to crack from the centre outwards, margin involute. Gills crowded, small, decurrent, whitish to light hazel with blackish edge. Stipe 6–12 × 2–5 cm, squat, solid, pointed at the base, whitish or ochreous, with two membranous rings, the upper deriving from the partial veil, the lower from the universal veil. Flesh firm, hard and white. Strong mealy and watermelon-like odour, flavour pleasant but slightly astringent. Spores white, elliptical, smooth, 12–15 × 5–7 microns.
Edibility Mediocre; good when preserved in vinegar or oil.
Habitat Beneath conifers, in groups.
Season Autumn. Rare in Europe. Not known in Britain.

53 LYOPHYLLUM DECASTES

Synonyms *Tricholoma aggregatum; Lyophyllum aggregatum; Clitocybe multiceps.*

Etymology From the Greek, 'a company of ten men', from its tufted habit.

Description Cap 5–15 cm, greyish or leather-coloured, fleshy, convex then expanded, often depressed and wavy, smooth. Gills whitish, crowded, adnate. Stipe 4–7 × 0.5–1.5 cm, cylindrical, tough, whitish, pruinose at top, solid. Flesh whitish, firm, fairly leathery in stipe. Slightly mealy odour, sweetish flavour. Spores white, roundish, smooth, 5–7 × 5–6 microns.

Edibility Very good, ideal for preserving in liquid.

Habitat In tufted groups, rarely isolated, in woods and open places near trees.

Season Autumn. Common.

Note *L. loricatum* has a cap that is initially blackish, then the cuticle breaks up into tiny granules as the surface expands, revealing the white background and giving the fungus a spotted or speckled look. *L. fumosum* has a cap that fades and the gills tend to become greyish. The stipes can be found growing together or ramified. Poisonous *Entoloma* species have salmon pink prints.

---

54 TRICHOLOMA BATSCHII

Etymology After the German mycologist Batsch.

Description Cap 6–9 cm, chestnut brown, reddish, convex becoming flattened, initially viscous, then faintly fibrillose when dry, with smooth margin. Gills adnate, whitish then developing dense reddish spots. Stipe 5–10 × 1–2 cm, solid, cylindrical or slightly narrowing towards top, white and furfuraceous uppermost, the rest cap-coloured. Flesh white, spotted reddish at edge or where eaten by larvae. Odour of watermelon or bugs, very bitter flavour. Spores white, round, smooth, 5–6 microns.

Edibility Inedible because of flavour.

Habitat In broadleaved woods, especially oak and chestnut.

Season Summer and autumn. Not yet identified in Britain but may occur.

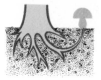

Note The clearly two-coloured stipe delimits the whitish top in the form of a ring. Similar species include *T. aurantium*, orange-red with a sometimes pungent green-corn odour; *T. albobrunneum*, reddish-brown with conspicuous zonation, a dry, fibrillose cap, somewhat bitter, beneath conifers in mountainous areas; *T. pessundatum*, smelling of flour, beneath conifers; *T. ustaloides* (**66**); *T. ustale*, beneath broadleaved trees, bitter. The last three species have a viscous cap and inconspicuous zonations.

55 TRICHOLOMA COLUMBETTA

Etymology From its former name in France.

Description Cap 6–10 cm, snowy white, first ovoid or campanulate, then flat, sometimes a central umbo, fleshy, slightly viscous, shiny, silken, cuticle detachable, margin at first curled towards the gills then unfolding and becoming undulate, sometimes splitting in the direction of the gills. Gills white, crowded, unequal, fairly small, adnate. Stipe 4–8 × 0.8–2 cm, white with pale bluish-green areas or more rarely reddish at the base where it is often more slender, more rarely with a squat base, solid, fibrous and sericeous. Flesh very white, soft, fibrous in stipe, unchanging. Slight odour, flavour sweetish. Spores white, elliptical, smooth, 5–7 × 4–5 microns.

Edibility Good but slightly fibrous.

Habitat In groups in woods, beneath broadleaved species.

Season Autumn. Occasional.

Note The absence of strong odour and sharp flavour should prevent confusion with *T. album* (**56**), also lacking the typical greenish-blue marking at base of stipe. *T. resplendens* is also white, although the cap has fairly bright shades of ochre, with no markings at base, and the odour is pleasant and aromatic.

---

56 TRICHOLOMA ALBUM

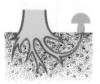

Etymology From Latin, meaning 'white'.

Description Cap 5–12 cm, white, sometimes ochreous at the disc, convex turning flat, fleshy, glabrous, with the margin initially incurved. Gills white, not very crowded, adnate. Stipe 7–8 × 1–1.5 cm, sometimes very long, narrowing towards the top, at times sinuate and also narrowing towards the base when growing deep in the leaf litter, mealy at the tip, rarely striate, solid. Flesh white, soft and fragile in the cap, fibrous in the stipe, with a strong smell of gas and flour when broken. Flavour at first just a little bitter, then hot. Spores white, elliptical smooth, 4.5–7 × 3–4.5 microns.

Edibility Inedible, probably slightly poisonous.

Habitat Broadleaved or mixed woods.

Season Summer and autumn. Common.

Note *T. inamoenum* grows underneath conifers in mountainous areas; it also has a strong smell of coal gas. Stipe and gills, which are fairly distant, are both white, whereas the cap has a deeper ochreous colour at the disc. Other species with a strong mealy or rancid smell include *T. suphureum* (**68**) and *T. lascivum* (**60**), which are described in detail, and *T. bufonium*.

57 TRICHOLOMA FLAVOVIRENS

Synonym *Tricholoma equestre.*
Etymology From Latin, 'greenish-yellow'.
Description Cap 5–10 cm, sulphur or olive yellow, reddish at the centre due to tiny scales covering it, convex then becoming flattened and undulate, fairly raised umbo, cuticle detachable, fleshy, smooth, slightly viscid especially when immature, margin thin and curled. Gills lemon yellow or sulphur yellow, crowded, of average size, unequal, edge undulate. Stipe 3–8 × 0.6–1.8 cm, sulphur yellow and olive-coloured areas, sturdy, squat at the base, solid, fibrillose. Flesh whitish, pale yellow beneath the cuticle, thick at the centre, thin at the edge, soft. Odourless, with a mealy flavour. Spores white, elliptical, smooth, 6–7 × 4–5 microns.
Edibility Very good and much sought after.
Habitat In lowland and mountains, especially under conifers, more rarely under broadleaved species, prefers sandy soil.
Season Autumn. Rare in Britain, less so in Scotland.

58 TRICHOLOMA CALIGATUM

Synonym *Armillaria caligata.*
Etymology From Latin, 'with the foot covered'.
Description Cap 11–20 cm, first hemispherical with an involute edge; then convex, obtusely umbonate, grey-, ochreous-, or reddish-brown, with radial coloration, smooth with markedly adpressed fibrous scales on a white background, viscous in wet weather, shiny when dry. Gills adnate-rounded, cream-coloured, with reddish-brown spots when older, large and crowded. Stipe 9–20 × 2–3 cm, cylindrical or tapered towards bottom, white above membranous ascending ring, below it cap-coloured with age, with scaly areas resembling girdles. Flesh white, soft, fairly fibrous in stipe. Pleasant, slightly fruity odour, sweetish flavour with a somewhat bitter aftertaste. Spores white, oval, smooth 5.5–8 × 4–5.5 microns.
Edibility Excellent.
Habitat Gregarious in coniferous woods.
Season Summer and autumn. Central and southern Europe. This species does not occur in Britain.

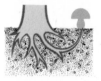

59 TRICHOLOMA IMBRICATUM

Etymology From Latin, 'like roof tiles', from scaly cap.

Description Cap 4–10 cm, reddish-brown, convex then expanded, obtusely umbonate, smooth and fleshy at centre, culticle dry, scaly, cracked, edge involute then thin and woolly. Gills white with reddish spots, quite distant, large, notched near stipe. Stipe 5–10 × 1–1.5 cm, white and pruinose at top, whitish with brown at the base, cylindrical but quickly becoming hollow, fibrillose. Flesh white, brownish at base of stipe, thick only at the centre. Odourless, sometimes with a slightly bitter aftertaste. Spores white, oblong, smooth 5–7 × 4–5 microns.

Edibility Mediocre.

Habitat In small groups in pinewoods, also beneath larch, in lowland and mountains.

Season Autumn. Occasional.

Note Other species are common in coniferous woods and have distinctive features: *T. aurantium* has an orange-red cap and almost the entire stipe is covered with small scales of the same colour, which form a band at the glabrous top, and its flesh is bitter and reddens in the stipe; *T. psammopum*, occasional under larch, has an ochreous-red cap, downy with tufted fibrils. The stipe is covered with orchreous or orange cottony scales.

60 TRICHOLOMA LASCIVUM

Etymology From Latin, 'licentious', from its odour of cheap face powder.

Description Cap 5–9 cm, light ochreous-brown at the disc, fading to white at the edge, fleshy then flat, eventually slightly depressed, delicately pubescent then smooth, dry, with the margin initially involute. Gills whitish, curved and adnexed, eventually adnexed-decurrent, not always straight, crowded. Stipe 7.5–11 × 1 cm, whitish, turning slightly darker when rubbed or with age, rigid, fibrillose, the top white and pruinose, downy at the base. Flesh thick, firm and white. Very pervasive odour of lilacs, flavour somewhat bitter. Spores white, elliptical, smooth, 6–7 × 3.5–5 microns.

Edibility Can be eaten. See **Note**.

Habitat In the litter of beech and oak woods.

Season Autumn. Common.

Note *T. inamoenum*, another member of this genus, emits a very strong but not unpleasant smell of acetylene. It grows in coniferous woods in mountains, with a whitish cap and yellow shading. Very liable to be confused with *T. album* (**56**) and so best not eaten.

61 TRICHOLOMA PORTENTOSUM

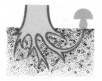

Etymology From Latin, 'monstrous'.
Description Cap 4–12 cm, dark grey with olive yellow coloration, fine radial striations throughout changing from violet to black, convex then flat and umbonate, edge thin, often cracked radially, cuticle sticky and easily detachable. Gills initially whitish then pale yellow, distant, unequal, quite large, sinuate at stipe. Stipe 5–10 × 1–2 cm, whitish with pale yellow or greenish-grey shades, cylindrical, enlarged at base, first solid then hollow, fibrillose. Flesh pale yellow or white, greyish beneath cuticle, thick at centre, thin at edge, fragile. Slight odour and flavour of flour. Spores white, elliptical, smooth, 6–8 × 3–4.5 microns.
Edibility Very good.
Habitat Grows alone or in groups in coniferous and broad-leaved woods.
Season Autumn. Occasional.
Caution Some grey-capped species of *Tricholoma* are poisonous, so identify with great care.

62 TRICHOLOMA SAPONACEUM

Etymology From Latin, 'soapy', because of the odour.
Description Cap 5–10 cm, grey-brown or greenish or of various other colorations, convex becoming flat, with a tendency to crack in dry weather, slightly greasy or viscous if wet, with curled margin. Gills white shading to pale blue, with a tendency to develop reddish spots, distant and adnate. Stipe 5–10 × 1.5–2 cm, whitish, reddish from base, often curved, narrowing at the base, rooting. Flesh white, sometimes reddening particularly at the base, soft. Odour sometimes of lavender or soap, flavour sweetish. Spores white, elliptical, smooth, 5–6 × 3–4 microns.
Edibility Can be eaten, but not very pleasant.
Habitat Gregarious, sometimes almost tufted in coniferous and broadleaved woods.
Season Autumn. Common.
Note A very variable species, *T. saponaceum* is always identifiable by the reddish area at the base of the stipe.

63 TRICHOLOMA SEJUNCTUM

Etymology From Latin, 'separate'.

Description Cap 7.5–10 cm, pale greenish-yellow with blackish fibrils arranged radially, darker at disc, pale yellow or whitish towards margin, which is curled or involute, turning from convex to expanded, humped, rarely umbonate, slightly viscid in damp weather. Gills white, often with yellowish shading, quite distant, adnate. Stipe 6–12.5 × 1.5–2.5 cm, white with yellow markings, ventricose then almost cylindrical, minutely furfuraceous at top. Flesh white, pale yellow beneath cuticle and on sides of stipe, fragile. Mealy odour, slightly bitter flavour. Spores white, subglobose, smooth, 5–7 microns.

Edibility Edible but not tasty.

Habitat In broadleaved woods, especially with oak and chestnut, and in mixed woodland.

Season Autumn. Occasional.

Note The cap is the same colour as *Amanita phalloides* (**4**), and also streaked toward the edge. However, it is easily distinguished from the species in lacking both a ring and volva.

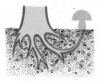

64 TRICHOLOMA TERREUM

Etymology From Latin, 'earth-coloured'.

Description Cap 4–8 cm, campanulate or conical, then flat, fairly umbonate, often cracked, covered with small silken radial scales, greyish or brownish, cuticle detachable, tough. Gills whitish then pale ash-coloured, fairly distant, long and large, unequal, sinuate at stipe, fragile, margin denticulate. Stipe 3–5 × 0.5–1 cm, cylindrical, solid then subfistular, fragile, white shaded with pale ash grey, greyish veil fairly conspicuous, quite long-lasting. Flesh greyish-white, thin, fragile. Mild odour, sweetish flavour, somewhat bitter when mature or old. Spores white, elliptical, smooth, 5–8 × 4–5 microns.

Edibility Very good, particularly when young.

Habitat In groups, almost tufted, or in rings in woodland, especially beneath conifers.

Season Autumn. Fairly common.

Note There are several similar species, not all of which are edible, having a dry greyish cap with radial scales or fibrils. *T. triste* has odourless flesh and a large partial veil shaped like a curtain that leaves no traces on the stipe but remains appendiculate from the cap edge. The status of the fungus in Britain is uncertain.

65 TRICHOLOMA PARDINUM

Synonym *Tricholoma tigrinum.*
Etymology From Latin, 'striped'.
Description Cap 6–8 cm, slate or silver-grey or dirty white, slightly suffused with violet, sometimes darker at centre, hemispherical or campanulate then convex-obtuse or slightly umbonate, sometimes depressed when old, fleshy, cuticle easily detachable with silky brownish scales, adpressed, rectangular, denser at the centre, fairly concentric, margin curled then straight, often cracked or split. Gills yellowish-white with olive green shading, crowded, unequal, long, worn near stipe, to which they are only slightly adherent, if at all. Stipe 4–10 × 1–4 cm, white and pruinose at top, fibrils half-way down or covered with small brownish scales, base often enlarged and fairly dark brownish, sturdy, solid and fibrous. Flesh greyish-white in cap, yellowish at base of stipe. Faint mealy odour and flavour. Spores white, ovoid, smooth, 8–10 × 6–7 microns.

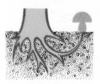

Edibility Poisonous.
Habitat Under conifers.
Season July to October. Although well-known in Europe, it does not occur in Britain.
Note Its close resemblance to *T. terreum* (**64**) makes this a particularly dangerous mushroom. It causes severe gastric upset.

---

66 TRICHOLOMA USTALOIDES

Etymology Similar to *T. ustale*, from its 'burnt' colour.
Description Cap 5–10 cm, thick, fleshy, compact, almost hard, almost hemispherical becoming eventually flat, slightly raised at disc but more often depressed, with incurved margin, quite often ribbed at edge, bright reddish-brown, not fading, shiny, viscid then dry, with innate scales resembling stains. Gills white with reddish highlights and reddish spots when mature, margin irregular, adnate, not very crowded. Stipe 6.5–10 × 1–1.5 cm, solid, slightly cavernous in upper part when mature, cylindrical or enlarged or fusiform at base, reddish-brown or reddish-ochre, darker towards base, which is shaded with white at top, pruinose, otherwise with darker squamulae and fibrils. Flesh white, tending to redden especially where eaten by larvae, thick and solid. Strong mealy odour and flavour. Spores white, subglobose or broadly elliptical, smooth, 6–7 × 4.2–5 microns.

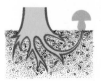

Edibility Fair.
Habitat Common in broadleaved woods.
Season Autumn. Common.
Note *T. ustale*, also edible, lacks a mealy smell and has a chestnut brown cap, ochreous-brown at the edge; its stipe is white with reddish fibrils when mature.

67　TRICHOLOMA VIRGATUM

Etymology From Latin, 'striped' or 'barred', because of the fibrils on the cap.

Description Cap 4–8 cm, ash grey with violet shading, darker at the centre, conical then expanded, fairly pointed umbo, cuticle detachable and dark, silky fibrils. Gills greyish-white, fairly crowded, uncinate. Stipe 5–10 × 0.5–1.8 cm, whitish, cylindrical, smooth and solid. Flesh whitish. Odourless, with a pungent flavour after prolonged chewing. Spores white, elliptical, smooth, 6–7 × 4–5 microns.

Edibility This species is suspected of causing mild cases of poisoning.

Habitat Grows in particular under fir and beech.

Season Autumn. Occasional.

Note The flesh has a particularly sharp taste, which nevertheless differs from that of other fungi like the *Russula* and *Lactarius* groups; the effect resembles being pricked with tiny needles on the tip of the tongue.

68　TRICHOLOMA SULPHUREUM

Etymology From Latin, 'sulphur-coloured'.

Description Cap 3–9 cm, sulphur yellow, often brownish at the centre, convex then flat, sometimes with a slight central umbo, sometimes slightly depressed, silky, dry, glabrous at the edge, which is involute. Gills sulphur yellow, quite distant, long and large, worn near the stipe. Stipe 2–8 × 1–2 cm, sulphur yellow, enlarged towards the base, striate lengthwise, solid at first becoming hollow, fibrous. Flesh sulphur yellow, sometimes lighter, fibrous. Odour of acetylene or coal gas, flavour mild. Spores white, elliptical, smooth, 8–10 × 5–6 microns.

Edibility Suspected of having caused cases of mild poisoning.

Habitat In broadleaved and coniferous woods.

Season Autumn. Occasional.

Note In rare cases the gills may be pinkish or lilac-coloured, typically in the variety *Rhodophyllum*. *T. bufonium*, which is very similar, can be considered a variety of *T. sulphureum*, with a brown or reddish-brown cap. The strong smell distinguishes it from *T. flavovirens* (**57**), one of the most sought-after species.

69 CALOCYBE IONIDES

Synonyms *Tricholoma ionides; Lyophyllum ionides.*
Etymology From Greek, 'violet-like'.
Description Cap 3–6 cm, deep violet, often brownish-blue at disc, fading with age, fleshy, convex-campanulate then flat, often obtusely umbonate, initially pruinose, soon becoming smooth except at incurved cap edge. Gills white tending to turn pale yellow, adnate, crowded, thin. Stipe 3–6 × 0.7–1.2 cm, cap-coloured or paler, tough, elastic, narrowing or slightly enlarged at base, surface fibrillose or striate and fibrous, mycelium white, cotton or hairy at base, solid. Flesh white, violet beneath cuticle and at base of stipe. Mealy odour and flavour, at times strong. Spores white, elliptical smooth, 5–6.5 × 2–3 microns.
Edibility Good.
Habitat Gregarious, especially in leaf litter in beechwoods on chalk.
Season Autumn. Occasional in south-east England.
Note In rare cases the cap may be pinkish or cream-coloured. Especially beneath conifers, seldom in broad-leaved humus, is *C. obscurissima*, a more slender species with a violet-brown cap and stipe.

70 CALOCYBE CARNEA

Synonym *Tricholoma carneum.*
Etymology From Latin, 'flesh-coloured'.
Description Cap 2–3 cm, reddish then pale flesh-coloured, paling further, shiny, thin, hemispherical becoming flat, rarely raised at the centre, smooth and dry. Gills pure white, rounded near the stipe, virtually free, very crowded. Stipe 2–5 × 0.2–0.6 cm, same colour as cap, narrowing towards the base, tough, almost cartilaginous, sometimes pruinose at the top. Flesh white, thin. Odourless, no particular flavour. Spores white, elliptical, smooth, 4–6 × 2–3 microns.
Edibility Mediocre.
Habitat In meadows, fields and lawns.
Season Autumn. Common.
Note *C. persicolor* is very similar and has a distinctive pink coloration like peaches; it grows in tufts in well-manured fields or by the roadside. The cap and stipe are the same colour but the gills are white.

71 CALOCYBE GAMBOSA

Synonym *Tricholoma georgii.*
Common name St. George's mushroom.
Etymology From Latin, 'large-legged'.
Description Cap 5–10 cm or more, hemispherical then convex, very fleshy and thick, then distended, normally humped, dry, finely velvety, colour from white to buff to yellowish, margin smooth, pruinose, curled, only later expanded and often sinuate. Gills growded, thin, whitish then cream-coloured, very small at first, adnate. Stipe 3–6 × 1–2 cm or more, sturdy, cylindrical but more often enlarged at base, whitish with ochreous markings towards bottom, fibrillose, pruinose at top, solid. Flesh compact, thick, white. Strong, pleasant smell of fresh meal, similar flavour but with resinous aftertaste. Spores white, elliptical, smooth, 5.5–6 × 3.5–4 microns.
Edibility Excellent and highly prized.
Habitat In grassland or scrub, in groups, lines or rings, often beneath shrubs.
Season Spring. Common.

72 TRICHOLOMOPSIS RUTILANS

Common name Plums and custard.
Etymology From Latin, 'reddening'.
Description Cap 5–20 cm, yellowish, thickly covered with reddish granulations that become small scales, fleshy, campanulate then convex and flat, often umbonate with involute edge, slightly grooved. Gills sulphur yellow, adnate, crowded and broad. Stipe 4–14 × 1–2.5 cm, uniform or enlarged or tapered at base, yellow, fairly covered with small reddish scales, pruinose at top. Flesh thick, soft, leathery in stipe, yellow. No particular odour or flavour. Spores whitish, oval or spherical, smooth, 5–8 × 4.5–6 microns.
Edibility Can be eaten, but taste unpleasant.
Habitat Isolated or in groups on stumps or roots of conifers.
Season Autumn. Common.
Note Other less common and smaller species grow on wood. *T. decora*, which is found only in Scottish pinewoods, has a cap up to 12 cm in diameter with blackish-brown scales at the centre. *T. platyphylla* has a golden yellow cap striped with greyish-brown or blackish innate fibrils, very long and large gills, and a large pithy stipe with rhizomorphs at the base.

73 LEPISTA GLAUCOCANA

Synonyms *Tricholoma glaucocana; Clitocybe glaucocana; Rhodopaxillus glaucocana.*

Etymology From Latin, 'whitish, pale blue-green'.

Description Cap 6–12 cm, convex-campanulate or flat and slightly umbonate, fleshy, blue-grey, lilac, violet, all pale, tending to fade more with age, disc shaded ochreous, margin involute. Gills cap-coloured, quite crowded, crenulated and adnate, detachable from cap. Stipe 6–10 × 1–2 cm, cap-coloured, pruinose at top, otherwise somewhat fibrillose, with an enveloping felt-like mycelium at the enlarged base, solid. Flesh whitish with pale lilac, violet, pale blue-grey shading, thick. Odour often loamy with an acrid-sweetish flavour. Spores whitish, shaded pink in mass, elliptical, minutely roughened, 6–8 × 3–5 microns.

Edibility Good.

Habitat Gregarious, on leaf litter in woods.

Season Autumn. Rare.

Note *L. saeva* grows in open places and in grassland, during late autumn, often in lines or rings; it has a pale brownish-ochre cap, gills lacking lilac and the stipe violet-lilac. *L. irina,* which is creamy flesh-coloured all over, has a sweet smell of orange or iris flowers. It is an uncommon species in beechwoods in southern England.

74 LEPISTA NUDA

Synonyms *Tricholoma nudum; Clitocybe nuda; Rhodopaxillus nudus.*

Common name Wood blewit.

Etymology From Latin, 'naked', from its smooth cuticle.

Description Cap 4–12 cm, convex, almost flat, rounded at edge when young, moist, smooth, pale reddish-brown or violet, more or less tawny-shaded in dry weather, fading with age. Gills thin, crowded, sinuate at stipe, fairly decurrent, light violet then brownish-violet. Stipe 5–10 × 1–2 cm, sturdy, fibrous, solid, with enlarged fleecy base with lots of mycelial hyphae, lilac or lilac-grey, covered with light, floccose fibrils. Flesh violet-white, fragile in cap, fibrous in stipe. Odour pleasant, flavour sweetish. Spores faintly pinkish in mass, elliptical, minutely roughened, 6–8 × 3–4 microns.

Edibility Excellent cooked (parboiling recommended), slightly poisonous raw.

Habitat In humus-rich ground in broadleaved and coniferous woods, shrubberies and gardens.

Season Usually in autumn, but also occurring in early winter. Common.

Note This species is common and easily recognized, and is often eaten. It is sometimes offered for sale in country areas.

Caution Slightly poisonous when raw.

75   LACCARIA AMETHYSTEA

Common name   Amethyst deceiver.
Etymology   From Latin, 'amethyst-coloured'.
Description   Cap 1.5–8 cm, initially convex and fairly umbilicate then expanded, depressed, sometimes perforated at the centre, margin thin, somewhat irregular when mature, often split, slightly striate, dark violet or discoloured depending on age and state of saturation of the cap, finely felt-like-squamulose. Gills distant, violet, adnexed-decurrent. Stipe 4–10 × 0.4–1 cm, cylindrical in young specimens, then compressed, fistulous, tomentose at half-way level, hairy at base. Flesh thin, hygrophanous, elastic, pale lilac-violet. Slightly fruity odour, sweet flavour. Spores white, globose, aculeate, 8.5–9 microns.
Edibility   Good.
Habitat   In coniferous and broadleaved woods and in scrub.
Season   Autumn. Common.
Note   This is an easily identifiable fungus because of the lilac-violet coloration of the carpophore. *L. bicolor* has a reddish cap but pale lilac gills and base of stipe.

76   LACCARIA LACCATA

Common name   Deceiver.
Etymology   From Persian, 'painted' or 'varnished'.
Description   Cap 1.5–5 cm, pale pinkish if wet or moist, ochreous when dry, convex then unevenly flat, fairly umbilicate-depressed, moist becoming dry, cuticle thick, broken up into small mealy scales, sometimes silky, undulate-wrinkled when mature. Gills flesh-coloured, powdery when mature, adnexed-decurrent, broad, thick and distant. Stipe 7–10 × 0.6–1 cm, cap-coloured, tough, fibrous, often supple, base whitish and hairy, fibrillose and striate, solid then hollow at cap attachment. Flesh cap-coloured, thin, quite tough in stipe. Insignificant odour and flavour. Spores white, globose, aculeate, 8–9 microns.
Edibility   Fair.
Habitat   Common in woods and heaths.
Season   Autumn.
Note   There are many similar species and a microscope is necessary for identification. We should mention *L. proxima*, which prefers marshy or boggy areas; the cap is relatively large, orange and squamulose; *L. tortilis*, a small fungus growing in damp or wet places with a striate, translucent cap; and *L. striatula* which grows in peat bogs. This, like the *L. tortilis*, has two-spored basidia.

77 LEUCOCORTINARIUS BULBIGER

Etymology From Latin, 'bulbed'.
Description Cap 5–10 cm, light brick yellow, often with velar remains, especially at the edge, in the form of cobweb-like or slightly membranous brownish scales, on a brown-ochreous background with pinkish shading, or reddish-brown or leather-coloured, at first hemispherical, moist, becoming almost flat. Gills white then cream-coloured, dirty reddish-brown, barely adnate, quite crowded. Stipe 5–10 × 1–1.2 cm, enlarged at the base in the form of an abrupt bulb, up to 2.5–3 cm wide, marginate, and with ringed remains of a cobweb-like veil, thick, whitish, occasionally with blackish fibrils, solid. Flesh white, reddish beneath cuticle and at cap attachment. No particular odour or flavour. Spores white, elliptical, roughened, 6–7 × 4–5 microns.

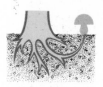

Edibility Quite good.
Habitat Coniferous woods.
Season Autumn. A rare species; in Britain occurring in Scotland.
Note The large conspicuous veil in young specimens and certain other characteristics suggest a *Cortinarius*, although this species has white, not rusty-orchre, spores.

---

78 CLITOCYBE PHYLLOPHILA

Synonym *Clitocybe cerussata* of some authors.
Etymology From Greek, 'leaf-loving'.
Description Cap 5–10 cm, convex then flat-depressed, co-vered as if with a silky white layer, especially near the edge, which conceals an ochreous, cream-coloured background appearing with age in the form of uneven speckling. Gills white, turning yellowish or pinkish-cream, adnexed-decurrent, fairly distant. Stipe 5–8 × 0.5–0.8 cm, cap-coloured, elastic, fibrous, cylindrical, hairy at the base, often curved. Flesh white, thin. Strong odour of rancid meal, flavour similar. Spores whitish, oval or subglobose, smooth, 4–5 × 3–4 microns.
Edibility Poisonous.
Habitat In groups on leaves, especially of beech.
Season Autumn. Common.
Note This species may be confused with *Clitopilus prunu-lus* (**162**), an edible pink-spored mushroom with long, decur-rent gills. Ingestion causes muscarine poisoning.

79 CLITOCYBE FLACCIDA

Etymology From Latin, 'limp', from flesh texture.
Description Cap 5–8 cm, rust ochre, reddish, or reddish-brown, shiny, not very fleshy, quite tough, limp when dry, always umbilicate then funnel-shaped, smooth, rarely squamulose. Gills whitish tending to turn yellow especially at the ends, decurrent, crowded, straight. Stipe 2.5–5 × 0.5–1 cm, reddish-brown, rust-coloured, elastic and tough, solid, cylindrical, enlarged and hairy at base. Flesh pale, thin, fragile, limp when dry. Cyanic odour and sweetish flavour. Spores white, globose, minutely warty, 3–4 microns.
Edibility Good.
Habitat Gregarious, often in rings, in broadleaved woods.
Season Autumn and winter. Common.
Note *C. gilva* (syn. *C. splendens*) grows in large groups in conifer woods and is further distinguished by having a yellowish cap. Similar but microscopically different fungi include *C. sinopica*, conspicuous red or reddish-brown, with a preference for coniferous burnt areas and *C. vermicularis*, flesh-red when wet, with white mycelial threads at the base.

80 CLITOCYBE GEOTROPA

Etymology From Greek, 'erect', because of its stance.
Description Cap 8–30 cm, chamois brown tending to turn pale, fleshy, broadly funnel-shaped with a central umbo, downy at the centre, margin involute, pubescent. Gills whitish, long and decurrent, pointed at the tips, quite crowded, soft. Stipe 5–10 × 1–4 cm, whitish, fibrillose-striate, elastic, narrowing towards the top, solid then pithy. Flesh whitish, thick, soft. Smell aromatic, flavour sweetish. Spores white, subglobose, smooth, 4–6 × 3–4 microns.
Edibility Very good when young.
Habitat In groups, sometimes in fairy-rings, in woodland.
Season Autumn. Occasional.

81 CLITOCYBE CLAVIPES

Etymology From Latin, 'club-footed'.

Description Cap 4–6 cm or more, amber to ash grey, sometimes whitish at the margin, rarely white all over, fleshy, slightly convex then flat, becoming eventually slightly concave, sometimes umbonate, smooth, although under the microscope it shows a fine covering of fibrils. Gills white, sometimes yellowish, long and decurrent, soft. Stipe 3.5–10 × 0.6–1.2 cm, at the base up to 4 cm, markedly club-shaped, soft, spongy, tough, sometimes fibrillose. Flesh ash grey then white, soft, thin at margin of cap. Pleasant smell, quite specific, flavour sweetish. Spores white, elliptical, smooth, 5–7 × 3–4 microns.

Edibility Mediocre, but see **Caution**.

Habitat In broadleaved and coniferous woodland.

Season Autumn. Common.

Note This species is quite distinctive because of its club-shaped stipe, which is soft and spongy. Some forms of *C. nebularis* (**83**) and *C. alexandri* may be similar.

Caution Should not be eaten with or followed by alcholic beverages: some people develop a headache and transient upper body rash, a 'poisoning' similar to but not the same as that caused by the ink cap *Coprinus atramentarius* (**223**).

---

82 CLITOCYBE LANGEI

Etymology After the Danish mycologist Lange.

Description Cap 1–3 cm, grey-brown tending to turn hazel when drying, or chamois- or cream-coloured, depressed, glabrous when mature, in young specimens covered with a fine pruinescence, striate when moist. Gills adnexed, slightly decurrent, grey or yellowish, unequal. Stipe cylindrical, greyish-brown, then light brown, slightly fibrillose, elastic, solid. Flesh thin, hygrophanous. Strong fragrant odour and flavour of meal. Spores white, tear-shaped, smooth, 5–6.5 × 2.7–3.2 microns.

Edibility Good.

Habitat In groups, beneath conifers and birch.

Season Autumn. Occasional.

Note This is a small aromatic fungus, not unlike *C. vibecina*, which grows in the same habitat, but is distinguished by its more elliptical spores.

83   CLITOCYBE NEBULARIS

Common name   Clouded clitocybe.
Etymology   From Latin, 'mist-grey'.
Description   Cap 7.5–20 cm, light, brownish, or dark grey, rarely white, sometimes as if covered with a whitish pruinosity but in fact glabrous, smooth, thick, convex then flat, eventually slightly depressed at disc. Gills whitish, sometimes with yellowish shades, short and decurrent, curved, crowded, thin. Stipe 7–12 × 2–3 cm, whitish, enlarged at base, narrowing at top, spongy and elastic. Flesh white and thick. Strong odour and flavour. Spores yellowish, elliptical, smooth, 7–8 × 3–4 microns.
Edibility   Good when cooked, but best avoided. May cause allergic upset.
Habitat   Common in woodland, gregarious, often in fairy-rings.
Season   Autumn and early winter.
Note   *C. alexandri* is a similar fungus which grows in woods; it has a brownish cap with grey or ochre shading, finely pubescent, with a club-shaped base with a mycelial tuft that envelops the substratum and leaves, and ochreous, light brown gills.

---

84   CLITOCYBE ODORA

Etymology   From Latin, 'perfumed'.
Description   Cap 3–9 cm, typically sea green; it fades on drying and is paler growing under leaves, from convex to flat, rarely depressed, or slightly umbonate, margin incurved, pubescent. Gills white to green-tinged, quite distant, adnexed-decurrent. Stipe 3–5 × 0.6–0.8 cm, cap-coloured, cylindrical, supple, floccose-fibrillose then smooth, hairy and enlarged at the base. Flesh dirty white, elastic. Very strong odour of anise, similar flavour. Spores white, elliptical, smooth, 6–8 × 3–4.5 microns.
Edibility   Good.
Habitat   Usually in broadleaved woods.
Season   Autumn. Occasional.
Note   Its presence is often given away by the strong odour of anise. Other species have the same odour, although to different degrees: *C. subalutacea*, pale yellowish; *C. obsoleta*, tufted; *C. fragrans*, whitish, non-umbilicate cap, growing in moss; *C. suaveolens*, very similar to the previous species with an umbilicate cap, darker at the centre, with margin striate.

85 ARMILLARIA MELLEA

Synonym *Armillariella mellea.*
Common names Honey fungus; boot-lace fungus.
Etymology From Latin, 'like honey', from its colour.
Description Cap 3–15 cm, globose, expanding, cuticle brownish-ochre with green and red shades, disc covered with erect brown hairs, spreading out towards the edge. Gills quite crowded, adnate, decurrent, whitish then yellowish, eventually with reddish spots. Stipe 10–20 × 1.5–5 cm, long, club-shaped, often curved, colour variable, darker towards the base, similar to cap colour, white ring, striate at top, yellowish and floccose at bottom. Flesh fine, fibrous in stipe, white. Oily odour, quite unpleasant, flavour somewhat bitter, slightly astringent. Spores white, elliptical, smooth, 7–9 × 5–6 microns.
Edibility Good when cooked, suitable for drying. Somewhat poisonous: parboiling is recommended.
Habitat Parasitic or saprophytic, typically clustered, in woodland, parks and gardens. A very destructive parasite of all woody plants.
Season Autumn. Common.
Note Differing only in its lack of a ring, *A. tabescens* is equally edible, given the above precautions.
Caution Somewhat poisonous.

86 OMPHALOTUS OLEARIUS

Synonyms *Clitocybe olearia; Clitocybe illudens.*
Common name Copper trumpet.
Etymology From Latin, 'of the olive (tree)', because of its habitat on this host in Europe.
Description Cap 6–14 cm, convex becoming funnel-shaped, with radial innate fibrils, dry, from light orange-yellow to mahogany brown, margin thin, often lobate and split. Gills very decurrent, crowded, unequal, orange-yellow, arcuate. Stipe 8–16 × 1–2 cm, central or eccentric, narrowing at base, striate-fibrillose, tough, cap-coloured. Flesh orange-yellow, staining, tough. Odour strong and oily, flavour astringent. Spores pale yellow-white, globose, smooth, 5–7 × 4.5–6.6 microns.
Edibility Poisonous.
Habitat At the foot of stumps or unhealthy trees or on the ground on roots, parasitic on broadleaved species, especially olive and oak.
Season Autumn. Very rare in Britain, occasional in central and southern Europe.
Note In the dark the gills of fresh fruit-bodies give off a greenish glow. Can be confused with the chanterelle (*Cantharellus cibarius*, **154**), which grows on the ground and has thick-edged forked ridges instead of gills, or with *Hygrophoropsis aurantiaca*, which has clearly forking gills.

87   LEUCOPAXILLUS GIGANTEUS

Synonym   *Clitocybe gigantea.*
Etymology   From Greek, 'gigantic', because of its size.
Description   Cap 30–40 cm, or more, convex then flat, depressed, eventually funnel-shaped, soft to touch, white with minute adpressed scales, silky, turning slightly brown, margin markedly involute, first pubescent then revolute and smooth and grooved with sometimes pale ochre small depressions, rarely split at grooves. Gills whitish then slightly ochreous, subdecurrent, often ramified and anastomosing, crowded, detachable from flesh. Stipe 3–7.5 × 2–5 cm, cylindrical or narrowing at top, with enlarged base, smooth or slightly pubescent, white. Flesh white, solid. Pleasant, mealy odour, sweet flavour. Spores whitish, broadly elliptical, smooth, 7–8 × 5–6 microns, amyloid.
Edibility   Very good.
Habitat   Gregarious, often in rings, in fields and meadows.
Season   Autumn. Uncommon.

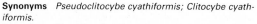

88   CANTHARELLULA CYATHIFORMIS

Synonyms   *Pseudoclitocybe cyathiformis; Clitocybe cyathiformis.*
Etymology   From Greek, 'cup-shaped'.
Description   Cap 2–7 cm, flat-depressed, eventually cup-shaped, sometimes undulate, ash grey/brown or dark grey, fading when dry, shiny when wet, opaque when dry, very hygrophanous, fairly striate at margin. Gills ash grey, greyish sometimes with reddish spots, adnate or decurrent, connate at stipe, rarely forked. Stipe 5–10 × 0.6–0.9 cm, greyish, elastic, narrowing towards top, fibrillose-reticulate, with white hairs at the base. Flesh watery, thin, greyish. Cyanic odour, sweetish flavour. Spores white, elliptical, 7.2–12 × 4–7.5 microns, amyloid.
Edibility   Fair.
Habitat   Especially on rotten wood; also in grass or moss in meadows, near trees and under bushes, often gregarious.
Season   Late autumn, winter, and spring. Common.
Note   This genus includes two other species that are likewise grey with amyloid spores: *C. expallens*, with deeply umbilicate cap, markedly striate, gills pointed at tips; and *C. obbata*, with very dark cap and gills and much lighter brown stipe.

89 MYCENA RIBULA

Synonym *Omphalina fibula; Rickenella fibula.*
Common names Little nail fungus.
Etymology From Latin 'pin-shaped'.
Description Cap 0.4–2 cm, usually orange-yellow, tending to turn paler when drying, membranous, campanulate soon becoming umbilicate and eventually funnel-shaped, glabrous, striate when wet. Gills whitish or yellowish, very decurrent, distant. Stipe 3–8 × 0.1–0.2 cm, cap-coloured, delicate, wavy in appearance, often pubescent under the microscope. Flesh very thin, cap-coloured. Spores white, elliptical, smooth, 3–4 × 2 microns.
Edibility Of no value because of size.
Habitat Typically in moss, in lawns or short grass.
Season Autumn. Common.
Note A very similar species, *Xeromphalina campanella*, is smaller, often gregarious and grows on the bark of conifer stumps. *Mycena swartzii* is a very common fungus found on lawns which has a pallid brown cap with a darker centre and a yellowish stipe, brown or dark violet at the top.

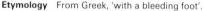

90 MYCENA HAEMATOPUS

Etymology From Greek, 'with a bleeding foot'.
Description Cap 2–4 cm, greyish with brownish and purple shades, tending to fade with age, dark at disc, conical then campanulate, obtuse, glabrous, with over-reaching margin in young specimens, slightly striate. Gills white then pinkish or violet, adnate. Stipe 5–10 × 0.2–0.5 cm, white, greyish, pinkish or violet, eventually ash grey, rigid but fragile, often curved at base, hairy, initially with a thick powdery pruinescence, short-lived, then smooth, producing droplets of blood red latex on cutting. Flesh fine, turns red. No odour or flavour. Spores white, elliptical, smooth, 8–11 × 5–7 microns, amyloid.
Edibility Can be eaten, but of poor quality.
Habitat In fairly large groups, tufted on rotting wood, particularly birch or oak.
Season Autumn. Occasional.
Note The yield of coloured or white latex occurs in several species in this genus. *M. sanguinolenta*, terrestrial, with a brownish cap and a conspicuously red edge to the gill, yields a red latex. The latex produced by *M. crocata* is bright orange.

91 MYCENA EPIPTERYGIA

Etymology From Greek, 'surmounted by a small wing', from the pellicle of the cap.

Description Cap 1–3 cm, grey, ash grey or yellow, tending to whiten, campanulate, membranous, striate, covered with a viscid transparent pellicle, completely separable, margin often denticulate. Gills white and adnate. Stipe 5–8 × 0.1–0.2 cm, cap-coloured, also covered with viscid, separable pellicle, small rhizomorphs at base. Flesh fine, whitish. No particular smell or flavour. Spores white, elliptical, smooth, 8–12 × 5.5–7.5 microns, amyloid.

Edibility Of no value because of size.

Habitat Amongst grass.

Season Autumn. Common.

Note *M. viscosa* grows beneath conifers, among the needles or on stumps, has reddish markings on the cap and emits a strong smell of rancid fat. *M. epipterygioides* has greenish coloration on the stipe, the pale yellowish cap and the gills.

92 MYCENA INCLINATA

Etymology From Latin, 'not straight' or 'bent'.

Description Cap 2–3 cm, grey-brown, quite dark, globose, campanulate, obtuse, smooth, margin striate, fairly salient, slightly crenate. Gills whitish, greyish at attachment, sometimes pinkish, adnate, crowded. Stipe 6–10 × 0.2–0.4 cm, whitish or brownish becoming orange-yellow from base upwards, eventually reddish-brown at base of old specimens, initially elastic and leathery then fragile, slightly pruinose and fibrillose, with hairy base. Flesh whitish in the cap, light ochre-brown in the stipe. Slightly rancid odour, flavour slightly astringent, rancid. Spores white, elliptical, smooth, 7–10 × 5–7 microns, amyloid.

Edibility Caps edible, but quality inferior.

Habitat In dense tufts on stumps of oak.

Season Autumn. Common.

Note Many similar species grow clustered on wood but they lack a crenate cap margin or have a stipe that is otherwise coloured.

93 MYCENA GALERICULATA

Etymology From Latin, referring to a particular sort of headgear worn in ancient times.

Description Cap 2–5 cm, brownish-grey, sometimes white, conical-campanulate then expanded and striate to the umbo, dry and smooth. Gills whitish then pinkish, adnate, sometimes connected by veins. Stipe 5–12 × 0.3–0.5 cm, cap-coloured, smooth, often curved with hairy base, white, and rooting. Flesh fine, greyish. Mealy odour and flavour. Spores white, broadly elliptical, smooth, 10–11 × 6–8 microns, amyloid.

Edibility Can be eaten, but of little interest.

Habitat Tufted, with the base of stipes connected by hairs, on coniferous and broadleaved stumps and trunks.

Season Autumn to early winter. Common.

Note *M. polygramma*, growing on wood, has a bluish-grey, conspicuously striate stipe. *M. alcalina*, also forming tufts on dead wood, resembles *M. galericulata*: it is brownish-grey with ash grey (not pinkish) gills and a strong alkaline odour. This odour and a carpophore with reddish-brown markings especially on the gills are also typical of *M. maculata*, which is more gregarious than tufted, with base of stipe often rooting if the wood is soft and decomposed.

---

94 MYCENA PURA

Etymology From Latin, 'clean'.

Description Cap 2–8 cm, purple to pale lilac, campanulate then expanded, eventually flat, sometimes slightly umbonate, margin striate. Gills cap-coloured but paler, adnate, broad, ventricose, connected by veins. Stipe 3–10 × 0.2–1 cm, cap-coloured, tough, leathery, hollow, narrowing at top, smooth with fibrils running lengthwise, white and hairy at base. Flesh whitish. Odour and flavour of radish. Spores white, elliptical, smooth, 6–9 × 2.5–4 microns, amyloid.

Edibility Edible in small quantities.

Habitat Gregarious in woodland, in leaves and moss.

Season Autumn. Common.

Note There are many varieties of *M. pura*, all identifiable by the strong smell of radish and the fact that the gill edges are not blackish. *M. alba* is entirely white; *M. lutea* has an ochreous-yellow cap and violet stipe; *M. multicolor* has a greenish blue-grey cap with a yellow umbo and pinkish purple stipe; *M. rosea* is sturdier with a pink cap and paler or whitish stipe. A similarly radish-scented species, *M. pelianthina*, is entirely violet or purple and has dark purple-brown gill edges.

95   MYCENA VULGARIS

Etymology From Latin, 'common'.

Description Cap 0.6–1 cm, fairly dark greyish-brown, sometimes whitish except at the centre, or reddish-ochre in old specimens, campanulate then convex, depressed at the centre with papilla, slightly striate, covered with a thin viscid pellicle, separable. Gills white or grey, slightly decurrent, thin. Stipe 2.5–5 × 0.1–0.2 cm, ash-coloured, very viscid, has a rooting base with white hairs. Flesh whitish. No special odour or flavour. Spores white, elliptical, smooth 6–9 × 3–4 microns, amyloid.

Edibility Of no value because of size.

Habitat Gregarious, grows in large numbers in needle litter in coniferous woods.

Season Autumn. Rare.

Note *M. strobilicola* grows on cones of Norway spruce; *M. seynii*, found on maritime pinecones, has a very hairy base. Only the latter occurs, very rarely, in Britain.

96   MYCENA ROSELLA

Etymology From Latin, 'small rose'.

Description Cap 0.7–1 cm, membranous, campanulate then hemispherical, obtusely umbonate, slightly hygrophanous, pinkish, striate. Gills pinkish, adnate, quite distant, edge darker blackish-purple. Stipe 2–3.5 × 0.1 cm, soft, pinkish with white, tomentose base. Flesh very fine, white, reddish in stipe. No particular smell or flavour. Spores white, elliptical, smooth, 6.5–10 × 4–5 microns, amyloid.

Edibility Of no value because of size.

Habitat Gregarious, on conifer needles.

Season Autumn. Occasional.

Note A principal characteristic of the species is the fact that the colour of the gill edge differs from the rest of the fungus. Other small fungi with this feature include *M. citrinomarginata*, found on wood, with yellow gill edges; *M. flavescens*, with a smell of radish; *M. chlorantha*, with an iodized smell; *M. elegans* has bright orange-red gill edges. Many species have darker gill edges, including *M. avenacea*, with a brown cap; *M. albidolilacea*, with a whitish cap with pale lilac-pink shading; *M. atromarginata*, which is entirely brownish-grey; *M. capillaripes*, found in needles, with an alkaline odour; and *M. viridimarginata*, with greenish gill edges.

97 HYGROPHORUS LIMACINUS

Etymology From Latin, 'mucous'.
Description Cap 5–10 cm or more, olive grey to soot brown, darker at disc, convex then expanded, slightly raised at centre, covered with a separable glutinous pellicle, cuticle also detachable, shiny in dry weather, glabrous or with innate fibrils. Gills white with greyish or pale yellowish shading, distant, adnate-decurrent. Stipe 5–8 × 1–1.5 cm, sturdy, ventricose, sometimes with pointed base, viscous and at the same time floccose-squamose, greyish in lower half, white and squamulose at top. Flesh white, soft. No particular smell or flavour. Spores white, elliptical, smooth, 9–13 × 5.5–7.5 microns.
Edibility Very good if cuticle is removed.
Habitat In woodland in leaves and moss, prefers pine.
Season Summer and autumn.
Note *H. olivaceoalbus* is more slender and grows in spruce and fir woods.

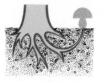

98 HYGROPHORUS MELIZEUS

Etymology From Greek, 'honey-coloured'.
Description Cap 2.5–4 cm, very light leather yellow, pale hazel ochre, uniformly coloured, at least in central area, very viscid, convex then flat with raised edge, margin at first pubescent. Gills yellowish cream-coloured, decurrent, distant, connected by veins. Stipe 7–8 × 0.6–1 cm, cap-coloured, narrowing towards base, conspicuously flocculose and white at the top in wet weather, dry, non-glutinous even if wet. Flesh light cream-coloured. Inconspicuous odour and flavour. Spores whitish, ellipsoid, smooth, 6.5–9 × 4.5–5 microns.
Edibility Can be eaten.
Habitat Gregarious, in grass usually beneath birch.
Season Late summer and autumn.
Note Not known in Britain and rarely collected in Europe.

99 HYGROPHORUS AGATHOSMUS

Etymology From Greek, 'nice-smelling'.

Description Cap 4–7 cm, uniform pale brownish-grey, often viscid, especially at centre covered with small raised papillae, convex then flat, humped, margin first involute, hairy, eventually spreading and undulating. Gills pure white, decurrent, distant, soft, sometimes venose at base. Stipe 5–12 × 0.6–1.5 cm, white, cylindrical or slightly enlarged at base, sometimes striate with fibrils, with mealy granulations at top tending to turn brownish-grey, solid, full. Flesh whitish, soft. Strong odour of celery with a hint of anise or bitter almonds, flavour sweetish. Spores white, broadly oval, smooth, 8–10 × 4–6 microns.

Edibility Good, although the smell is not to everyone's liking.

Habitat Grows among spruce and pine.

Season Autumn. Rare. In Britain found chiefly in Scotland.

Note *H. pustulatus*, brownish-grey with darker cap disc, is umbonate and normally covered with papillae; top of stipe has black spots; the gills, sometimes with pale green highlights, are adnexed-decurrent; no particular odour.

100 HYGROPHORUS CAMAROPHYLLUS

Synonym *Hygrophyllus caprinus*.

Etymology From Greek, 'vaulted leaf'.

Description Cap 3–10 cm, sooty black or blackish, with pale bluish shades, convex then flat and depressed, at times fairly umbonate, especially when immature, solid, moist or dry, with fairly radial, innate, blackish fibrils, pellicle separable only at margin, at first white, pruinose and involute, then expanded and at times recurved, same colour as the rest of the cap, and undulate. Gills white, tending to turn pale green or grey, very decurrent, distant, often connected by veins. Stipe 4–8 × 1–1.5 cm, sooty grey, cylindrical or narrowing at the base, whitish at top, full. Flesh white. Strong indefinable odour, sweet flavour. Spores white, elliptical, slightly pointed at one end, smooth, 6–9 × 4–5 microns.

Edibility Very good.

Habitat In heathland and meadows beneath fir.

Season Autumn. Occasional to rare. Perhaps more common in parts of Europe than Britain.

101 HYGROPHORUS RUSSULA

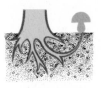

Etymology From Latin, 'reddish'.
Description Cap 10–20 cm, flesh-coloured or pale purple with more deeply coloured speckling, paler and whitish at tomentose margin, slightly viscid, humped, flat-convex, eventually depressed, slightly undulating. Gills whitish, often with deep red markings, sinuate to adnexed becoming decurrent, thin, quite crowded. Stipe 6–12 × 1–2 cm, white, spotted red, with the upper part white, mealy, solid, fairly cylindrical, often curved. Flesh white, compact, fibrous in stipe. No particular odour or flavour, sometimes slightly bitter. Spores white, elliptical, smooth, 6–8 × 4–5 microns.
Edibility Good.
Habitat Beneath broadleaved trees, especially oak.
Season Autumn. Rare.
Note A similar species is *H. erubescens*, which prefers conifers. The flesh is pale yellow, slightly bitter; the decurrent gills are, at most, suffused with pale flesh pink; the stipe is red but takes on a yellow coloration when touched; the viscid cap has pink markings. This species is very rare in Britain, more or less restricted to Scotland.

102 HYGROPHORUS MARZUOLUS

Etymology From Latin, 'of March'.
Description Cap 3–10 cm, fairly dark ash grey, sometimes with ochreous shading, becoming speckled blackish-grey with age, at first convex, soon becoming flat and depressed, irregularly humped, with margin expanded, wavy-lobate, cuticle initially moist, drying out rapidly. In young specimens gills are crowded, large, short, distant; they then become thinner, arcuate, decurrent, connected by veins and ramified, white tending to turn grey or blackish. Stipe 4–8 × 1.2–3 cm, squat, full, cylindrical, straight or curved, or tapered at base, furfuraceous, white at top, otherwise silvery-grey, solid. Flesh thick, white, faintly grey beneath cuticle, tender, slightly fibrous in base. No particular odour or flavour. Spores white, elliptical, smooth, 7–9.5 × 5.5–6.5 microns.
Edibility Excellent.
Habitat Gregarious, beneath litter of leaves and moss in coniferous and broadleaved woods, especially in mountainous areas.
Season Late winter, early spring, rarely in late autumn. It is not known in Britain.
Note Distribution is generally limited to central Europe and north Africa.

103   CAMAROPHYLLUS VIRGINEUS

Synonym *Hygrophorus virgineus.*
Etymology From Latin, 'virginal', because it is snow white.
Description Cap 3–7 cm, convex, obtuse, flat with a slight umbo, eventually depressed, cuticle moist, broken up into small adpressed scales, floccose, turning yellow when drying out. Gills white, decurrent, distant, quite thick, joined by veins at base. Stipe 5–11 × 0.5–1 cm, white, solid, pruinose and striate, narrowing at base, sometimes reddish. Flesh white, slightly fibrous. No particular odour or flavour. Spores white, elliptical, smooth, 8–12 × 5–6 microns.
Edibility Good.
Habitat In grassland, often gregarious.
Season Autumn. Common.
Note Another entirely white species, *Hygrophorus niveus*, is very similar, with a thin, fairly striate cap, yellowish or brown shading in old specimens. *H. russocoriaceus*, which is at first dirty white and then lighter-coloured as it dries, has a distinctive odour of leather.

104   HYGROPHORUS EBURNEUS

Etymology From Latin, 'ivory white'.
Description Cap 3–10 cm, pure white, shiny, disc at most cream-coloured or faintly yellowish, or else entirely cream-coloured, or the colour of pale leather, never darker, very viscous, convex-flat with the peripheral part turned outwards when mature, margin at first involute, pubescent. Gills white, decurrent, distant, venose at the base. Stipe 3–8 × 0.6–1.5 cm, white, not always regular, smooth, viscid except at the top, floccose, emitting small watery droplets that do not turn yellow as they dry out. Flesh white. Strong distinctive odour (which lingers on the fingers) of sage, flavour similar. Spores white, elliptical, smooth, 8–10 × 4–5 microns.
Edibility Can be eaten, but of poor quality.
Habitat Gregarious, in broadleaved woods.
Season Autumn. Common.
Note A very similar species, *H. chrysodon*, has a white cap ornamented, like the stem apex, with bright yellow floccons. The flesh has no specific odour, merely mushroomy. Its flesh recalls that of *H. eburneus*, but the carpophores of that species are easily identifiable since both the cap and apex of the stem lack yellow floccons.

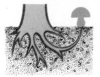

105 HYGROCYBE SPADICEA

Synonym *Hygrophorus spadiceus.*
Etymology From Greek, 'date brown'.
Description Cap 1–6 cm, olive ochreous-brown, blackish and shiny when dry, fragile, campanulate, but expanded, acute or obtuse, with radial innate fibrils, viscid in wet weather. Gills lemon yellow, broad, distant, quite sinuate, ventricose, adnate or almost free. Stipe 4–7 × 0.6–1 cm, yellowish, dry, striate with brown or lemon yellow fibrils, cylindrical. Flesh pale lemon yellow. No special odour or flavour. Spores white, elliptical, smooth, 8.5–12.5 × 4.5–7.5 microns.

Edibility Mediocre.
Habitat In moist grassland with moss, or near broadleaved trees.
Season Autumn. Rare.
Note This is one of the most easily identifiable of the *Hygrocybe* group because of the sharp contrast in colour between the cap and the yellow gills and stipe. *H. calyptraeformis* is also easily recognizable. It grows in meadows; the cap is conical, acute, pinkish with innate fibrils, or pale lilac-mauve, as are the gills; the stipe is up to 12 cm long, white or with pale lilac shading.

106 HYGROCYBE MINIATA

Synonym *Hygrophorus miniatus.*,
Etymology From Latin, 'red lead-coloured'.
Description Cap 0.5–2 cm, crimson, paling with age and becoming opaque, convex, often umbonate and eventually umbilicate, squamulose. Gills yellow or orange-yellow, adnate, distant. Stipe 3–5 × 0.2–0.4 cm, crimson, shiny, fibrillose, cylindrical. Flesh waxy, red. No special odour or flavour. Spores white, elliptical, smooth, 6–7 × 4–5 microns.

Edibility Can be eaten but of little value.
Habitat Typically in moss.
Season Autumn. Occasional.
Note Although it is small, this fungus is easily spotted because of the bright colour that stands out sharply from the surrounding environment. *H. cantharellus* has a squamulose cap and decurrent gills, colour ranging from whitish to pale yellow. *H. turundus* has a markedly flocculose cap and grows in sphagnum moss in peat bogs. *H. coccineus* and *H. reai*, two more red species with glabrous caps, tend to fade to orange and yellow with age. The latter species usually has bitter flesh.

107 HYGROCYBE PUNICEA

Synonym *Hygrophorus puniceus.*
Etymology From Latin, 'of pomegranate' or 'garnet red'.
Description Cap 5–11 cm, scarlet tending to turn pale with age starting from the centre, campanulate, obtuse, margin normally involute, lobate, viscid. Gills yellow, often red at base, ascending and apparently free, ventricose, broad, thick, and distant. Stipe 7–11 × 1–2.5 cm, cap-coloured or bright yellow, base invariably white, fusiform, often curved, fibrillose, striate, squamulose at top, solid, quickly becoming hollow. Flesh cap-coloured, initially white, slightly watery, waxy, slightly fibrous in the stipe. No particular odour or flavour. Spores white, broadly elliptical, smooth, 8.5–11 × 5–5.5 microns.
Edibility Good.
Habitat Meadows.
Season Autumn. Occasional.
Note This fungus is one of the largest and brightest members of its genus. *H. coccinea*, also red but turning orange with age, has a stipe that is almost smooth and non-striate. Most of the many red, orange or yellow species are small in comparison.

108 HYGROCYBE PSITTACINA

Synonym *Hygrophorus psittacinus.*
Common name Parrot fungus.
Etymology From Greek, 'parrot', because of the colours.
Description Cap 2–5 cm, initially olive green, bright light bluish-green, shiny, then yellowish, pale yellow, finally brick-coloured before turning purple-brown, campanulate then partially expanded, umbonate, striate, viscid. Gills yellow, greenish at base, adnexed, ventricose, quite distant. Stipe 4–7 × 0.4–0.7 cm, cylindrical, bright green because of the mucus, which eventually only persists at the top, otherwise turning yellowish. Flesh thin, waxy, watery, white shaded with green or yellow. No particular odour or flavour. Spores white, elliptical, smooth, 8–9 × 4–5.7 microns.
Edibility Mediocre.
Habitat In grassland.
Season Autumn. Common.
Note *H. sciophana* has different red shading, with pale greenish markings and yellow-edged gills. *H. laeta* also forms carpophores with different colours. The cap and stipe may be yellow, orange, salmon pink or pinkish, although the very top of the stem may be pale lilac or greenish. The decurrent gills are salmon-coloured then pale lilac.

109 HYGROCYBE BREVISPORA

Synonym *Hygrophorus brevisporus.*
Etymology From Latin, 'with short spores'.
Description Cap 3–6 cm, yellow, pale greenish yellow, conical, campanulate, margin unevenly lobate, central area mammillate, sulcate-striate (radially), dry, at most, damp. Gills whitish then pale yellow, broad, ventricose, quite distant, almost free. Stipe 4–6 × 0.8–1.2 cm, cap-coloured, soon becoming hollow, compressed, with lengthwise grooves, often forming fissures, briefly floccose at top, with orange shading at base, not viscous. Flesh pale yellow, watery, fibrillose, but fragile in stipe. No particular odour or flavour. Spores white, oval or globose, smooth, 6–8.5 × 5–6 microns.
Edibility Mediocre.
Habitat In grassland.
Season Late summer and autumn. Occasional.
Note Other very similar species are *H. citrinovirens*, which has a slightly more slender stipe, 6–10 × 0.3–1 cm; *H. obrussea*, with a conspicuously compressed stipe, sulcate, up to 3 cm maximum width, smooth all over, dry, cap golden-yellow, and yellow gills with white edge; and *H. chlorophana*, all yellow with very viscid stipe.

110 HYGROCYBE CONICA

Synonym *Hygrophorus conicus.*
Etymology From Latin, 'cone-shaped'.
Description Cap 3–6 cm, scarlet, yellow, hazel, yellow-green, grey-brown, or sooty grey and yellow, tending to blacken all over, conical with a pointed apex, often lobate and split when expanded, viscid when wet, silky when dry. Gills white or yellow, sometimes reddish at base, becoming black, semi-free, ventricose, thin, crowded. Stipe 6–9 × 0.4–0.9 cm, red, yellow or pale green, turning black, cylindrical, striate-fibrous, rigid and straight. Flesh thin, watery, same colour as outside surface, blackening. No particular odour or flavour. Spores white, broadly elliptical, smooth, 9–14 × 4–8 microns.
Edibility Rather mediocre.
Habitat In grassland and by the roadside.
Season Autumn. Common.
Note This initially bright fungus changes colour with age and immediately after being picked. A similar species that does not blacken is *H. intermedia*, with reddish-orange, fibrillose scaly cap, and yellow, strongly fibrillose stipe.

111 PLEUROTUS ERYNGII

Etymology From the name of the host plant.
Description Cap 5–10 cm, reddish-brown to dark brown or ochreous-brown, slightly squamulose, striped with adpressed fibrils, greyish-brown, eventually glabrous, convex then flattened, faintly depressed, sometimes irregular, eccentric or concentric, margin thin, recurved. Gills fairly crowded, rarely ramified, very decurrent, whitish then ochreous-grey, edge darkening with age. Stipe 4–6 × 1–2 cm, usually eccentric, but sometimes central, cylindrical or narrowing and rooting at the base, sometimes curved, full, soft, elastic, fibrillose lengthwise, whitish, eventually ochreous-grey, with brownish mycelium at the base. Flesh thick, not hygrophanous, solid, white. Slight, indistinct but pleasant odour and sweet flavour. Spores white, elliptical, smooth, 10–12.5 × 5–5.5 microns.

Edibility Excellent.
Habitat On leaves of plants in the genus *Eryngium* and some related genera in the parsley family.
Season In warmer regions from spring onwards, then late summer and autumn. In Mediterranean areas of Europe. Not known in Britain.

Note *P. ferulae*, just as delicious, often grows in tufts at the base of giant fennel. Tasty *P. opuntiae* grows on prickly-pear cactus, agave and yucca. Neither of these two species occurs in the wild in Britain.

112 PLEUROTUS DRYINUS

Etymology From Greek, 'of oaks'.
Description Cap 5–10 cm, lateral, oblique, convex then quite flat, whitish, covered with dirt brown down, often lighter, which breaks up into spot-like adpressed scales, becoming greyish-brown, sometimes with edge appendiculate because of membranous and downy velar remains. Gills white, yellowish with age, decurrent with slight edge on stipe, often anastomosed, but never joining together at base, short and single. Stipe 2.5–10 × 1–1.5 cm, solid, full, tough, eccentric, white, almost woolly, downy, squamulose, with tapered base, at times with ring-like velar remains. Flesh white, thick, solid. Pleasant odour and flavour, like cultivated field mushrooms. Spores white, extended, cylindrical, smooth, 12–13 × 3–4 microns.

Edibility Good.
Habitat On trunks, living or dead, of broadleaved trees.
Season Late summer, autumn.

113 PLEUROTUS OSTREATUS

Common names Oyster fungus; oyster mushroom.

Etymology From Latin, 'oyster', because of cap shape.

Description Cap 6–14 cm, often imbricate, superposed, violet-black to brownish-grey, fading with age, eccentric and asymmetrical, shell- or spatula-shaped, slightly depressed at attachment to stipe, smooth, shiny and glabrous. Gills initially creamy white, then ivory white, long, fairly crowded, unequal, decurrent along stipe. Stipe 2–8 × 1–2 cm, white, smooth, oblique, lateral, rarely central, enlarged at top, rudimentary, hairy base. Flesh white, thick, at first tender then slightly tough. Fairly pleasant odour, tasty flavour. Spores pale cream-coloured or shaded with pale lilac, cylindrical, smooth, 8–11 × 3–4 microns.

Edibility Good, sought after.

Habitat In tufts, on stumps and trunks of various broad-leaved trees, rarely on conifer trunks.

Season Late autumn up to first frost, reappearing in mid-winter (if mild), then in spring and summer with rains. Common.

Note This species is also cultivated on poplar wood or various vegetable remains in Europe.

114 PLEUROTUS CORNUCOPIAE

Etymology From Latin, 'horn of plenty'.

Description Cap 5–12 cm, briefly convex and funnel-shaped, whitish or light grey, pale ochreous-brown or yellowish, glabrous. Gills whitish or cap-coloured, but much paler, crowded, very decurrent on stipe, anastomosing to form a net. Stipe 3–8 × 0.7–1.5 cm, often ramified, nearly central to fairly eccentric, whitish, full, almost completely covered by the usually anastomosed extension of gills. Flesh white, soft, becoming rather tough. Distinctive mealy odour, sweetish flavour. Spores whitish in mass, then pale lilac-grey, elliptical, smooth, 7.5–11 × 3.5–5 microns.

Edibility Very good when young.

Habitat On stumps and trunks, living and dead, of broad-leaved trees, in tufts.

Season Summer and autumn. Common.

115 PANELLUS STIPTICUS

Etymology From Greek, 'astringent'.
Description Cap 1.5–4 cm, brownish-ochre, yellowish or cinnamon-coloured, downy-floccose or pruinose then breaking up into small furfuraceous scales, elastic, kidney-shaped, sometimes funnel-shaped and lobate. Gills ochreous or cinnamon-coloured, thin, straight and crowded, connected by veins. Stipe 0.5–2 × 0.2–0.3 cm, whitish, enlarged at top, pubescent, short and lateral. Flesh cinnamon ochre-coloured, elastic, thin, leathery in stipe. Somewhat acid odour and very astringent flavour. Spores white, elliptical, smooth, 3–6 × 2–3 microns, amyloid.
Edibility Inedible, possibly poisonous.
Habitat On trunks, stumps and dead branches, particularly on broadleaved trees, mainly oak.
Season All year. Common.
Note In North America there is a markedly luminescent variety of *P. stipticus*. *P. mitis* has a white, glabrous cap, stipe of the same colour, downy-velvety, grows mainly on conifers, flesh sweetish. *P. serotinus* is a rather large species, cap olive green with fine downy hair, gills pale straw yellow or orange, stipe yellowish, covered with small, brown, cottony scales. The latter is common in late autumn.

---

116 LENTINUS TIGRINUS

Synonym *Panus tigrinus*.
Etymology From Latin, 'marked like a tiger'.
Description Cap 3–8 cm, thin, supple, fairly leathery, silvery white or cream-coloured, variegated with small fibrillose scales, adpressed, brown or blackish, margin often split in dry weather. Gills white then yellowish, decurrent, thin and crowded. Stipe 3–5 × 0.5–1.5 cm, whitish, blackish-brown at base, tough, often narrowing towards the base and rooting, thinly squamulose, with a short-lived ring at top, residual, with a white veil, often curved. Flesh white, blackish-brown at base of stipe. Strong milk-like odour, flavour somewhat acid. Spores white, elliptical, smooth, 8–12 × 3–3.5 microns.
Edibility Inedible because of the texture.
Habitat In frequently tufted groups, on the stumps of broadleaved trees or on buried rotting wood.
Season Autumn. Rare.
Note *Lentinus lepideus* is more robust and has a cap that is never funnel-shaped but rather flat-topped; it is ochreous, with brownish, particularly coarse scales, and the scaly stipe has a ring at the top; it has a smell of anise and grows on conifers and worked wood.

117 LENTINELLUS COCHLEATUS

Etymology From Greek, 'spiralled'.
Description Cap 2.5–9 cm, initially flesh-coloured, tending to turn paler, often chamois-coloured or reddish-brown, usually eccentric, irregular, lobate and contorted, funnel-shaped, edge faintly spiralled, open on one side, imbricate. Gills white then cream-coloured with pinkish shading, very decurrent, very crowded, small, edge serrate when mature. Stipe 3–9 × 0.5–1.5 cm, pale flesh-coloured or reddish-brown, darker towards base, central or lateral, sulcate, often connate at base, normally hollow. Flesh thin, whitish turning to pinkish or reddish, tough, elastic, leathery. Pleasant odour of anise, sweet flavour. Spores white, globose, minutely warted, 5–6 microns, amyloid.

Edibility Can be eaten, but leathery.
Habitat On or at foot of stumps, mainly beech, tufted.
Season Autumn. Occasional.
Note *Lentinus* and *Lentinellus* are two similar genera easily recognized by their serrate gill edges. *Lentinus* has a mostly central stipe and spores that are elliptical, smooth and non-amyloid. *Lentinellus* has an eccentric to lateral or rudimentary stipe and spores that are nearly round, minutely spiny and amyloid (turn blue-black in Melzer's reagent).

---

118 LACTARIUS BLENNIUS

Etymology From Greek, 'viscid'.
Description Cap 4–10 cm, olive grey to grey-green, with darker concentric spots, flat then depressed at centre, surface viscous. Gills white with slight red shading when mature, developing olive grey spots when touched, crowded, thin, adnate. Stipe 4–6 × 1–1.5 cm, greyish or olive grey, lighter than the cap, hollow. Flesh white, becoming slightly grey when exposed to air, fragile. Odourless, flavour acrid. Latex white, acrid. Spores pale cream-coloured, elliptical, cristate, partly reticulate, 7.5–8.5 × 5.5–6 microns, amyloid.

Edibility Not recommended because of the acrid flavour.
Habitat Very frequent in broadleaved woods, especially beech, often hidden among dead leaves.
Season Autumn. Common.
Note This is a member of the *Lactarius* group with the cuticle fairly or very viscous; flesh and drops of latex take on greenish-grey or olive-coloured shades when exposed to air. A similar species is *L. pallidus*, ochre with pale pinkish shading.

119   LACTARIUS FULVISSIMUS

Etymology   From Latin, 'deep reddish-white'.
Description   Cap 2.5–7 cm, at first red-brown, paling gradually with age, retaining a darker coloration at centre, convex, depressed at disc, then funnel-shaped or crater-like, surface dry, finely rugose. Gills cream-coloured, with pale flesh- or orange-coloured shading, averagely crowded, decurrent. Stipe 3–4 × 0.9–1.6 cm, orange, reddish-orange at base, short, squat. Flesh reddish-white, thick, hard. Bug-like odour. Latex white, constant, not plentiful, with a mild flavour but a little harsh on the throat. Spores cream-coloured, almost spherical, spiny, often with crests and connecting lines, 7.5–8.5 × 6.5–7.5 microns, amyloid.

Edibility   Can be eaten, but flavour mediocre.
Habitat   In broadleaved woods, especially on clayey-calcareous ground.
Season   Autumn. Occasional.
Note   Easily confused with very similar species. *L. ichoratus* has a brighter, more fibrillose cap; the cap of *L. mitissimus* is decidedly more orange in colour; *L. subdulcis* has softer coloration; *L. rubrocintus* is much larger and has a distinctive reddish ring-like zone on the stipe immediately below the gills.

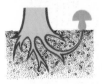

---

120   LACTARIUS GLAUCESCENS

Synonym   *Lactarius piperatus glaucescens*.
Etymology   From Latin, from the blue-green colour of its flesh when cut.
Description   Cap 5–15 cm, whitish, initially convex, then funnel-shaped, surface bare, not rough, at most cracked. Gills yellowish-white, crowded, decurrent, almost anastomosed. Stipe 2–6 × 1.5–2.5 cm, whitish, full, may have small pits with blue-green spots. Flesh creamy white, turning blue-green when cut, hard. Odourless, with a hot, acrid flavour. Latex white, becoming greenish like the flesh when drying out. Spores white, subspherical, slightly and incompletely reticulate, 7–8.5 × 6–7 microns, amyloid.

Edibility   Not recommended because of the acrid flavour and it has been reported to cause poisoning.
Habitat   Grows in large numbers in broadleaved woods.
Season   Late summer and autumn. Rare.
Note   This species is very similar to *L. piperatus* (**121**). The latex of these two fungi does, however, react differently to KOH treatment: it quickly turns bright yellow in the case of *L. glaucescens*, but does not alter in the case of *L. piperatus*.

121 LACTARIUS PIPERATUS

Etymology From Latin, 'peppery', from the flavour.
Description Cap 5–13 cm, whitish, may develop ochre spots with age, initially convex, then flattening and eventually becoming funnel-shaped, surface dry, rugose near margin. Gills creamy white with pinkish shading, decurrent, crowded, forked near stipe. Stipe 3–8 × 1.5–2.5 cm, same colour as cap, cylindrical, irregular, rugose, finely pruinose. Flesh white, hard. No odour, acrid flavour. Latex white, immediately hot and acrid. Spores white, subspherical, light, imperfect reticulum, 7–8.5 × 5.5–6.5 microns, amyloid.
Edibility Not recommended because of the acrid flavour.
Habitat In broadleaved woods, rarely beneath conifers.
Season Autumn. Common.
Note This fungus, like *L. glaucescens* (**120**), has flesh and latex with an acrid flavour that burns the tongue, which is why neither can be used in cooking. But in some eastern European countries they are eaten after a lengthy period of treatment similar to the preparation of sauerkraut.

---

122 LACTARIUS LILACINUS

Etymology From Latin, 'lilac-coloured'.
Description Cap 4–7 cm, from brown-pink to pink-lilac, flat-depressed, cuticle dry, finely furfuraceous, then squamulose. Gills ochre-pink, then very like cap colour, not very crowded, slightly decurrent. Stipe 4–8 × 0.6–0.8 cm, slender, enlarged at base, solid then hollow, ochre-pink. Flesh whitish-lilac. Slight odour of chicory. Latex whitish, watery, turning greenish-grey when drying on gills, quite sweet. Spores white, ovoid, incompletely reticulate, 7.5–8 × 6 microns, amyloid.
Edibility Not recommended though not poisonous.
Habitat This species grows exclusively under alder.
Season Autumn. Occasional.
Note A very similar species is *L. spinosulus*, growing in the same habitat; it is smaller, more conspicuously violet in colour, with a small pointed umbo at the centre of the cap, which is slightly scaly. Both belonging to the *Lactarius* group, having a completely dry, downy-hairy cap.

123 LACTARIUS PORNINSIS

Etymology After the French mycologist Pornin.
Description Cap 3–8 cm, orange, with brighter red or orange zonations, convex, becoming slightly depressed at centre, cuticle slightly viscous as a result of humidity. Gills first ochreous-cream-coloured, then ochreous-orange, crowded, slightly decurrent. Stipe 3–6 × 0.8–1.5 cm, orange but lighter than cap, soon becoming hollow. Flesh slightly reddish. Unpleasant smell and bitter flavour. Latex white, unchanging. Spores white, ovoid, reticulate, 7.5–9.5 × 5.5–7 microns, amyloid.
Edibility Can cause mild stomach troubles.
Habitat Grows exclusively in larch woods.
Season Summer and autumn. Unknown in Britain. It occurs in Europe and is sometimes plentiful.
Note Many bitter or acrid species of *Lactarius* are known to cause stomach upsets. However, in Europe certain species are sold in markets and are prepared in ways that remove the irritant compounds.

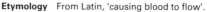

124 LACTARIUS SANGUIFLUUS

Etymology From Latin, 'causing blood to flow'.
Description Cap 6–15 cm, orange- or wine red, sometimes with darker zonations, developing green spots, flattened, margin involute. Gills winy-orange, may develop some green markings, crowded, barely decurrent. Stipe 4–6 × 1.5–2.5 cm, orange with wine-coloured markings, covered with whitish pruinosity, may have small wine red pits. Flesh only faintly coloured, whitish, becoming blood red when touched. Latex wine red, slightly bitter. Spores white, sub-spherical, cristate, reticulate, 8–9.5 × 6.5–8 microns, amyloid.
Edibility Excellent cooked.
Habitat In coniferous woods, especially beneath pines, and prefers warmer latitudes.
Season Autumn. Unknown in Britain, but occurs in Europe.
Note All *Lactarius* with wine or carrot red latex are edible. It is a good rule to consume only this group of *Lactarius*, excluding those with latex initially white or watery; although non-toxic, they often taste acrid.

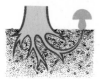

125 LACTARIUS DELICIOSUS

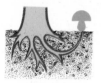

Common names Saffron milk cap; milk agaric.
Etymology From Latin 'delicious'.
Description Cap 5–12 cm, bright orange, deeper coloured zonations, may turn slightly green with age, convex, slightly depressed at centre, margin involute. Gills bright orange, sometimes green when mature, crowded, slightly decurrent. Stipe 3–6 × 1–2 cm, cap-coloured, with small and more brightly coloured pits. Flesh whitish, orange at edge because of latex, soft. Odour fragrant, flavour slightly bitter. Latex orange, carrot red. Spores creamy white, rounded, cristate, reticulate, 7.5–9.5 × 6.5–7 microns, amyloid.
Edibility Good.
Habitat In coniferous woods, especially pine.
Season Autumn. Common.
Note This species belongs to the *Lactarius* group, with latex that is coloured from the first, rather than changing from milky white or watery to a brighter colour.

---

126 LACTARIUS CONTROVERSUS

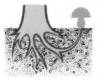

Etymology From Latin, 'turned the other way'.
Description Cap 7.5–25 cm, whitish with concentrically placed pink spots, convex becoming funnel-shaped, often irregular, cuticle moist and viscous, usually with inconspicuous zonations. Gills a distinctive flesh pink colour, crowded. Stipe 3–5 × 1.5–3 cm, whitish, squat, hard. Flesh white. No odour, acrid flavour. Latex white, does not change when exposed to air, flavour very acrid. Spores cream-coloured, subspherical, finely reticulate, interrupted, 6–6.5 × 5 microns, amyloid.
Edibility Not recommended.
Habitat Beneath broadleaved trees, prefers poplars, may occur under willows or on sand dunes.
Season Autumn. Rare.
Note An easily identifiable fungus because of its exceptional size and, above all, by the pink gills that single it out from the other white *Lactarius* species, from which it also differs because of the cap zonations. It is one of the largest and the most fleshy of this *Lactarius* group; the flesh of the cap is much thicker than the width of the gills.

127 LACTARIUS VOLEMUS

Etymology From Latin, 'filling the palm of the hand', an adjective used to describe a very large variety of pear.

Description Cap 7–15 cm, red-brown to reddish-orange, convex then flat, depressed at centre, surface dry, cracked in old specimens. Gills pale ochre-cream, spotted with brown when rubbed, averagely crowded, slightly decurrent. Stipe 6–12 × 1.5–2.5 cm, cap-coloured, tough, full, pruinose. Flesh whitish, darkening slightly, thicker in cap than the width of the gills. Strong distinctive odour of herring or Jerusalem artichoke. Latex white, very plentiful, mild. Spores white, spherical, cristate-reticulate, 8–12 × 7–11 microns, amyloid.

Edibility Good and popular.

Habitat Grows in coniferous and broadleaved woods.

Season Autumn. Rare.

---

128 LACTARIUS ACERRIMUS

Etymology From Latin, 'very acrid'.

Description Cap 5–13 cm, yellow-ochre, somewhat tinged with orange, zonation often distorted, massive, convex, slightly depressed at disc, then conspicuously funnel-shaped. Gills from whitish to yellow-ochre, decurrent, forked and anastomosed near stipe. Stipe 3–7 × 2–3 cm, whitish with small, scattered, cap-coloured markings, soft, massive, irregular, tapering at base. Flesh whitish, may turn yellow at base of stipe when cut, then turns slowly reddish and finally blackish-grey. Odour fruity, flavour very acrid. Latex white, unchanging, slight hot-acrid flavour. Spores cream-coloured, subspherical, cristate, 10–13 × 8–10 microns, amyloid.

Edibility Not recommended because of the flavour.

Habitat In broadleaved woods, especially oak.

Season Autumn. Rare.

Note This fungus differs from the other members of the *L. zonarius* group by its much larger spores and the two-spored basidia. *L. zonarius* has similar coloration and a very strong fruity smell; *L. insulsus* has a much more orange and zoned cap, and the stipe is covered with conspicuous small pits. *L. zonarioides* grows only beneath conifers in mountainous regions; when touched, the gills become marked with green. The last occurs in Europe but not in Britain.

129 LACTARIUS CILICIOIDES

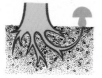

Etymology From Greek, 'resembling cilice' (a goat-hide fabric).

Description Cap 3–7 cm, whitish, tending to turn ochre, convex then flattened with centre slightly depressed, margin very involute and covered with a felt-like layer of woolly hairs a few millimeters in length, centre bare, though slightly viscid. Gills cap-coloured, crowded and adnate. Stipe 2–4 × 1–1.5 cm, whitish then ochreous, with a few pits narrowing towards base. Flesh white. Slight odour of geranium, acrid. Latex white, then yellow, acrid. Spores pale cream-coloured, elliptical, cristate, 6–7.5 × 4.5–5.5 microns, amyloid.

Edibility May cause very serious intestinal disorders.

Habitat In broadleaved woods, beneath birch or near birch trees in grassland.

Season Autumn. Very rare.

Note This may be considered a pale form of *L. torminosus* (**131**), differing in colour and in the slightly smaller size of the spores. Very similar *L. pubescens* is smaller and grows almost exclusively in northern Europe.

130 LACTARIUS SCROBICULATUS

Etymology From Latin, 'pock-marked' or 'pitted'.

Description Cap 6–20 cm, yellow or reddish-yellow, faintly zoned, large, fleshy, convex, depressed at centre, margin conspicuously involute, woolly with numerous short hairs. Gills yellowish, lighter than cap, crowded, slightly decurrent. Stipe 3.5–6 × 2–3.5 cm, whitish, with numerous yellow or yellowish-red pits, hard and hollow. Whitish flesh, yellowing when cut because of the latex, tending to blacken with time, quick to rot. Odour slightly fragrant, flavour acrid to burning. Latex white, turning immediately sulphur yellow when exposed to the air. Spores pale cream-coloured, rounded, finely reticulate, 8–8.5 × 6.5–7.5 microns, amyloid.

Edibility Inedible, possibly poisonous.

Habitat In coniferous woods in mountains.

Season Autumn. Rare. In Britain mostly found in Scotland. Occasional in northern Europe.

Note This is a very beautiful *Lactarius* in form, colour and above all for the way its white latex turns immediately yellow when exposed to air. Very similar species include *L. resimus* and *L. citriolens*, with the latex also turning yellow, but without pits on the stipe. *L. representaneus* looks like *L. scrobiculatus*, but the white latex turns violet on exposure to air.

131   LACTARIUS TORMINOSUS

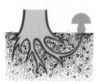

Etymology   From Latin, 'causing colic'.

Description   Cap 4–12 cm, varying in colour from pale orange to brick red, convex then flattened, depressed at centre; the surface is covered with dense long hairs and has fairly conspicuous dark orange-red zones. Gills light salmon ochre, crowded, slightly decurrent. Stipe 2–6 × 1–2 cm, whitish to orange-red, soft. Flesh whitish, thick. Slightly fruity odour. Latex white and very acrid. Spores pale cream-coloured, elliptical, cristate, reticulate, 7.5–10 × 6–8 microns, amyloid.

Edibility   Causes severe gastro-intestinal disorders unless thoroughly cooked.

Habitat   Beneath or near birch.

Season   Autumn. Common.

Note   This is the commonest of the hairy-capped *Lactarius* species. In addition to *L. cilicioides* (**129**) and *L. pubescens*, which are much lighter in colour, there is *L. mairei*, which has a reddish-ochre cap with no hint of pink, a much stronger fruity smell and grows beneath oak.

---

132   LACTARIUS TURPIS

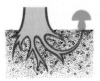

Synonyms   *Lactarius necator; Lactarius plumbeus.*

Common name   Ugly one.

Etymology   From Latin, 'foul', 'disgusting'.

Description   Cap 8–25 cm, olive greyish-brown, greenish at edge, very dark, convex, depressed at the centre, margin pubescent, surface viscous in wet weather. Gills creamy white becoming brown when rubbed, crowded. Stipe 4–8 × 2–5 cm, olive brown, paler than the cap, hard, soon becoming hollow, slightly viscous in wet weather. Flesh whitish, slightly brown-tinged when exposed to air, becoming black when drying out, thick, hard. Virtually odourless. Latex white and acrid. Spores pale cream-coloured, rounded, reticulum somewhat interrupted, 6.5–8 × 5–7 microns, amyloid.

Edibility   Not recommended because of acrid flavour.

Habitat   Always with birch.

Season   Autumn. Common.

Note   This fungus has dark blackish coloration and one can find old specimens that have become black all over. The cap surface turns a beautiful violet in contact with ammonia.

133 LACTARIUS VELLEREUS

Etymology From Latin, 'velvety'.
Description Cap 8–25 cm, white to ochre-tinged, at first convex then depressed at centre, eventually becoming funnel-shaped, irregular, surface finely velvety. Gills white, with pale blue highlights, then reddish cream-coloured, distant, fairly decurrent. Stipe 3–6 × 2–3 cm, cap-coloured and likewise velvety, soft, large, short and irregular. Flesh white, slightly yellow-brown when cut, with greenish shading, hard, thick. No odour, flavour peppery and acrid. Latex white, unchanging, very acrid. Spores white, subglobose, with slight reticulum, incomplete, 9–12 × 7.5–10 microns, amyloid.

Edibility Not recommended because of the acrid, peppery flavour.
Habitat In broadleaved woods, especially in calcareous ground.
Season Autumn. Occasional.
Note This species differs from *L. piperatus* (**121**) and *L. glaucescens* (**120**) by having much more distant gills and the velvety cap and stipe, and like the others, it is eaten in eastern Europe after fermentation.

134 RUSSULA LUTEA

Etymology From Latin, 'deep yellow'.
Description Cap 2–6.5 cm, lemon or chrome yellow, first uniform then fading to cream-coloured at the edge, globose then slightly depressed, with cuticle detachable, at first slightly viscid, shiny, with margin tuberculate-sulcate when mature. Gills eventually becoming fairly distant, sometimes with rare lamellae, forked, ochreous or orange-yellow, darkening slightly with age. Stipe 2–6 × 0.7–1.5 cm, white, quite rugose, slightly enlarged at the top, almost hollow, pithy. Flesh white, fragile. Slight smell of vinegar in old specimens, sweet flavour. Spores orchreous-yellow, elliptical, with isolated pointed warts, 7.5–11 × 6.2–9 microns, amyloid.

Edibility Can be eaten, but of little value.
Habitat Beech woods.
Season Autumn. Common.

135 RUSSULA ADUSTA

Etymology From Latin, 'burnt', from its colour.

Description Cap 5–15 cm or more, whitish becoming tinged with light reddish-brown tending to greyish or sepia brown, convex-expanded becoming eventually depressed at centre, cuticle adnate, shiny and smooth, viscous in damp weather, margin thick, undulate. Gills pale cream-coloured or ivory, with a few pale ochre highlights, crowded, distant when mature, interspersed with numerous lamellae, arcuate, rounded at stipe, narrowing frontwards. Stipe 3–10 × 1.5–4 cm or more, white, tinged with reddish at base, which is greyish-brown, cylindrical, narrowing or enlarged in the lower part, full, hard pruinose. Flesh creamy-white turning gradually pink then soot coloured, thick, firm. Slight but distinctive odour of old casks, flavour sweet. Spores white, hemispherical-ovoid, with crowded warts, 7–10 × 6–8 microns, amyloid.

Edibility Fairly poor quality.

Habitat In sandy pinewoods, also beneath Norway spruce.

Season Late autumn. Common.

Note This belongs to the *Russula* group characterized by blackening all over with age. Another, *R. nigricans*, has deep, distant gills and its flesh when cut turns red before becoming black.

---

136 RUSSULA FOETENS

Etymology From Latin, 'fetid-smelling'.

Description Cap 6–18 cm, pale ochre at edge, yellow-brown at disc, then tawny ochre-yellow, tinged with reddish-brown, at first globose then flattened at top, flat, eventually slightly depressed, cuticle fairly detachable, radially sulcate to margin, which is thin, undulate-lobate. Gills whitish then cream-coloured with reddish-brown markings, unequal, large, some forked, connected by veins; young specimens produce watery droplets in damp weather. Stipe 4–12 × 1–4 cm, whitish marked with brown starting at base, tough, first solid then hollow and fragile, cylindrical. Flesh whitish turning brownish when exposed to air. Odour and taste disagreeable. Spores pale cream-coloured, ovoid, with thick conical or obtuse warts, 7.5–10 × 6–9 microns, amyloid.

Edibility Inedible because of flavour.

Habitat In groups in broadleaved and coniferous woods.

Season Autumn. Common.

Note Similar species are *R. subfoetens*, smaller with a faint odour and taste; *R. fragrantissima*, with unpleasant odour with pleasant component smelling like marzipan; and *R. laurocerasi*, more yellow in colour and more fragrant with the smell of cherry laurel. None is palatable.

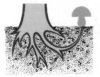

137 RUSSULA SARDONIA

Etymology From Greek, having to do with the acrid flavour.

Description Cap 3–10 cm, violet-purple, black at centre or fading to olive-cream, often all purple-red, hemispherical then flat, depressed, cuticle adnate, slightly viscous, smooth or slightly cracked, shiny, margin thin, slightly striate. Gills pale then cream-coloured, typically tinged with lemon yellow, crowded, rigid, thin, never obtuse frontwards, arcuate then straight, producing small droplets of water in young specimens. Stipe 3–8 × 1–3 cm, violet-purple, bluish-violet more marked at centre, and also whitish at base, solid, rigid, pruinose at top, rugose in mature specimens. Flesh whitish tinged with lemon yellow, wine red beneath cuticle, thick, hard, rigid, succulent. Odour of dried fruit, very acrid flavour. Spores orchreous-cream, hemispherical-ovoid, warty, reticulate, 6.5–8.5 × 6–7.5 microns, amyloid.

Edibility Inedible because of very acrid flavour.

Habitat Beneath conifers, prefers pine, on sandy soil.

Season Late summer and autumn. Common.

Note In contact with ammonia the flesh and gills give a typical and very marked pinkish-red reaction. It resembles two other species associated with conifers that do not react to ammonia, however, and which have white or whitish gills, *R. queletii* and *R. torulosa*.

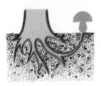

138 RUSSULA ATROPURPUREA

Synonym *Russula krombholzii*.

Etymology From Latin, 'black and purple-red'.

Description Cap 5–12 cm, dark purple-red with central part blackish, tinged with ochre-brown, hemispherical then convex, eventually slightly depressed and often undulate-lobate, cuticle detachable at edge, slightly viscid, shiny with tendency to discolour. Gills forked at base, whitish-cream, arcuate, almost pointed at margin. Stipe 7–7.5 × 1–2 cm, white, unchanging or sometimes slightly tinged with ochre-brown, especially at base, rarely tinged with pink, solid, quite regular, pruinose at top. Flesh whitish or sometimes tinged with ochre-brown in stipe, purple-red beneath cuticle. Slight fruity odour, acrid flavour, especially in gills. Spores white, ovoid, reticulate, 7.5–8 × 6–7 microns, amyloid.

Edibility To be avoided, like all the acrid species.

Habitat Beneath conifers and broadleaved trees, prefers oak and beech, especially on acid ground.

Season Autumn. Common.

Note The variety *depallens* usually grows in wetlands, is discoloured, ochreous, with flesh tending to turn greyish with age.

139   RUSSULA LEPIDA

Etymology From Latin, 'pretty', from its colour.
Description Cap 3–11 cm, beautiful red colour, sometimes, vermilion and crimson, lighter at edge, sometimes with discoloured areas, or even whitish and lemon yellow at disc in the variety *lactea*, rounded then convex, eventually fairly flattened, fleshy, hard, margin curved, regular or slightly undulate, cuticle not detachable. Gills gypsum white, with cream-coloured highlights, sometimes pinkish towards cap edge, crowded, with few lamellae, forked-anastomosed neai stipe, obtuse frontwards. Stipe 3–8 × 1–3 cm, white, fairly speckled with crimson, especially at base, hard, fragile, club-shaped, sometimes short and almost cylindrical, rugose lengthwise. Flesh white, pink beneath cuticle, thick, hard, compact granular when broken. Odour of cedar or menthol, similar flavour or resinous and somewhat bitter. Spores pale cream-coloured, subglobose-ovoid, with obtuse warts, 6–8 × 6–8 microns, amyloid.
Edibility Mediocre, must be parboiled.
Habitat Broadleaved woods, prefers beech.
Season Autumn. Occasional.
Note The flavour is sometimes remarkably minty and the cap cuticle is opaque, resembling coloured gypsum.

140   RUSSULA EMETICA

Common name Sickener.
Etymology From Greek, 'causing vomit'.
Description Cap 4–10 cm, varies greatly in colour, normally bright red, convex, eventually depressed with thin, briefly sulcate margin and viscid, shiny cuticle, may become slightly rugose as it dries, easily detachable with red subcuticle. Gills white then slightly cream-coloured, fairly distant, thin, rounded at stipe, almost free, fat towards margin. Stipe varies in length, up to 9–10 cm high in the variety *longipes*, fairly club-shaped at base, white. Flesh white, typically red beneath cuticle, fragile. Odour slightly fruity to puffball-like, acrid. Spores white, ovoid, warty, very reticulate, 7.5–12.5 × 6.2–9.2 microns, amyloid.
Edibility Slightly poisonous.
Habitat Typically in peat bogs in sphagnum, always close to conifers.
Season Autumn. Common.
Note There are many varieties. The distinctive features of the species are cuticle viscid, completely detachable, spores with conspicuous reticulum, flesh acrid, weak reaction to guaiacol.

141 RUSSULA DELICA

Etymology From Latin, from the absence of any latex.
Description Cap 6–15 cm, whitish, often with ochreous brown speckling, hemispherical then convex, finally with a wide, deep depression, cuticle not detachable, dry, pruinose, with radial fibrils, rugose, sometimes cracked, margin thick, curled then straight, cap-coloured. Gills whitish then pale ochre, tinged rust-coloured, distant, unequal, anastomosed, forked, broad, adnate. Stipe 2–5 × 1–3 cm, white and faintly brownish, hard, full, cylindrical, sometimes truncated-conical, shiny, pruinose, may become slightly rugose with age. Flesh whitish, thick, hard. Odour of fruit or fish, flavour sweet but gills acrid. Spores creamy-white, broadly ovoid, rounded, with mainly obtuse warts, 7–10 × 6–8.5 microns, amyloid.
Edibility Mediocre.
Habitat In broadleaved woods.
Season Autumn. Common.

---

142 RUSSULA AERUGINEA

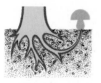

Etymology From Latin, 'copper-coloured'.
Description Cap 4–10 cm, with various shades of green or steel grey or, more especially, grey-green with centre dark, and even entirely pale ochreous, with a hint of grass green at centre, often with small rust-coloured spots, convex then flat and depressed, cuticle two-thirds detachable, slightly viscous when moist. Gills whitish with ochreous spots, crowded, forked at attachment, delicately intervenose, arcuate then faintly ventricose, obtuse at margin, crumbly. Stipe 5–7 × 1–2 cm, whitish, tinged with yellowish-brown at base, flared beneath gills, narrowing in lower part, full and sturdy. Flesh whitish tending to turn grey when exposed to air, thick, soft. Odour pleasant, flavour slightly peppery then sweet. Spores fairly markedly cream-coloured, elongated, ovoid, with obtuse warts, 6–7.5 × 5–6 microns, amyloid.
Edibility Edible, slightly poisonous when raw.
Habitat In groups beneath birch.
Season Autumn. Common.
Note The flesh reacts conventionally to ferrous sulfate, turning pinkish quite quickly. Other green *Russulas* are dry or have a cracked cap.
Caution Slightly poisonous when raw.

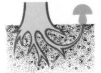

143 RUSSULA OCHROLEUCA

Etymology From Greek, 'white-ochre-yellow'.
Description Cap 4–11 cm, yellow but variously tinged, pale lemon yellow, yellowish-ochre spotted with orange or brownish at centre, late in season often light olive yellow or ochreous-greenish-grey at centre, convex-umbilicate then flat, slightly depressed, cuticle half detachable, moist and shiny, margin thick, curved, sometimes lobate. Gills pale cream-coloured or faintly pale yellow with a few small brownish markings with age, averagely crowded, unequal, intervenose, ventricose, slightly obtuse frontwards. Stipe 3–7 × 1.5–2.5 cm, white, slightly greyish, spotted with brownish-yellow from base upwards, cylindrical, sometimes club-shaped, flared beneath gills, full, soft, slightly pithy at top. Flesh white, greyish at top of stipe, thick, soft then tough. Odour pleasant, flavour varying from piquant to sweet. Spores white, ovoid, aculeate, 7–9 × 6.3–9 microns, amyloid.

Edibility In small quantities only, because of taste.
Habitat In coniferous and deciduous woodland.
Season Autumn. Common.
Note Another yellow *Russula, R. lutea*, has a clear yellow cap and yellow gills. Some varieties are so different from this typical variety that only a specialist can identify them.

---

144 RUSSULA OLIVACEA

Etymology From Latin, 'olive-like', from colour of cap.
Description Cap 8–18 cm, olive green especially at centre, speckled with ochre, brown, grey, purple- or wine red, at first hemispherical then convex, then flat-convex, eventually flat-depressed, cuticle quite adherent, thin, toughish, dry, with concentric cracking, margin thick, recurved. Gills cream-coloured then ochreous-yellow, crowded then distant, forked, intervenose, often ventricose, crumbly. Stipe 4–10 × 2–3.5 cm, white tinged with pink, spotted brownish towards base, sturdy, cylindrical or various forms, slightly obese, full, rugose, reticulate, sometimes even cracked. Flesh whitish turning yellowish, brownish with age, thick, compact. Pleasant fruity odour, hazel-nut flavour. Spores ochre-yellow, ovoid, with strong, long spines and obtuse warts, 8–11 × 6–10 microns, amyloid.

Edibility Good.
Habitat Grows beneath oak and in shady beech woods.
Season Summer and early autumn.
Note Identifiable by the cuticle, which is often concentrically cracked, and by the flesh, which produces a conspicuous crimson reaction to carbolic acid.

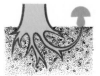

145   RUSSULA SORORIA

Etymology   From Latin, 'sister'.
Description   Cap 5–11 cm, dark brown and cigar brown at centre, fading to yellowish-brown, hazel brown at edge, sometime with olive markings, subglobose to convex, then flat, conspicuously depressed or split, connecting with hollow of stipe, cuticle detachable, elastic, viscous, pebbled, pruinose at disc, margin first curved then straight, then recurved, striate and tuberculate, translucent. Gills whitish, often with largish brown or greyish markings, crowded then distant, unequal, very intervenose, thin, very slightly obese, narrowing to the rear. Stipe 2–6 × 1–2.5 cm, white, starting from base tinged with brownish-grey and slightly flesh-coloured or reddish-brown, cylindrical, flared beneath gills, quickly becoming hollow, pruinose at top. Flesh whitish then slightly greyish, brownish in hollow of stipe, thick, rigid. Slightly fruity odour, fairly acrid, nauseous flavour. Spores pale cream-coloured, ovoid, with conical, obtuse, or truncated warts, 6.5–8.5 × 5–7 microns, amyloid.
Edibility   Not recommended because of taste.
Habitat   In sandy ground, under oak.
Season   Autumn. Common.
Note   Very similar to *R. pectinata*, margin deeply sulcate and tuberculate, cap light ochre-brown, flesh nauseous to taste, first acid then bitterish.

146   RUSSULA VIRESCENS

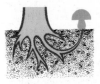

Common name   Green agaric.
Etymology   From Latin, 'turning green', from its colour.
Description   Cap 5–12 cm or more, grey- or bluish-green, then brownish in mature specimens, rarely entirely whitish, first globose then convex and open, slightly depressed at centre, cuticle detachable near edge, tough, dry, cracked into small areolae, mealy, darker than background, margin thin, curved then straight, obtuse, sometimes radially sulcate. Gills creamy-white with rose-cream-coloured iridescence, often with reddish-brown markings, crowded, unequal, forked, often anastomosed, intervenose, arcuate then ventricose, fragile. Stipe 3–9 × 1.5–4 cm, whitish, flared beneath gills, slightly narrowing at base, full then spongy, pruinose at top, slightly rugose. Flesh whitish, thick, soft. Odour initially slightly fruity, becoming unpleasant, flavour sweet. Spores whitish, broadly elliptical, with fairly distant warts, 6–8.5 × 5–6.5 microns, amyloid.
Edibility   Excellent.
Habitat   In broadleaved woods.
Season   Autumn. Occasional.

147 RUSSULA CYANOXANTHA

Etymology From Greek, 'blue-yellow', from its colour.

Description Cap 5–15 cm, blackish-violet, pale purple at edge and conspicuously green at disc, varying to slate grey with lighter areas, or bluish-violet or even a uniform green when mature, rounded then convex, flat, fairly depressed, cuticle two-thirds detachable, thin, viscous in damp weather, shiny, with radial fibrils and grooves, margin curved inwards then obtuse, sometimes striate when mature. Gills white tinged bluish-green, fairly crowded, unequal, forked, intervenose, ventricose. Stipe 5–10 × 1.5–4 cm, white, sometimes tinged lilac or reddish, with brownish markings, sturdy, narrowing and rooting at base, fleshy, soft then spongy, pruinose, slightly rugose. Flesh white, sometimes greyish when mature, thick, soft, moist. Odour pleasant, flavour first sweet then unpleasant. Spores white, elliptical, with small isolated warts, 7–10 × 6–7.5 microns, amyloid.

Edibility Excellent.

Habitat In broadleaved and coniferous woods.

Season Summer. Common.

Note Flesh shows no reaction to ferrous sulphate, which is a distinguishing factor when attempting to distinguish it from *R. ionochlota* and *R. parazurea*.

148 RUSSULA VESCA

Etymology From Latin, 'edible'.

Description Cap 6–10 cm, pale flesh pink to wine brown, or hazel, tinged with ochre or lilac, more conspicuous or lighter olive-coloured at disc, never violet, sometimes even all white in young specimens, subglobose then flat, depressed at centre, cuticle hot, very detachable, with fine radial venations especially at centre, margin obtuse, slightly striate. Gills whitish then cream-coloured, crowded, equal, forked around stipe, intervenose, narrowing, slightly decurrent. Stipe 3–10 × 1.5–4 cm, white tending to turn yellow or develop greyish markings, brownish at base, full then spongy, slightly flared beneath gills, narrowing at base, soft. Flesh white tending to develop rust-coloured or dirty yellow markings especially at base of stipe, soft, thick. Pleasant odour, tasteless or with sweet hazel-nut flavour. Spores white, subglobose, with small isolated warts, 6–8 × 4.5–6 microns, amyloid.

Edibility Good.

Habitat In broadleaved and coniferous woods.

Season Autumn. Common.

Note The cuticle often withdraws, revealing the flesh at cap edge. Reacts orange-pink to ferrous sulphate.

149   RUSSULA XERAMPELINA

Etymology   From Greek, 'colour of dried vine leaves'.
Description   Cap 5–11 cm, crimson, purple, pale lilac-red with centre blackish, often brownish-wine-coloured, with olive-ochre discolouration, convex then flat, slightly depressed when mature, cuticle not detachable, slightly viscous when damp, shiny in mature specimens, velvety, finely pebbled, margin thin and grooved in adult specimens, curved. Gills whitish-cream-coloured then pale ochre, distant when mature, intervenose, ventricose, obtuse frontwards, not crumbly, slightly lard-like to the touch. Stipe 3–7 × 1.5–3 cm, whitish or tinged with glowing red-pink, or even wine red in some forms, developing brownish spots beneath gills, cylindrical or narrowing from base to top, flared at top, soft then pithy, pruinose, venose-reticulate. Flesh whitish tending to darken when exposed to air, thick, soft. Odour of crab, flavour sweetish. Spores deep ochre, ovoid, with obtuse or conical warts, 8–10 × 6.5–8.5 microns, amyloid.
Edibility   Mediocre.
Habitat   In coniferous and broadleaved woods.
Season   Autumn. Common.
Note   To identify this very variable species, apart from odour, note that flesh turns brownish when exposed and has a greyish-green reaction to ferrous sulphate.

---

150   RUSSULA MAIREI

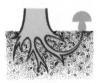

Etymology   After the French mycologist Maire.
Description   Cap 4–8 cm, scarlet, blood red, often paling, becoming yellow-ochre when rotten, very convex then flat, eventually slightly depressed, cuticle detachable only at margin, translucent, slightly viscous, slightly pebbled, as if velvety, even lobate at margin, which is curved, opaque, striate and tuberculate in mature specimens. Gills white or whitish, crowded then distant, unequal, rarely with lamellae, forked, intervenose, arcuate then straight, faintly obtuse frontwards. Stipe 2–6 × 1–2 cm, white, rarely with hint of red, ochre or brownish markings at base, even or enlarged half-way up, full, hard, striate and rugose. Flesh white, slightly yellowish in stipe, red beneath cuticle, thick, soft when mature. Odour of fruit or coconut, of honey when mature, flavour acrid. Spores white, ovoid, warts not crowded, 6–7.5 × 5.5–6.3 microns, amyloid.
Edibility   Inedible, but can be used for flavouring.
Habitat   In beechwoods.
Season   Autumn. Common.
Note   Very similar to *R. emetica* (**140**) and distinguished by growing under beech as well as by spore characters.

151 CANTHARELLUS CINEREUS

Etymology From Latin, 'ash-coloured'.
Description Cap 2–5 cm, funnel-shaped, depressed at the centre, margin undulate, dark greenish-brown, covered with adpressed scales. Decurrent hymenial folds, ramified and anastomosed, greyish. Stipe 3–6 × 0.4–0.7 cm, cylindrical, compressed, sinuate, hollow. Flesh greyish, thin. Odour of dried plums, sweetish flavour. Spores white, elliptical, smooth, 8–10 × 5–6 microns.
Edibility Good.
Habitat In broadleaved woods.
Season Autumn. Rare.

152 CANTHARELLUS INFUNDIBULIFORMIS

Etymology From Latin, 'funnel-shaped'.
Description Cap 3–7 cm, funnel-shaped, pierced at the centre by a cavity that extends into the stipe, cuticle brownish-yellow, slightly villose, edge recurved and margin sometimes undulate. Decurrent hymenial folds, ramified, relatively long, anastomosed, yellow to greyish sometimes with amethyst coloration. Stipe 2–8 × 0.3–0.8 cm, hollow, cylindrical, compressed, smooth, yellowish, often curved. Flesh thin, white. No particular odour, and a sweetish flavour. Spores white, ovoid, smooth, 9–12 × 7–8 microns.
Edibility Good.
Habitat In broadleaved and coniferous woods.
Season Autumn. Common.
Note The gill-like folds vary considerably in colour, with some collections appearing very yellow and others deeply amethyst.

153 CANTHARELLUS AMETHYSTEUS

Etymology From Greek, 'amethyst-coloured'.

Description Cap 5–10 cm, flat or depressed, covered with adherent, pale lilac-violet scales, more numerous towards margin, giving glimpses of yolk yellow flesh, margin very curved. Hymenium with raised veins, resembling gills, anastomosed, ramified, decurrent, yellow. Stipe 3–4 × 2.5–3 cm, conical, turbinate, enlarged towards top. Flesh white then pale yellow. Fruity odour and flavour. Spores white, ovoid, smooth, 10 × 5–6 microns.

Edibility Excellent.

Habitat In beechwoods.

Season Autumn. Rare.

Note Some consider this a variety of *C. cibarius* (**154**). Although the genus *Cantharellus* would seem to have carpophores resembling some of those formed by some gilled fungi, it is related to the Clavariaceae. The fruit-body simulates a fungus with cap and stipe, and the hymenium, which is fairly rugose, resembles gills. *Hygrophoropsis aurantiaca* and *H. olida* are two cap-and-stipe species formerly included in the *Cantharellus* group. The first is entirely orange-red, with detachable, anastomosed gills; the second is pinkish-cream-coloured or orange with a lobate cap, sometimes very irregular, and has a strong odour.

---

154 CANTHARELLUS CIBARIUS

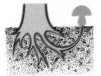

Common name Chanterelle.

Etymology From Latin, 'good to eat'.

Description Cap 2–10 cm, sometimes larger, convex then open and usually funnel-shaped, margin undulate, sinuate, cuticle extremely thin, transparent, yolk yellow, glabrous. Gill-like hymenial folds, very decurrent, short, anastomosed, ramified, yolk yellow. Stipe 3–6 × 1–2 cm, tapering from top to bottom, full, solid, cap-coloured. Flesh compact, quite fibrous in stipe, pale yellow. Odour strong, often like apricots, flavour sweet. Spores pale yellow, elliptical, smooth, 7–11 × 4–6 microns.

Edibility Excellent fresh or preserved by canning or short-cooking and freezing; drying not recommended because on rehydration they are usually tough.

Habitat Beneath coniferous and broadleaved species.

Season Late summer to autumn. Common.

Note There are many varieties of this fungus, which is one of the best known and most sought after. Despite its appearance it is not, systematically speaking, a gilled mushroom (agaric) because its 'gills' are actually folds that develop during expansion of the cap and are not pre-formed as in *Agaricus*. Like the French truffle it is used in liqueur-making.

155   CANTHARELLUS LUTESCENS

Etymology From Latin, 'turning yellow'.
Description Fruit-body shaped like small trumpet with upper part like a cap, 2–6 cm, consistency membranous, convex and umbilicate when immature, then open and funnel-shaped with central part closed or connecting with hollow part of stipe, cuticle fibrillose and scaly, glabrous with age, brown or brownish-grey on orange background, margin expanded, markedly lobate, undulate, curled. Hymenium from cap edge to upper third, at first smooth, then faintly sulcate with gentle folds. Stipe 5–8 × 0.5–1 cm, slender, irregular, narrowing towards base, compressed, grooved or ribbed, especially in the upper part, hollow, shiny, orange-yellow. Flesh thin, quite tough, pale yellow. Pleasant, fruity odour, somewhat of alcohol, flavour sweet. Spores white, elliptical, smooth, 10–12 × 6–7 microns.
Edibility Excellent.
Habitat Gregarious, sometimes almost tufted, in damp coniferous woodlands.
Season Autumn. Rare. In Britain it occurs only in Scotland.
Note Can easily be confused with *C. infundibuliformis* (**152**), with a more raised hymenium, with gill-like folds, ramified, fairly yellow but normally pale lilac-grey when mature.

156   CRATERELLUS CORNUCOPIOIDES

Common name Horn of plenty.
Etymology From Latin, 'like a horn of plenty'.
Description Cap 2–8 cm, initially almost tubular then open and trumpet-shaped, with a thin edge, rounded then flared with margin undulate and lobate, pierced at centre and hollow down to stipe, cuticle dark brown or slate black, covered with small brown adpressed scales. Hymenium with small ash grey wrinkles. Stipe no more than 1.5 cm wide, narrowing from top to bottom, tubulose, fibrillose, blackish. Flesh thin, blackish-grey, fairly elastic. Odour aromatic, flavour slightly astringent. Spores white, elliptical, smooth, 10–15 × 6–9 microns.
Edibility Excellent, much sought after.
Habitat In the litter beneath broadleaved trees.
Season Autumn. Occasional.
Note When dried and reduced to powder this is an excellent flavouring in soups, sauces, for roast meats, etc., and is known in Italy as 'the poor man's truffle'.

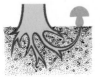

157 LEPTOGLOSSUM MUSCIGENUM

Synonym *Cantharellus muscigenus.*
Etymology From Latin, 'born from moss'.
Description Fruit-body fan- or spatula-shaped, 1–2.5 cm, slate grey when wet, ash-coloured or whitish and zoned when dry, membranous, elastic, slightly undulate when fully mature. Hymenium with ramified venations, broad, starting from stipe, same colour as fruit-body, anastomosed towards margin. Stipe 2–4 × 2–4 mm, small, lateral, horizontal and continuous with fertile part, villose at base. Flesh thin, greyish. No particular odour or flavour. Spores white, ovoid, smooth, 7–9 × 4–6 microns.
Edibility Of no value because of size.
Habitat On moss.
Season All year round during wet periods. Occasional.
Note This is a small, insignificant fungus with a specific habitat that it shares with other species in the genus. *L. lobatum*, growing in peat bogs at high altitude with spores of 8–10 × 6–7 microns, is larger (up to 6 cm) with clamped hyphae, and grows on *Carex*. *L. retirugum* is cup-shaped; *L. bryophilum*, funnel-shaped, is completely white.

---

158 VOLVARIELLA BOMBYCINA

Synonym *Volvaria bombycina.*
Etymology From Latin, 'silken'.
Description Cap 5–20 cm, ochre-white towards disc, silvery-white towards outside, at first parabolic then convex or almost flat, sometimes slightly umbonate, cuticle adnate, shiny, with fibrils or fibrous scales, silky, margin rounded and curved then straight and regular. Gills white then pink, eventually brownish, crowded, free, with numerous lamellae. Stipe 7–10 × 0.6–2 cm, satiny white, pale yellow in lower part, easily detachable from cap, or heterogeneous, narrowing from bottom to top, sometimes sub-bulbous, slender, full, smooth, slightly fibrous in adult specimens. Volva whitish or ochre-white, outer cuticle often with yellowish-brown or brownish markings, persistent, free, wide, large and membranous. Flesh pure white, thin at edge, not hygrophanous, tender. Strong odour of radish or wood, flavour pleasant. Spores pale pink, elliptical, smooth, 7–9 × 5–6 microns.
Edibility Mediocre to good.
Habitat Usually solitary, on rotting broadleaved tree trunks, in holes in living trees, sometimes some yards above ground, and in hollow stumps, especially elm.
Season Autumn. Rare.

159 VOLVARIELLA VOLVACEA

Synonym *Volvaria volvacea*.
Common name Padi-straw.
Etymology From Latin, 'with a volva'.
Description Cap 4–10 cm, ovoid then campanulate-conical, eventually flattened, first blackish, which persists to maturity towards disc, then with dark brown or blackish-brown fibrils on a whitish or silvery-white background. Gills long, white then pinkish, free. Stipe 5–12 × 1 cm, white, hairy, hollow when mature, volva membranous, brown or dark brownish-grey externally (at least in part), whitish background, uniformly felt-like. Flesh white, soft, slightly fibrous in stipe. Very slightly earthy odour, insignificant flavour. Spores pink, elliptical, smooth, 7–9 × 5–6 microns.
Edibility Good when young.
Habitat In loam in greenhouses or gardens, on sawdust or other vegetable residue, also with field mushrooms.
Season Spring to autumn; with heat, all year. Occurs in above situations in Europe, but not known in Britain.
Note Easy to cultivate. *V. speciosa* and *V. speciosa gloiocephala* grow in grassy areas or ploughed fields and have a viscid cap (whitish in the former and sooty grey in the latter). *V. surrecta* (*V. loveiana*) is easily identifiable because it forms small fruit-bodies on other fungi, especially on *Clitocybe nebularis* (**83**).

160 PLUTEUS CERVINUS

Etymology From Latin, 'deer-like', from its colour.
Description Cap 6–15 cm, brown to sooty brown, convex-flat, often umbonate, viscid in damp weather, fibrillose when mature, sometimes split radially, fragile, glabrous. Gills whitish then pinkish, crowded, broad, free. Stipe 5–10 × 0.7–1.5 cm, whitish with brownish or blackish, sometimes raised fibrils, full, rigid. Flesh white, tender, fragile. Slight root-like odour, flavour mild. Spores pinkish-salmon, ovoid, smooth, 6–8 × 5–6 microns.
Edibility Mediocre. See **Caution**.
Habitat On decomposing coniferous and broadleaved woods, also on sawdust, where it grows larger.
Season Summer and autumn. Common.
Note *P. atromarginatus* closely resembles the above species although much more fibrillose and darker on cap and stipe, especially when young. It differs markedly by having floccose and blackish gill edges. *P. salicinus* has a white stipe with a base tinged with bluish-green, cap grey, glaucous, with tiny insignificant scales on disc.
Caution Do not confuse with poisonous *Entoloma* species, which are mostly terrestrial with attached gills and pink angular spores.

161 PLUTEUS AURANTIORUGOSUS

Synonym *Pluteus coccineus.*
Etymology From Latin, 'golden- yellow and wrinkled'.
Description Cap 2–6 cm, first bright red then bright orange-red, deeper-coloured at the disc, golden towards the margin, edge thinly striate in mature specimens. Gills white then pink, free. Stipe 4–6 × 0.5–0.8 cm, faintly narrowing towards top, often curved, white, often tinged with orange towards base. Flesh thin, whitish, orange beneath cuticle and in stipe. No particular odour or flavour. Spores pink, roundish or subglobose, smooth 5–7 × 4–5 microns.
Edibility Can be eaten, but of little value.
Habitat Isolated or in small groups on trunks, stumps, or dead branches of broadleaved trees.
Season Autumn. Rare.
Note Easily identified by the bright cap colour. *P. leoninus* also grows on broadleaved trees, cap bright yellow, finely pruinose or velvety, stipe white with yellow base, gill edges also yellow. *P. lutescens* has a markedly yellow stipe, while the smooth cap, which is at most rugose, is brown or brownish-ochre.

162 CLITOPILUS PRUNULUS

Common name Miller.
Etymology From Latin, 'small plum'.
Description Cap 3–11 cm, white or pale yellow, or more rarely light grey, convex then flat, eventually depressed, undulate, margin involute, often lobate, thin, mealy, cuticle smooth, barely viscid if wet. Gills white then pinkish, very decurrent, narrowing at both ends. Stipe 2–6 × 1–1.5 cm, white, full, tapered towards base, pruinose or pubescent, villose at the base. Flesh white, fragile. Strong mealy odour and flavour. Spores pink, elliptical with longitudinal ridges, angular in endview, 9–13 × 5–7 microns.
Edibility Good, but see **Note**.
Habitat In woodland.
Season Autumn. Common.
Note May be confused with certain poisonous white species of *Clitocybe*, but they have a whitish spore-print. Certain toxic *Entoloma* species, which have a pinkish spore-print, do not typically have long decurrent gills.
Caution When in doubt, do not eat.

163   ENTOLOMA SINUATUM

Synonym *Entoloma lividum.*
Etymology From Latin, 'sinuate', from gill attachment.
Description Cap 6–20 cm, varying in colour and texture, white, greyish with ochre shades, brown, pinkish, ash-coloured, innate fibrils, fairly conspicuous, fleshy, not hygrophanous, convex or globose-campanulate, then flattened, barely depressed, slightly humped, dry and glabrous. Gills initially pale yellow then salmon-coloured starting from stipe, retaining original colour for some time at edge, fairly crowded, sinuate. Stipe 7–13 × 1.5–3.5 cm, sturdy, solid, rarely slightly hollow when old, sometimes faintly curved or enlarged at base, whitish, with some yellow marking. Flesh thick, soft, slightly fibrous in stipe. Strong odour of meal turning to rotting walnut when older, sweetish, mealy flavour. Spores pink, polyhedral, 8–11 × 7–8 microns.
Edibility Very poisonous. See **Note**.
Habitat In groups, in sparse, dry woodland beneath broad-leaved trees, especially oak.
Season Autumn. Rare.
Note This large fleshy *Entoloma* is often eaten by mistake by people who think it is a *Pluteus*, which has free gills and grows on wood. It causes severe gastric upset.

---

164   ENTOLOMA NIDOROSUM

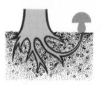

Etymology From Latin, 'reeking', from its smell.
Description Cap 3–7 cm, dirty white and shiny in dry weather, ochre-ash-coloured, slightly striate at margin, transparent when wet, convex then expanded, eventually concave, cuticle split radially. Gills whitish then pinkish, adnate or semi-free. Stipe 3.5–9 × 0.3–1 cm, whitish or light grey, fragile, striate-fibrillose, soon becoming hollow, cylindrical, the top pruinose. Flesh white, fragile. Strong nitrous odour, fairly strong, mealy, unpleasant flavour. Spores pinkish, polyhedral, 7–10 × 6–7.5 microns.
Edibility Poisonous. See **Note**.
Habitat Gregarious, in broadleaved woods and in scrub.
Season Autumn. Common.
Note There are many species of *Entoloma* with a mealy smell and many of them are poisonous. In spring the poisonous *E. clypeatum* is found in tufted groups beneath plants belonging to the Rosaceae family (apple, pear, plum, etc.); its cap has a conspicuous umbo like an ancient shield. Although some species of *Entoloma* are edible, these fungi are difficult to identify and differentiate from similar poisonous species; therefore, **no species of *Entoloma* should be eaten**.

165 ENTOLOMA INCANUM

Synonym *Leptonia incana*.
Etymology From Latin, 'turning white with age'.
Description Cap 2–3 cm, olive brown to grass green, sometimes variegated with brown fibrils or small scales, thin, fragile, convex then expanded, umbilicate, slightly striate, tending to become silky and greyish with age. Gills whitish or tinged with pale yellow-green, then pinkish, fairly distant, adnexed then detached from stipe. Stipe 2.5–5 × 0.2–0.4 cm, smooth, fistular, fragile, green, greenish-yellow, turns blue-green towards the base when touched, as does the surrounding white mycelium. Flesh thin, greenish. Strong unpleasant odour of mice, flavour disagreeable. Spores pink, polyhedral, 8–14 × 7–9 microns.
Edibility Of no value because of flavour.
Habitat In fields and meadows with low grass.
Season Autumn. Uncommon.
Note Those species with slender, tapering, smooth stipes, thin, often umbilicate caps, and gills not entirely grey or brown belong to the subgenus *Leptonia* and are of no interest gastronomically. Several related species, such as *E. serrulatum*, have bluish caps and stipes, and blue-grey gills, pinkish at maturity.

166 RHODOTUS PALMATUS

Etymology From Latin, 'hand-like', from its shape.
Description Cap 5–12 cm, apricot pink, orange-hazel, flesh pink, convex then flattened, horizontal, fairly eccentric relative to stipe, margin that remains involute for a long period, covered by a thick, wrinkled, gelatinous cuticle, emitting small, clear, orange droplets, very astringent. Gills pinkish, crowded, broad, soft, sinuate, connected by veins. Stipe 3–7 × 1–1.5 cm, whitish then orange-brown, cap-coloured, fibrillose-striate, pruinose, full, eccentric or lateral. Pleasant odour but bitter, acid-astringent flavour. Spores pinkish, salmon-coloured (in the spore-print on paper, if the gills touch the paper, spores become dark ochre or rust-coloured), subspherical, spinose, 5–7 microns.
Edibility Non-toxic but very bitter.
Habitat Normally tufted with imbricate caps on trunks, especially elm.
Season Summer to early winter. Occasional.
Note A distinctive and unmistakable species, formerly rare, much less so since the advent of Dutch elm disease.

167 TERMITOMYCES LETESTUI

Etymology After the Frenchman Le Testu.
Description Cap 9–25 cm, fleshy, campanulate then convex, eventually fairly expanded with a conspicuous cylindrical umbo that is dark brown from the small brown scales about disc. Cuticle dry and whitish, fairly pale pinkish-grey, squamulose and cracked except towards margin, which is usually appendiculate. Gills white, almost free, crowded, unequal. Stipe 12–18 × 2–3 cm or more, solid, fusiform, deeply rooting, whitish, pubescent beneath membranous ring, which is large, double, variable but complete and persistent, pendent or sheath-like. Flesh whitish, soft. Odour faint, flavour insignificant, sometimes slightly bitter. Spores white, elliptical, smooth, 6–9 × 3–5 microns.
Edibility Good.
Habitat On termite nests in tropical Africa. This species does not occur in Britain or Europe.
Season All year.
Note The gill fungi growing on termite nests belong to the genera *Podabrella* (pink-spored) and *Termitomyces* (white-spored). The fruit-bodies form inside the tunnels and bore through the very hard layer of inner matter, forcing their way through it with a special umbo, sometimes quite pointed, called a 'driller'.

168 INOCYBE PATOUILLARDI

Etymology After the French mycologist Patouillard.
Description Cap 3–7 cm, white but soon flushed ochre, bruising red, conical-campanulate, cuticle dry, silky, with radial fibrils, margin split. Gills initially whitish or pinkish, then olive brown or rusty brown, adnexed or semi-free, crowded and ventricose, edge irregular, white. Stipe 4–7 × 1–1.5 cm or more, variable, often cylindrical, sturdy, enlarged at base; bulb sometimes faintly marginate, solid, consistent, pruinose at top, fibrillose, with velar remains, white with fibrils that redden with age, turning red then brown if touched. Flesh white, faintly reddening at base. Odour quite fruity and flavour sweetish. Spores rust ochre, elliptical, smooth, 10–13 × 5–7 microns.
Edibility Poisonous.
Habitat Often gregarious, on calcareous ground, in open beechwoods.
Season Late spring and throughout the summer. Rare.
Note The carpophores can be recognized by the fact that they turn from their initial pale colours to red. This slow and spontaneous colour change is accelerated when the fungus is rubbed with the hands. Ingestion causes muscarine poisoning.

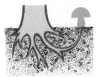

169 INOCYBE SPLENDENS

Etymology From Latin, 'shining'.
Description Cap 3–5 cm, first conical with edge raised, then convex with umbo, covered with radial fibrils, adpressed, orange-brown or pale lilac-brown, pale purple, split towards edge, joined at disc, flesh beneath cuticle pale yellow, margin soon incised. Gills whitish then brownish-ochreous, margin paler, adnate, sometimes slightly decurrent. Stipe 7–11 × 3–3.5 cm, sturdy, cylindrical or suddenly enlarged into an almost marginate bulb, pure white, finely striate or furfuraceous at top, full. Flesh compact, fibrous in stipe, white. Slight earthy odour and slightly nauseous flavour. Spores ochreous-brown, elliptical, smooth, 9.5–11.2 × 5.5–6.2 microns.
Edibility Not certain.
Habitat Gregarious and often almost tufted, on humus-rich ground or in grassland at the edge of woods.
Season Summer and autumn. Rare in Europe and unknown in Britain.
Note A rare species showing clear distinctive features under the microscope, but not always identifiable in the wild. Most of the *Inocybe* species, unless with specific organoleptic or morphological features, are difficult to identify with the naked eye.

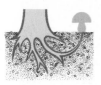

---

170 INOCYBE GEOPHYLLA

Etymology From Greek, 'earth-coloured gills'.
Description Cap 1–3.5 cm, white, sometimes pale yellow in old specimens, conical then convex, flat with smallish pointed umbo, silky then fibrillose, often split or cracked at the margin. Gills whitish, then dirty grey or brownish, semi-free, crowded. Stipe 4–8 × 0.2–0.6 cm, white, cylindrical, slightly enlarged at base, often supple, satiny. Veil cobweb-like, fugacious. Flesh white. Spermatic odour, flavour slightly acrid. Spores brownish, elliptical, smooth, 7–10 × 4–6 microns.
Edibility Poisonous.
Habitat Gregarious in coniferous and broadleaved woods, also beneath bushes.
Season Autumn. Common.
Note Young specimens have a conical cap connected with the stipe by a cobweb-like veil. Often found growing with it is a violaceous, or lilac-capped, variety, *lilacina*. A distinctive species, *I. pudica*, is white but readily bruises reddish-orange.

171 INOCYBE FASTIGIATA

Etymology From Latin, 'inclined', because of the shape of the cap.

Description Cap 2–7 cm, pale straw or ochreous-yellow, sometimes darker at the disc, conical then raised at the edge with distinct umbo; surface dry, very fibrillose, margin soon split. Gills greyish, tinged with olive, then brownish, crowded, narrow, adnexed, with lighter edges. Stipe 3–8 × 0.4–1 cm, whitish or light ochre, cylindrical or enlarged at the base, never bulbous, tapering, fibrillose. Flesh whitish, fibrous in the stipe. Spermatic odour, no flavour. Spores brownish, elliptical, smooth, 7–10 × 4–5 microns.

Edibility Poisonous.

Habitat In woods and nearby grassland.

Season Autumn. Common.

Note One variety, *I. superba*, has a cap covered with abundant silky white, silvery fibrils. *I. obsoleta* has a faint mealy odour and greyish gills. *I. cookei*, another distinctive member of the group, has a small but conspicuous bulb at the base. Most species of *Inocybe* cause muscarine poisoning.

---

172 CORTINARIUS COTONEUS

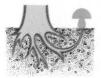

Etymology From Greek, 'the colour of wild olive'.

Description Cap 3–8 cm, olive brown or olive yellow tending to darken at disc, hemispherical becoming flattened, typically velvety and tomentose with fine, adpressed scales, dry. Gills more rusty, olive yellow, slightly distant, adnexed, broad, with lighter and slightly denticulate edge. Stipe 4–8 × 1–3 cm, pale olive yellow, darkening towards base until becoming almost cap-coloured, characterized almost invariably by a ring-shaped mark, club-shaped and enlarged at base. Veil olive yellow, cobweb-like, fugacious. Flesh pale olive yellow, darker at base of stipe. Distinctly radish-like odour and flavour. Spores rusty brown, almost globose or slightly elliptical, coarsely warty, 7–9 × 6.5–7.5 microns.

Edibility Suspect.

Habitat In broadleaved woods, particularly under beech.

Season Late summer and autumn. Rare.

Note The *Cortinarius* group is large, so its division into clearly defined subgenera is important. *C. cotoneus* is part of the subgenus *Leprocybe*, which includes fungi that are neither viscid nor hygrophanous, with fibrous, scaly or silky caps (cuticles have a specific microscopic structure), usually red, orange, yellow or olive-coloured.

173 CORTINARIUS ORICHALCEUS

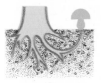

Etymology From Greek, 'copper-coloured'.

Description Cap 4–10 cm, coppery red or tawny brick-coloured, darker at disc with a greenish or blue-green area at margin, eventually entirely tawny red, convex then flattened, fleshy, smooth, viscid in damp weather. Gills greenish-yellow then rusty olive, crowded, broad, emarginate, with undulate edge. Stipe 4–8 × 1.5–2 cm, greenish-yellow, fibrillose, ending at base with a reddish-tinged marginate bulb. Veil greenish-lemon yellow, cobweb-like. Flesh whitish, tinged and greenish-yellow towards margin. No odour, sweet flavour. Spores rust brown, elliptical, warty, 11–13 × 6.5–7 microns.

Edibility Not certain.

Habitat In coniferous and mixed woods in mountains.

Season Autumn. Uncommon.

Note All *Cortinarius* have warty spores, rusty brown in mass, finally hiding original colour of gills; they also have a cobweb-like veil, hence the name (*cortina*, 'curtain', 'veil'); the remains, coloured by spores, are usually visible on stipe when mature. *C. orichalceus* is part of the subgenus *Phlegmacium*, with a smooth and viscid cap in wet weather and a dry stipe.

---

174 CORTINARIUS BULLIARDII

Etymology After the French mycologist Bulliard.

Description Cap 4–8 cm, red-brown in damp weather and light clay brown somewhat tinged with reddish in dry, convex, slightly humped, smooth. Gills pale amethyst or purple then rusty brown, slightly distant, broad, sinuate-adnate, with edge denticulate and whitish. Stipe 6–8 × 1–2 cm, pale lilac-white at top, reddish below, becoming a magnificent fiery red, cinnabar red at base, which is enlarged. Veil whitish, cobweb-like, fugacious. Flesh pale lilac-whitish, then reddish, cinnabar red at base of stipe. No particular odour or flavour. Spores rusty brown, elliptical, warty, 8.5–10.5 × 5–6 microns.

Edibility Suspect.

Habitat In dense, shady broadleaved woods, especially beneath beech, generally gregarious.

Season Autumn. Rare.

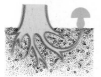

Note Part of the subgenus *Telamonia* (which includes fungi that are hygrophanous in damp weather), it is distinguished from the other red-based members of this group by its larger size and by the presence of pale lilac markings on gills, at top of stipe and in the flesh of young specimens.

175 CORTINARIUS SUBPURPURASCENS

Etymology From Latin, 'resembling *purpurascens*'.

Description Cap 5–7 cm, at first lead-coloured with violet shades at margin, then brownish-ochre tending to darken when rubbed, convex then flattened, fibrillose, smooth, viscid in wet weather. Gills pale violet then rust-coloured, turning purple-violet if bruised, slightly crowded, emarginate-adnate. Stipe 5–7 × 1–1.5 cm, pale lilac darkening towards base, with a strong tendency to turn purple-violet when rubbed, fibrillose, not very fleshy, with a not very conspicuous marginate bulb. Veil pale lilac, cobweb-like, fugacious. Flesh whitish-pale lilac, unchanging. Specific, not unpleasant odour and sweet flavour. Spores rusty brown, elliptical, warty, 8–9 × 4.5–5.5 microns.

Edibility Inedible.

Habitat In beechwoods.

Season Autumn. Uncommon.

Note *C. purpurascens* and its varieties can be identified by their fuller colours, their more massive appearance and the flesh turning purple-violet. This latter feature also singles out *C. porphyropus*, which is smaller, lighter in colour and has no marginate basal bulb. These mushrooms all belong to subgenus *Phlegmacium*.

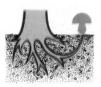

176 CORTINARIUS VIOLACEUS

Etymology From Latin, 'violet-coloured'.

Description Cap 6–15 cm, dark violet sometimes tinged with pale purple-violet, hemispherical then convex-flattened, entirely velvety-tomentose, dry and fleshy. Gills dark violet then cinnamon brown, sinuate-adnate, distant, broad, often joined at base by veins. Stipe 6–12 × 1.5–2 cm, cap-coloured but slightly lighter, at first tomentose-velvety then just fibrillose, club-shaped, full then hollow. Veil violet, cobweb-like, fugacious. Flesh violet, soft, spongy. Often a distinctive odour of cedarwood, flavour sweet. Spores rusty brown, elliptical, warty, 11–14 × 7–9 microns.

Edibility Can be eaten but not tasty.

Habitat In damp broadleaved woods, prefers oak and chestnut.

Season Autumn. Rare. In Britain found mostly in Scotland, but common in some parts of Europe.

Note An absolutely unmistakable species because of its uniform colour and the conspicuously velvety appearance of the cap cuticle; identification is also helped by the odour.

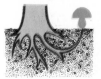

177 CORTINARIUS MULTIFORMIS

Etymology From Latin, 'changing in appearance'.
Description Cap 4–10 cm, tawny ochre, brown-ochre, tending to darken with age, hemispherical then convex-flattened, smooth, fibrillose with whitish velar remains, not striate, viscid in damp weather. Gills initially whitish then clayey and eventually rust-coloured, crowded, emarginate, edge undulate and slightly serrate. Stipe 9–6 × 1.5–2 cm, whitish with tendency to turn ochreous towards base, full, with a bulb of varying shape, generally globose or almost marginate. Veil whitish, cobweb-like, fugacious. Flesh whitish. Odour initially faint then slightly honey-like, flavour sweet. Spores rusty brown, elliptical, finely warty, almost smooth, 10–11.5 × 5–6.5 microns.
Edibility Can be eaten.
Habitat Decidious woods, especially beech.
Season Autumn. Uncommon.
Note This *Cortinarius* of subgenus *Phlegmacium* is not always easy to recognize because of its variable shape and the large number of similar species.

178 CORTINARIUS SPECIOSISSIMUS

Etymology From Latin, 'most beautiful-looking'.
Description Cap 2–8 cm, reddish-brown or reddish-tawny, immature specimens sometimes yellowish at margin because of velar remains, initially conical then flattened with an evident pointed umbo, finely felt-like, dry. Gills first cap-coloured then rusty-brown, distant, sometimes venose on the surfaces, broad and adnexed. Stipe 5–11 × 0.6–1 cm, reddish-tawny, slightly lighter than the cap, cylindrical or enlarged at the base, almost invariably with velar remains in the form of a yellowish band, solid then hollow. Veil yellowish, cobweb-like, fugacious. Flesh reddish-ochre. Odour mushroomy or slightly radish-like, flavour sweet. Spores rusty brown, ovoid, finely warty, 9–12 × 6.5–8.5 microns.
Edibility Deadly poisonous.
Habitat In coniferous woods, especially beneath Norway spruce.
Season Autumn. Rare. In Britain found mostly in Scotland.
Note This fungus is as lethal as *C. orelanus* (**186**), from which it is distinguishable by the yellowish band around the stipe, the distinctive umbo and its occurrence under conifers.

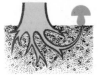

179 CORTINARIUS ALBOVIOLACEUS

Etymology From Latin, 'white and violet'.

Description Cap 3–9 cm, pale lilac-white turning paler, fibrillose, silky, convex then flattened with a central umbo, opaque, dry. Gills light violet-blue, then clayey violet, eventually rusty, slightly distant, broad, emarginate, edge denticulate. Stipe 5–10 × 1–2 cm, pale lilac-white then whitish, club-shaped, also almost cylindrical. Veil whitish, cobweb-like, fugacious. Flesh at first pale violet-blue then whitish-lilac, soft. No odour or flavour. Spores rusty brown, elliptical, warty, 8–9.5 × 5–6 microns.

Edibility Edible but not usually pleasant-tasting, usually earthy.

Habitat In broadleaved woods, especially beech and oak, often gregarious.

Season Autumn. Occasional.

Note This is a typical member of the subgenus *Sericeocybe*, whose members have generally smooth and dry to moist but not slimy caps, and never have red, yellow, olive or orange coloration.

---

180 CORTINARIUS TRAGANUS

Etymology From Greek, referring to its goat-like odour.

Description Cap 4–10 cm, a violet-amethyst colour tending to turn ochreous from the disc, hemispherical then convex, fleshy, first slightly squamulose then smooth, dry. Gills saffron ochre when immature, then cinnamon-rust-coloured, emarginate, thin, slightly distant, sometimes denticulate. Stipe 6–9 × 1–2.5 cm, cap-coloured, sometimes with ochreous bands, then brownish-ochre, downy at base, club-shaped and bulbous, fleshy. Veil pale lilac-violet-coloured, cobweb-like, fugacious. Flesh yellowish in cap, ochreous-yellow in stipe. Strong, penetrating smell of billy-goat or acetylene, sometimes fruity, flavour sweet. Spores rusty brown, elliptical, warty, 8–10 × 5–6 microns.

Edibility Inedible, but may be used for flavouring.

Habitat In coniferous woods, isolated or gregarious.

Season Autumn. Rare. In Britain found especially in Scotland.

Note Like *C. alboviolaceus* (**179**), this mushroom is a purplish member of subgenus *Sericeocybe*. It is distinguished by its ochre-cinnamon-coloured flesh, especially in the stipe, and its goat-like odour.

181 CORTINARIUS GLAUCOPUS

Etymology From Greek, 'with light blue leg'.

Description Cap 5–10 cm, tawny ochreous tinged with olive, particularly at edge, hemispherical then flattened, soft, conspicuously fibrillose, viscid in damp weather. Gills bluish or pale lilac, then tinged with a clayey coloration, eventually turning light cinnamon-coloured, crowded, thin, emarginate, edge undulate or slightly denticulate. Stipe 4–8 × 1–2 cm, bluish or pale lilac, then ochreous from base upwards, fibrillose, with a rounded marginate bulb usually narrowing after margin. Veil whitish to pale lilac, cobweb-like, fugacious. Flesh whitish-ochre in cap, pale lilac in stipe and more intensely ochre at base. Slightly mealy odour, sweet flavour. Spores rusty brown, elliptical, with small wart, 7–9 × 4.5–5.5 microns.

Edibility Can be eaten.

Habitat In coniferous and deciduous woods, gregarious, often in large groups.

Season Autumn. Occasional.

Note Unlike subgenus *Myxacium*, which has a slimy cap and stipe, subgenus *Phlegmacium*, to which this species belongs, has a slimy to sticky cap (shiny when dry) and dry stipe; its species are further divided into those with a conspicuous marginate bulb at the base of the stem, and those in which it is club-shaped to equal.

182 CORTINARIUS PRAESTANS

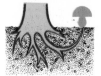

Etymology From Latin, 'prominent' or 'outstanding'.

Description Cap 7–20 cm, reddish or wine brown, margin sometimes violet, covered by a whitish-violet veil that may leave scaly remains of the same colour, hemispherical then convex, soft and fleshy, striate at margin in mature specimens, viscid in damp weather. Gills whitish-grey tinged with pale lilac, then rust-coloured, crowded, adnexed, edge slightly eroded. Stipe 10–15 × 3–6 cm, pale lilac-white, turning paler, bluish-white, band-shaped velar remains on adults, club-shaped and bulbous, fibrillose, sturdy. Veil pale blue-white, cobweb-like, fugacious. Flesh whitish in cap and bulb, pale blue in stipe. No odour or flavour. Spores rusty brown, elliptical, warty, very large, 12–17.5 × 8–9 microns.

Edibility Very good.

Habitat In broadleaved and deciduous woods on calcareous soil.

Season Autumn. Rare.

Note *Cortinarius* is not a genus much sought after for eating despite its relative abundance and the many different species (about 800 in North America, over 1000 in Europe). Unlike *C. praestans*, few are particularly tasty; some are lethal; many are mildly toxic; most are unknown.

183 CORTINARIUS TRIVIALIS

Etymology From Latin, 'common'.

Description Cap 3–8 cm, olive ochre-yellow or tawny brown, turning from campanulate-convex to flattened, often with an obtuse umbo, smooth, glutinous in damp weather, edge involute for a long period. Gills clay-coloured or pale amethyst-coloured, then rust cinnamon-coloured, not very crowded, thin, broad, adnate or decurrent with a small tooth. Stipe 4–10 × 1–1.5 cm, white at top, brownish-ochre lower down, slender, tall, usually tapered and almost truncated at base, covered in wet weather by a glutinous universal veil, which, as it dries, leaves behind numerous scaly bands. Veil glutinous, whitish, cobweb-like, fugacious. Flesh whitish-ochre, dark ochre at base of stipe. No odour, flavour sweet. Spores rusty brown, elliptical, warty, 10–15 × 6–8 microns.

Edibility Can be eaten.

Habitat In broadleaved woods, often with willow or beech.

Season Autumn. Occasional.

Note Typically, members of the subgenus *Myxacium*, to which *C. trivialis* belongs, are entirely viscid in wet weather. *C. mucosus*, a similar species, grows under conifers.

184 CORTINARIUS PSEUDOSALOR

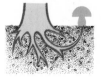

Etymology From Greek, 'resembling *salor*', from its resemblance to that species.

Description Cap 4–7 cm, varying from yellow-ochre to tawny-olive green, almost hemispherical then flattened-convex, sometimes campanulate, with or without umbo, very viscid in damp weather; margin smooth or slightly rugose, also raised in mature specimens. Gills creamy-ochre then tinged with rust, broad, averagely crowded, adnate, with edge paler and uneven. Stipe 6–10 × 1–1.5 cm, pale blue-violet, glutinous below, paler when mature, slender, almost cylindrical or narrowing at base, which may have ochreous floccose zones; striate at apex. Veil glutinous, whitish, cobweb-like, fugacious. Flesh whitish with ochreous shading. Slightly honey-like odour, flavour sweet. Spores rusty brown, elliptical, warty, 11–15 × 7–8 microns.

Edibility Uncertain.

Habitat In broadleaved woods, especially with beech, more rarely with conifers.

Season Autumn. Very common.

Note *C. elatior*, also a *Myxacium*, is similar in odour and colouring, with stipe sometimes pale blue, but it differs in the cap, which is deeply sulcate at margin; the gills, which are venose; and the stipe, which is conspicuously spindle-shaped.

185 CORTINARIUS METRODII

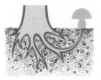

Etymology After the French mycologist Metrod.
Description Cap 4–7 cm, yolk yellow or orange-yellow, conical-campulate then convex and also slightly depressed at disc, smooth, viscid in wet weather. Gills light violet then rust-coloured, thin, crowded, straight, adnate or slightly decurrent. Stipe 7–9 × 1–1.5 cm, whitish, long, club-shaped or with a distinctive bulb at base, which may also narrow into a point, often recurved, covered by a whitish glutinous sheath, solid then hollow. Veil whitish, cobweb-like, fugacious. Flesh whitish turning slightly yellow, especially at base. No particular odour or flavour. Spores rusty brown, elliptical, warty, 10.5–11.5 × 5.5–6.5 microns.
Edibility Uncertain and best avoided.
Habitat In coniferous woods.
Season Autumn. Very rare.
Note Other *Myxacium* fungi that may have the cap tinged with orange are *C. vibratilis* (small, stipe slender, gills cream-coloured with very bitter flesh), and *C. collinitus* (stipe almost cylindrical and pale blue in colour, with pale gills).

186 CORTINARIUS ORELLANUS

Etymology After *Bixa orellana*, a plant from which a dye is extracted.
Description Cap 3–8 cm, tawny brown, reddish-brown or reddish-orange, convex-campanulate then flattened with a low, obtuse umbo, finely felt-like, dry. Gills tawny-saffron coloured then rusty brown, distant thick, broad, adnexed or decurrent with a small tooth. Stipe 4–9 × 1–2 cm, yellow then saffron yellow, cylindrical or narrowing at base, fibrillose with reddish or cap-coloured fibrils, soft. Veil pale yellow, cobweb-like, fugacious. Flesh light yellow then tawnyish, thin at cap margin. Slight odour of radish, sweet flavour. Spores rusty brown, elliptical, warty, 8.5–12 × 5.5–6.5 microns.
Edibility Deadly poisonous.
Habitat Broadleaved woods.
Season Autumn. Rare in Britain, widely distributed in Europe.
Note The number of species of *Continarius* known to be poisonous is increasing as more research is undertaken. *C. orellanus* belongs to the subgenus *Leprocybe*, as does lethal *C. speciosissimus* (**179**).

187 HEBELOMA CRUSTULINIFORME

Common name Poison pie.

Etymology From Latin, 'biscuit-like', from its colour.

Description Cap 5–15 cm, light ochre, yellowish, or bri[e] coloured, disc a deeper colour, brownish-ochre, conic[ ] convex, convex-flat, typically with large obtuse umbo[ ] slightly humped; when mature sometimes raised at marg[ ] smooth, initially slightly viscid in damp weather. Gills wh[ ] ish then ochreous-brown, eventually brown, short, sinua[te] crowded, with edge denticulate, irregular and lighter. T[he] gills produce small watery droplets in young specimens i[n] in damp weather; when dry they look spotted. Stipe 4–7[ ] 1–2.5 cm, white, finely floccose towards top (sometimes[ ] base also), solid, cylindrical or enlarged at base, alm[ost] bulbous. Flesh whitish. Radishy odour and slightly bit[t] flavour. Spores, elliptical, warty, 10–12 × 5–6 microns.

Edibility Poisonous.

Habitat In groups, beneath broadleaved trees.

Season Autumn. Common.

Note In Europe there are numerous species of *Hebelom[a]* few are well known and for this reason none should [be] eaten. The genus is recognized by the smooth, pallid, slim[ ] cap, becoming shiny when dry, clay brown gills, oft[en] radishy odour, and its terrestrial habitat.

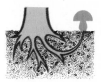

188 HEBELOMA SACCHARIOLENS

Etymology From Latin, 'smelling of sugar'.

Description Cap 2–6 cm, whitish, brown at disc, entir[e] surface darkening with age, campanulate then conve[x] smooth, quite viscid in damp weather. Gills whitish the[n] brown-ochre, eventually rust-coloured, adnate, long, edg[e] whitish, split. Stipe 4–5 × 1 cm, white, then tinged wit[h] ochre or brownish starting at base, fibrillose, white an[d] pruinose at the top, solid, narrowing towards top. Fles[h] yellowish, sometimes brown-ochre in stem. Distinctiv[e] odour of orange blossom or caramel, flavour sweetis[h] Spores brownish, elliptical, finely ornamented, 12–17 × 7–[ ] microns.

Edibility Not known.

Habitat In woodland.

Season Autumn. Occasional.

Note The carpophores of *H. anthracophilum* are foun[d] among charcoal remains; the flesh is elastic and bitter, stip[e] floccose, whitish and darkening from base upwards.

189   HEBELOMA RADICOSA

Synonym *Myxocybe radicosum.*
Etymology From Latin, 'with a root'.
Description Cap 5–15 cm or more, whitish ochre-brownish, never uniformly coloured, also with reddish markings, in wet weather covered with an abundant shiny viscous layer tending to dry off revealing adpressed fibrillose scales, fleshy, convex then fairly expanded, edge faintly sulcate or recurved. Gills whitish then rust brown, rounded at base, semi-free, crowded. Stipe 7.5–25 × 1–2.5 cm, whitish with inferior membranous ring, white then brownish, above which stipe is white and mealy, below which covered with floccose scales that become reddish-brown, sturdy, enlarged below and prolonged into a long rooting base, solid. Flesh whitish. Pleasant odour of bitter almonds or cherry laurel, flavour sweetish. Spores ochreous, elliptical, slightly roughened, 9–10 × 5–6 microns.
Edibility Can be eaten, although of mediocre quality.
Habitat Solitary or gregarious, in humus-rich woods.
Season Autumn. Rare.
Note A large and easily identifiable species. Species of *Phaeocollybia*, a related genus, have deeply rooting stipes and occur under conifers; they have rust brown spores and lack a veil.

190   PHOLIOTA ADIPOSA

Etymology From Latin, 'fat'.
Description Cap 3–17 cm, yellow, covered with floccose-gelatinous scales, dark rust-coloured on yellow background, concentrical and dropping off, cap thus eventually flat, sometimes humped, viscid in wet weather. Gills yellowish then rust-coloured, adnate, broad. Stipe 6–16 × 1–2.5 cm, first whitish then yellow, covered beneath the ring by pointed rust-coloured scales, gelatinous-viscous, enlarged toward base. Membranous ring, yellow then rust-coloured scales, gelatinous-viscous, enlarged towards base. Membranous ring, yellow then rust-coloured. Flesh yellowish, light brown at base. Odourless, with a slightly bitter flavour. Spores rust brown, elliptical, smooth, 5–7 × 3–4 microns.
Edibility Mediocre.
Habitat At base of trunks, often still living, of broadleaved species such as beech.
Season Autumn.
Note In *P. aurivella* the cap scales are entirely adpressed on rusty yellow background, broad and brownish. The stipe is not even slightly viscous, but fibrillose and floccose, whitish at the top tinged with yellowish-brown from the base upwards.

191   PHOLIOTA SQUARROSA

Etymology From Latin, 'covered with scales'.

Description Cap 3–10 cm, rust yellow or ochre, dry, convex-campanulate, flattened, barely raised at the centre or humped, covered with evident warts, which are crowded, tall, persistent, darker. Gills pale green then rust-coloured, adnate, crowded. Stipe 7–20 × 1–2.5 cm, cap-coloured, narrowing towards the base, though sometimes enlarged at base, covered with scales, raised, crowded, dark brown below ring. Ring dependent, dark brown. Flesh pale yellow. Odour of rotting wood, sometimes odourless, flavour not unpleasant. Spores rusty brown, elliptical, smooth, 6–8 × 3.5–4 microns.

Edibility Can be eaten, but see **Caution**.

Habitat In dense tufts on tree stumps, trunks or roots of broadleaved species, less often on conifers. A parasitic species.

Season Autumn. Common.

Note *P. squarrosoides* has an erect to recurved cap and stalk scales, and is somewhat slimy in wet weather. *P. squarrosoadiposa*, with viscid yellow cap, has adpressed cap scales, but raised scales on the stipe.

Caution Causes some people to experience mild to severe digestive upset.

---

192   PHOLIOTA ALNICOLA

Etymology From Latin, 'living on alder'.

Description Cap 3–11 cm, bright yellow and almost transparent when wet, also mucilaginous, ochreous when dry tending to become reddish or tinged with green, fleshy, convex then flat, margin initially fibrillose. Gills ochreous-brown, pale then rust-coloured, slightly adnate. Stipe 4–9 × 0.4–1.2 cm, lemon yellow then invariably darkening from base, fibrillose or slightly floccose, top pale yellow eventually darkening, tapering towards bottom if tufted, otherwise slightly enlarged, usually curved or supple. Veil abundant, pale, fibrillose, remaining mostly adherent to cap edge. Flesh cap-coloured, soft, rather fibrous in stipe. Odour pleasant, fruity, flavour bitter.Spores rust red, elliptical, 8–10 × 4–5.5 microns.

Edibility Inedible because of the bitter flavour.

Habitat Isolated but more often clustered on dead alder stumps and trunks, also on other broadleaved species in damp places.

Season Autumn. Common.

193 PHOLIOTA DESTRUENS

Etymology From Latin, 'destroying'.
Description Cap 6–20 cm, yellowish-white tending to brown-ochre at disc, covered with white scales, woolly fungacious, sometimes slightly viscid, convex then flat slightly umbonate or, rarely, humped, margin fibrillose initially involute. Gills white becoming gradually brownish rounded at stipe or fairly adnate, crowded. Stipe 5–17 × 2–3 cm, cap-coloured, darker at enlarged, rooting stipe, covered by same type of scales, even if raised, below a white ring floccose, fugacious. Flesh white, cinnamon brown at stipe. Odour of malt, flavour somewhat bitter, but sometimes sweetish. Spores brownish, elliptical, smooth, 7–10 × 4–6 microns.
Edibility Edible, but of poor quality.
Habitat On dead broadleaved trunks, especially poplars.
Season Autumn. Rare.
Note This is commonly seen where poplars have been cut. Its mycelium readily penetrates and breaks down the soft wood and mushrooms develop on stumps and out of the cut surfaces of logs.

---

194 PHOLIOTA CARBONARIA

Etymology From Latin, 'of coal', because of its habitat.
Description Cap 3–9 cm, ochreous-red, orange-brown, viscid in damp weather, fairly shiny when dry, glabrous or finely squamulose towards edge, recurved, convex then flat and slightly depressed at disc. Gills clay-coloured, then tinged with pale straw yellow eventually turning greyish-brown, adnate, crowded. Stipe 2.5–11 × 0.2–1.4 cm, whitish or pale lemon yellow at top, reddish lower down, blackish at base, elastic and tough, cylindrical or tapering towards base, fibrillose and squamose, with a mycelium that incorporates the substratum in a spheroidal mass at the base. Veil fibrillose and fugacious. Flesh yellowish, whitish towards stipe, firm. Slightly earthy odour, flavour sweetish. Spores dark rusty brown, elliptical, smooth, 6–8 × 3.5–4 microns.
Edibility Edible, but of poor quality.
Habitat Isolated or in small tufts on the remains of charcoal kilns or fires, or on burnt ground.
Season Early spring to the first winter frosts.
Note This fungus is easily identified by its habitat, which also hosts other fungi such as *Hebeloma anthracophilum* (see **Note** to **188**), *Geopetalum carbonarium* and some cup-shaped Ascomycetes belonging to the genera *Anthracobia*, *Geopyxis*, *Peziza* and *Ascobolus*.

195 AGROCYBE CYLINDRACEA

Synonyms *Pholiota aegerita; Agrocybe aegerita; Pholiota cylindracea.*
Etymyology From Latin, 'cylindric'.
Description Cap 3–12 cm, pale ochre-brown tending to fade to whitish from margin, convex then rugose and flat, slightly viscid and opalescent if wet, silky when dry, often cracked and aerolated at disc. Gills whitish then greyish-brown, adnate or adnate-decurrent, fairly crowded. Stipe 8–15 × 1.5–3 cm, whitish tinged with pale ochre-brown, narrowing towards base, fistular, fragile and fibrillose. Ring white, membranous, superior, pendant. Flesh whitish, brown beneath cuticle and at base. Pleasant cheese-like odour and flavour. Spores brown, broadly elliptical, smooth, 8–10 × 5–7 microns.
Edibility Very good.
Habitat In tufts or gregarious on dead wood, stumps and trunks of broadleaved species (prefers elm), also on living wood.
Season Late summer to autumn. Occasional.
Note Well known since antiquity, this was probably the first fungus to be cultivated artificially. Easily grown using small poplar trunks, straw or other vegetable remains, in the right conditions it will form its first fruit-bodies in 2–3 months. In order to bear fruit the mycelium needs sunlight.

196 GALERINA MUTABILIS

Synonyms *Pholiota mutabils; Kuehneromyces mutabilis.*
Etymology From Latin, 'changeable'.
Description Cap 3–6 cm, reddish to dark brown, very hygrophanous when wet, fading to ochreous on drying, smooth, convex then flat or faintly umbonate, sometimes depressed or irregularly humped when old. Gills pale yellow then cinnamon-coloured, adnate-decurrent, crowded, quite broad. Stipe 4–8 × 0.5–1 cm, rust brown, blackish towards base, covered up to ring with raised scales, smooth or very pale at top, rigid, cylindrical or narrowing towards base, curved. Ring membranous, brownish, persistent. Flesh whitish. Strong pleasant odour, flavour sweetish. Spores brownish-ochre, ovoid, smooth, 6–7.5 × 3–5 microns.
Edibility Caps very good, but see **Note**.
Habitat In tufts, sometimes quite extensive, on broadleaved and conifer stumps and logs.
Season Autumn. Common.
Note There is a **deadly look-alike** in Europe, also quite tasty. *Galerina autumnalis* and related species grow on decaying logs, in groups, and spores are ornamented. Poisoning is the same as that caused by the destroying angel (**8**).
Caution See **Note**.

197 ROZITES CAPERATA

Synonym *Pholiota caperata*.

Etymology From Latin, 'wrinkled', from cap appearance.

Description Cap 5–12 cm, yellowish, fleshy, soft, first campanulate then convex, eventually flat, shiny, cuticle with scattered silvery pruinescence, detaching along edge, persistent at centre, thin irregular grooves, especially at the margin, making it slightly wrinkled or puckered. Gills yellowish, crowded, of average length, adnate. Stipe 6–15 × 1–2.5 cm, whitish-cream, sturdy, fibrous, solid, cylindrical or narrowing from bottom to top, with soft, membranous, yellowish-white ring. Flesh creamy-white, soft and fragile. Odour faint, flavour sweet. Spores rusty brown, elliptical, warty, 11–14 × 7–9 microns.

Edibility Good; turns water yellow when boiled.

Habitat With pine and fir, in moss and *Calluna* (heather).

Season Autumn. Rare. In Britain found mostly in Scotland.

Note Although superficially resembling an *Agrocybe* or *Pholiota* in appearance, this mushroom is classed separately because of its slightly roughened-warty spores.

198 GYMNOPILUS JUNONIUS

Synonyms *G. spectabilis*; *Pholiota spectabilis*.

Etymology From Latin, 'of Juno'.

Description Cap 5–15 cm or more, semi-globose, fairly convex, expanded, slightly undulate, compact, fleshy, with fibrils or innate small fibrillose scales, adpressed, orange-yellow against a golden yellow background, eventually leather yellow. Gills yellow then rust-coloured, adnate, very crowded. Stipe 6–13 × 2–3 cm or more, sulphur yellow or cap-coloured, sturdy, fairly enlarged at middle, normally with rooting base, fusiform, sometimes squamulose, fibrillose, sometimes smooth, shiny, mealy at top, with full membranous ring, yellowish then rust-coloured, inferior, persistent. Flesh sulphur yellow, reddish when touched, thick, compact. Pleasant odour, bitter but aromatic flavour. Spores rust-coloured, almond-shaped, warty, 7.5–9 × 5.5–7 microns.

Edibility Quite bitter; reported to cause temporary alteration in visual perception.

Habitat Tufted, on stumps or at the base of unhealthy coniferous and broadleaved trees.

Season Autumn. Common.

Note This widely distributed species is more common on some trees than others, depending on the environment, although it can adapt to any type of wood.

199 PHAEOLEPIOTA AUREA

Synonym *Pholiota aurea.*
Etymology From Latin, 'gold-coloured'.
Description Cap 4–15 cm, golden ochre-yellow, first powdery because of small and quite crowded scales, then velvety and darker, hemispherical then convex, eventually expanded with inconspicuous umbo. Gills rounded towards stipe, ochreous then rust-coloured, crowded. Stipe 6–28 × 1–3.5 cm, sturdy, almost cylindrical, slightly enlarged at base, solid, with large ring, ascendant, permanent, almost cap-coloured, similarly powdery and then squamulose-velvety, with conspicuous darker radiating lines, whitish above ring, pale ochre and pruinose. Flesh soft, whitish and pale yellow when exposed to air, reddish towards base. Strong, aromatic odour, distinctive flavour. Spores golden ochre, elliptical, roughened, 9–15 × 4–6 microns.
Edibility Good, but can cause stomach upset.
Habitat Broadleaved woods.
Season Autumn. Rare.
Note This is a large, uncommon mushroom, resembling both *Pholiota* and *Cystoderma.*

200 CONOCYBE TENERA

Etymology From Latin, 'tender' or 'delicate'.
Description Cap 1–2 cm, pale rust-coloured, fading when dry, hygrophanous, thin, conical-campanulate, smooth. Gills cinnamon-coloured, adnexed or free, straight and quite crowded. Stipe 7.5–10 × 1.5–2 cm, cap-coloured, fragile, cylindrical, straight and rigid, silky, striate lengthwise, pruinose. Flesh membranous in cap, slightly fibrous in stipe, but almost non-existent. Spores pale rust-coloured, elliptical, smooth, 8–15 × 5.5–8 microns.
Edibility Of no value because of its size, and possibly poisonous, like some other species in the genus.
Habitat In soil in woods, grassland and gardens.
Season Autumn. Common.
Note *C. tenera* belongs to a group of small fungi of no gastronomic interest; most of these require microscopic examination to establish the precise species. One species, *C. lactea,* has a white cap and stalk and cinnamon-coloured gills; it comes up overnight on lawns after rains and usually disappears by noon.

201 PHOLIOTINA TOGULARIS

Synonyms *Conocybe togularis; Pholiota togularis.*
Etymology From Latin, 'with a small cloak'.
Description Cap 0.5–2 cm, pale ochre, darker at disc, campanulate then expanded, slightly convex, sometimes striate. Gills yellow, light rust-coloured when mature, crowded, narrowing at both ends. Stipe 1–4 cm × 0.5–1.5 mm, yellowish tending to darken towards base which is enlarged, fibrillose lengthwise, pruinose at top. Ring whitish, membranous, central, broad. Flesh very thin, pale yellow. Spores rust-ochre, smooth, varying in size becasue they are produced by two- and four-spored basidia, by the former 10.5–12.6 × 5.4–6.8 microns, in the latter 8–10 × 4.5–5.5 microns.
Edibility Poisonous, possibly fatal.
Habitat In grassland, gardens and pastures.
Season Spring to late autumn.
Note *Pholiotina filaris*, an allied species, has recently been found to contain amanitins, toxic compounds causing the same lethal poisoning as that of the destroying angel group of *Amanita.*

---

202 AGARICUS AUGUSTUS

Synonym *Psalliota augusta.*
Etymology From Latin, 'majestic'.
Description Cap 10–20 cm, initially subglobose, flat at top, then convex and eventually flattened, cuticle dry and detachable, broken up into small fibrillose scales, adpressed, reddish-brown on a yellow-cream background. Gills crowded, free, white then grey, pink and eventually chocolate brown.Stipe 10–20 × 2–3 cm, cylindrical, enlarged at base, solid then slightly hollow, white turning yellowish with age, pinkish above ring, which is large, membranous and double with brownish enlargement in lower part. Flesh white, turning yellow then brown when exposed to air, reddish at end of stipe. Odour of almonds, flavour sweet. Spores brown, ovoid, smooth, 7.5–9 × 5–5.5 microns.
Edibility Excellent.
Habitat Deciduous woods.
Season Autumn. Rare.
Note The gills, which remain white for a long period, may cause it to be confused with a *Lepiota.*

203 AGARICUS XANTHODERMUS

Common name Yellow-staining mushroom.

Etymology From Greek, 'yellow-skinned'.

Description Cap 6–12 cm, globose-cylindrical then truncated-conical, finally convex but flattened at top and expanded; cuticle dry, white, at times tinged greyish or brownish, or with small adpressed scales; normally the surface has chrome yellow markings. Gills free, crowded, whitish then pinkish, eventually blackish-brown. Stipe 8–15 × 0.8–1.2 cm, cylindrical, often curved towards base, with conspicuous basal bulb, fistular, smooth, silky, white but chrome yellow when touched, especially lower down. Ring membranous, slightly floccose and denticulate in lower part, white with margin turning yellow then darkening. Flesh white, turning slightly yellow beneath cuticle, decidedly chrome yellow at base of stem. Strong odour of carbolic acid, iodine or ink, flavour sweetish. Spores blackish-brown, ovoid, smooth, 5–6.5 × 3.5–5 microns.

Edibility Poisonous, causing severe symptoms resulting in coma in some people. Others can eat it with impunity.

Habitat In groups, in open woods or grassland, meadows and gardens.

Season Summer and autumn. Common.

204 AGARICUS ARVENSIS

Synonym *Psalliota arvensis*.

Common name Horse mushroom.

Etymology From Latin, 'of fields', from its habitat.

Description Cap 7–15 cm, subglobose becoming flattened, silky, white, turning yellow when touched, frayed with velar remains at margin. Gills crowded, greyish turning pinkish and eventually blackish, with white edge, free. Stipe 8–13 × 1.5–3 cm, club-shaped, fistular when mature, white, turning yellow, ring descendant, cog-wheel-like below. Flesh white, with age or when drying out becoming ochre-yellow starting from the base. Odour of anise, flavour sweet. Spores dark brown, oval, smooth, 7–8 × 4–5 microns.

Edibility Excellent, but see **Note**.

Habitat In groups of fairy-rings in fields, pastures, grassy areas.

Season Autumn. Occasional.

Note Some similar species that grow in woodland are often confused with *A. arvensis* because of their appearance and the smell of anise. Before eating any species of *Agaricus* one should always make sure there is no yellow coloration in the base of the stem when broken and the flesh rubbed. The cap surface should always be bruised to see whether a vivid chrome yellow colour results; if so **do not eat**.

205 AGARICUS SILVICOLA

Synonym *Psalliota silvicola.*
Common name Wood mushroom.
Etymology From Latin, 'growing in woods'.
Description Cap 5–12 cm, first globose then campanulate becoming expanded, cuticle dry, shiny, whitish, yellowing with age or when touched. Gills crowded, free, initially dirty white then pinkish, sepia brown when mature. Stipe 6–11 × 1.5–2.5 cm, slender, faintly hollow, fragile, basal bulb white turning yellowish, pinkish above ring, ring double, cogwheel-like. Flesh white, pinkish in stipe. Faint smell of anise, flavour pleasant. Spores cocoa-coloured, oval, smooth, 5–6 × 3–4 microns.
Edibility Good, but see **Caution.**
Habitat In broadleaved woods.
Season Autumn. Common.
Note *A. abruptibulbus* is a very similar species, but the bulb is clearly marginate and slightly curved at the base, and the spores are larger.
Caution When collecting woodland species of *Agaricus*, be especially careful with buttons or immature specimens: they can be confused with the immature buttons of the death cap group of *Amanita.*

---

206 AGARICUS BISPORUS

Common name Cultivated mushroom.
Etymology From Latin, 'with two spores'.
Description Cap 5–10 cm, white then rose, brownish when mature, fleshy, globose or hemispherical then convex and also completely expanded, flat, young specimens with white, soft, denticulate, fugacious fringe at edge. Gills rose-white in young specimens, reddish-brownish in mature fungi, crowded, not adherent. Stipe 3–5 × 1–1.5 cm, white, sometimes rose above ring in young specimens, squat, pithy then somewhat hollow; ring white, thick, soft, membranous, descending. Flesh white; when exposed to air young specimens are tinged rose, older specimens tinged brownish; thick, soft. Pleasant odour and flavour. Spores cocoa or violet-brown, elliptical, smooth, 6–9 × 4–6 microns.
Edibility Excellent.
Habitat In grassland, gardens, orchards, meadows, beside roads, in open places, on horse droppings.
Season Autumn. Occasional.
Note Cultivated since the eighteenth century and giving rise to a flourishing agricultural industry in all countries with a temperate climate. This is virtually the only fresh mushroom sold throughout Britain; other kinds can sometimes be found locally in delicatessens.

207 AGARICUS LANGEI

Etymology After the Danish mycologist Lange.

Description Cap 6–12 cm, semi-globose then expanded, covered with brownish fibrillose scales, thinning out towards edge, cuticle joined and darker at centre, dry. Gills free, pinkish, finally blackish-brown, crowded, short, margin sterile and whitish. Stipe 7–12 × 1.5–2.5 cm, almost cylindrical or faintly enlarged at base, smooth above ring, white and floccose below, tinged with red and then darkening if touched, hollow. Ring descending, large, membranous, with small brown scales below. Flesh at once crimson when cut. Slightly acid but pleasant odour and flavour. Spores blackish-brown, ovoid, smooth, 7–9 × 3.5–5 microns.

Edibility Good.

Habitat Gregarious, in coniferous and broadleaved woods.

Season Autumn. Common.

Note A. haemorrihoidarius has smaller spores, brownish scales on stipe and grows in broadleaved woods. A. silvaticus is similar but generally smaller and bruises red more slowly.

208 STROPHARIA AERUGINOSA

Common name Verdigris fungus.

Etymology From Latin, 'copper-green'.

Description Cap 3–7 cm, bluish-green, tending to turn yellow or pale with age as viscous gluten washes off; while hydrated, bluish, cuticle beneath, yellowish; rather fleshy, campanulate-convex, then flat, slightly umbonate or obtuse, often with whitish fugacious squamules. Gills brownish, finally purplish-brown, adnate, not very crowded. Stipe 4–10 × 0.4–1.2 cm, cap-coloured though paling more quickly. Ring often blackish above due to trapped spores. Flesh bluish, fading to whitish. No odour or flavour. Spores violet-brown, elliptical, smooth, 7–9 × 4–5 microns.

Edibility Quite good without the viscous cuticle.

Habitat On litter in broadleaved woods, sometimes under conifers and in open grassy areas or under nettles.

Season Autumn. Common.

Note The pale green coloration also marks the small S. albocyanea, green then whitish with colourless mucus, stipe not viscid, whitish or pale green, with incomplete white ring. S. cyanea is much more similar, ring floccose and evanescent, gills brownish with lighter edges.

209 PSILOCYBE SQUAMOSA

Synonyms *Stropharia squamosa; Naematoloma squamosum.*
Etymology From Latin, 'scaly'.
Description Cap 3–5 cm, hemispherical or campanulate, eventually almost flat, hygrophanous, olive grey, orange-yellow at disc, turning straw yellow when drying, starting at edge; detachable viscous layer, with vaguely concentric pale yellow scales, fugacious, initially making margin appendiculate. Gills violet then dark grey, white-edged, quite crowded, adnate. Stipe slender, 3–16 × 0.3–0.8 cm, rigid, straight to curved at slightly enlarged base, covered up to frayed membranous ring by a fibrillose veil, broken up into small raised scales, yellowish then reddish at base, white and finely pruinose-striate at top, fistular. Flesh pale yellow in cap, fibrous and reddish-yellow towards stipe. No odour or flavour. Spores violet-brown, elliptical, smooth, 12.5–14.5 × 7–8 microns.
Edibility Uncertain.
Habitat In broadleaved litter, basal mycelium closely associated with vegetable remains, dead wood or leaves.
Season Autumn. Occasional.
Note *P. thrausta* is very similar but has a bright reddish cap. Although both mushrooms are now considered to be species of *Psilocybe*, neither is hallucinogenic.
Caution Edibility is uncertain.

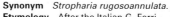

210 STROPHARIA FERRII

Synonym *Stropharia rugosoannulata.*
Etymology After the Italian G. Ferri.
Description Cap 5–20 cm, ochreous to brick red, with pale purple shades, first semi-globose, convex with involute margin, then flattened, very often split at margin, fleshy, fibrillose, dry. Gills violet-grey, adnate, crowded, thin. Stipe 7–14 × 0.9–1.5 cm, cylindrical, faintly narrowing towards top, solid, slightly tinged with yellow lower down, large membranous ring, sulcate higher up, where it soon becomes coloured by spores. Flesh white, soft. No odour or particular flavour, sometimes slightly earthy. Spores violet-charcoal grey, elongated-ovoid, smooth, 10–12 × 6–8 microns.
Edibility Delicious.
Habitat In wood-chip mulch and humus-rich soils.
Season Autumn. Rare.
Note Easy to cultivate on ground with plenty of straw, this robust, choice edible species is found in the mulch around garden shrubbery. It is easy to confuse with some species of *Agaricus* (they have free gills) and some species of *Agrocybe* (they have brown gills and give a brown spore-print).

211 STROPHARIA SEMIGLOBATA

Etymology From Latin, 'like a half sphere'.
Description Cap 1–5 cm, light yellow, hemispherical, obtuse, smooth, viscid. Gills very broad, up to 1.3 cm long, flat, adnate, greyish with black marks. Stipe 5–15 × 0.2–0.4 cm, pale yellow, paler at top, straight, rigid, faintly enlarged at base, covered by a glutinous transparent veil beneath ring, which is thin, viscid and incomplete. Flesh pale yellow, thin. Odour mealy, flavour sweetish. Spores violet-brown, elliptical, smooth, 16–21 × 8–10 microns.
Edibility Of no value because of size.
Habitat Directly on manure, mainly of horses or cattle, and among tall grass in meadows.
Season Spring to late autumn. Common.
Note This is one of the many dark-spored, gilled fungi that grow on dung, including species of *Coprinus* (**227**), *Panaeolus* (**217, 218, 219**), and *Psilocybe*. Their identification of species is often difficult without microscopic examination.

212 STROPHARIA CORONILLA

Etymology From Greek, 'with a small garland'.
Description Cap 2–5 cm, ochreous-yellow, lemon yellow, fleshy, hemispherical then convex, eventually flat, smooth with white, floccose margin. Gills pale yellow then violet, white-edged, adnate, crowded. Stipe 3–4 × 0.4–1 cm, white, cylindrical, ring white, persistent, striate, in central part of stipe. Flesh white and soft. No particular odour or flavour. Spores violet-brown, elliptical, smooth, 6.5–10 × 4–6 microns.
Edibility Possibly mildly toxic.
Habitat Common in lawns and grassy areas.
Season Autumn.
Note Resembles a small field mushroom (*Agaricus*), but the gills are not free. *S. melanosperma* is very similar, but rarer, with whitish cap, pale yellow at disc, stipe white and striate at top, ring well developed and spores blackish-violet. Another species, *S. inuncta*, is first yellowish then purplish-red on cap, which is covered with a viscous, detachable layer. The supple white stipe, with thin ring, is pruinose at top, dry and fibrillose beneath ring. It grows in fields. Similar is *S. albonitens*, which is completely white in the stipe and has a viscous cap.
Caution Possibly toxic.

213 HYPHOLOMA CAPNOIDES

Synonym *Naematoloma capnoides*.
Etymology From Greek, 'smoky' or 'smoke-coloured', referring to the gills.
Description Cap 2.5–8 cm, ochreous-yellow, convex then flat, dry, smooth, sometimes rugose, margin appendiculate with whitish velar remains. Gills whitish then ash grey, eventually violet-grey, adnexed, easily detachable from flesh, fairly crowded. Stipe 5–7 × 0.4–0.8 cm, pale ochre, then rust brown and darker at base, top whitish, cylindrical, normally curved and supple, unevenly striate, veil white then violet-brown. Flesh whitish, often rust-coloured towards base of stipe. No particular odour or flavour. Spores violet-brown, elliptical, smooth, 7–8 × 3–4 microns.

Edibility Fair to good.
Habitat Normally tufted on coniferous wood.
Season Autumn. Common.
Note This is the tastiest of the group. Unlike the other more common species, it grows exclusively in coniferous woods. Another species, *N. sublateritium*, has brick red caps and grows on logs and stumps of broadleaved woods; it is very palatable when young.

214 HYPHOLOMA FASCICULARE

Synonym *Naematoloma fasciculare*.
Common name Sulphur tuft
Etymology From Latin, 'in small bundles'.
Description Cap 2–5 cm, bright yellow, often darker at centre, convex then flat, rarely with a slight raised area at disc, smooth, dry margin sometimes appendiculate with velar remains. Gills sulphur yellow then pale green, greyish-brown when mature, adnexed, crowded. Stipe 5–22 × 0.4–1 cm, yellow, tapering or enlarged at base, curved or supple, fibrillose towards base, veil first pale yellow, cobweb-like, then covered with spores. Flesh thin and yellow. Faint distinctive odour, flavour bitter. Spores violet-brown, elliptical, smooth, 5–7 × 3.5–4 microns.

Edibility Inedible, possibly poisonous.
Habitat On stumps or buried roots of both conifers and broadleaved species, sometimes apparently parasitic, normally tufted.
Season All year round. Common.
Note *H. fasciculare* is easily recognized by its clustered growth pattern, the greenish tint of its gills and its bitter taste. In Europe and Asia there are reports of serious, even fatal poisonings from eating this species.

215 HYPHOLOMA DISPERSUM

Synonym *Naematoloma dispersum.*
Etymology From Latin, 'scattered'.
Description Cap 2–4 cm, honey brown, campanulate then convex, finally flat, smooth, with white velar fragments on the surface. Gills pale straw-coloured, eventually slightly pale greenish-grey, adnexed, ventricose, crowded, white-edged. Stipe 5–7 × 0.4–0.6 cm, cylindrical, erect, tough, sometimes rust brown, darkening at base, pale at top, with silvery-white, silky fibrils. Flesh yellowish, darker beneath cuticle and at base. No discernible odour, very bitter flavour. Spores violet-brown, oval, smooth, 7–9 × 4–5 microns.
Edibility Inedible.
Habitat Gregarious under conifers.
Season Autumn. Occasional.
Note Unlike other *Hypholomas*, this mushroom is not tufted; rather, it grows in large troops.

216 PANAEOLINA FOENISECII

Synonyms *Panaeolus foenisecil; Psathyrella foeniseci.*
Etymology From Latin, 'dry hay'.
Description Cap 1.5–3 cm, first almost hemispherical, convex or campanulate-convex, very rarely expanded and slightly umbonate, glabrous, smooth, hygrophanous, soot grey discolouring when drying out, starting from disc becoming light brownish-ochre, slightly cracked in very dry weather. Gills greyish, blackish-brown when mature, with greyish-white edge, broad, quite distant, soon detached from stipe, ventricose towards margin. Stipe 3.5–10 × 0.2–0.3 cm, brownish-grey then light ochreous, whitish, silky and fibrillose at top, pubescent at base, cylindrical, fistular, cartilaginous but fragile. Flesh thin, fragile, pale brownish-ochre in dry weather, greyish-brown when wet. Mushroomy odour, slightly acid flavour. Spores dark brown, not blackish, almond- or lemon-shaped, warty, 12–16.5 × 7.5–9 microns.
Edibility Slightly hallucinogenic when ingested in large quantities.
Habitat Gregarious in grassy areas.
Season Late summer to autumn. Common.
Note This is one of several lawn fungi that come up after rains.

217 PANAEOLUS ATER

Etymology From Latin, 'black'.
Description Cap 1–1.5 cm, subglobose, convex, obtuse, dark olive brown, sepia black, fading in dry weather from margin, turning ochreous grey-brown sometimes tinged reddish, faintly striate at margin in damp weather. Gills adnate, blackish-grey to black, ventricose, not very crowded, edge speckled with greyish. Stipe 3–7 × 0.1–0.3 cm, cylindrical, fistular, barely enlarged at top, finely striate, base pruinose, fistular, cap-coloured but lighter. Flesh thin, dark brown in moist carpophore, brownish-ochre when dry. No particular odour or flavour. Spores blackish, lemon-shaped, smooth, 10–12.5 × 6–7 microns.

Edibility Reputedly poisonous.
Habitat Isolated or in groups, on the droppings of herbivorous animals, or in fertilized grassland.
Season Late summer to autumn. Occasional.
Note Carpophores are easily recognizable while dark, but they resemble *P. fimicola* (which can be distinguished by its reddish-brown stipe, particularly near base) when turning lighter. Some species of *Panaeolus* have been found to contain compounds similar to those found in some *Psilocybe* mushrooms.

218 PANAEOLUS CAMPANULATUS

Etymology From Latin, 'bell-shaped'.
Description Cap 2–4.5 cm, with two different forms: hemispherical-convex with no umbo, white or light hazel; or conical-campanulate, campanulate-obtuse with umbo, soot brown. The cap form depends on colour, age and hygrophany of specimen. Cuticle smooth or scaly, cracked when dry in first form. Margin whitish, sometimes festooned and appendiculate with denticular velar remains, cuticle easily detachable in very wet specimens. Stipe 3–7.5 × 1.5–2.5 cm or more, slender, fistular, cylindrical, slightly enlarged at base, striate more conspicuously at top, pruinose, reddish-grey, flesh-coloured lower down, cream, ochreous at top. In first form stipe more white and pruinose, and shorter. Gills greyish speckled with black, white-edged, sometimes exuding droplets, fairly distant, adnate. Flesh faintly thicker in disc, but still thin, greyish or faintly reddish. No particular odour or flavour, but smells like burnt sugar when cut. Spores blackish, ovoid or lemon-shaped, smooth, 15–18.5 × 10–12.5 microns.

Edibility Difficult to distinguish and so should be avoided.
Habitat Isolated or in small groups, on or near droppings, normally in fields and grassland.
Season Late spring to early winter. Common.
Note This is most recognizable when the cap margin has velar remains resembling a row of white teeth.

219 PANAEOLUS SEMIOVATUS

Synonyms *Anellaria semiovata; Panaeolus separatus.*
Etymology From Latin, 'like a half-egg'.
Description Cap 2–6 cm, whitish or clay ochre, ovate-campanulate, never expanded, apex obtuse, viscid, shiny when dry, rugose and then also cracked when older, margin often appendiculate. Gills whitish, then ash black, adnate but virtually separate, ascending, up to 0.8 cm long, often whitish-edged. Stipe 5–20 × 0.4–0.8 cm, whitish, rigid and straight, faintly enlarged at base, finely striate, smooth, ring white, membranous, narrow, persistent, sometimes striate, some distance below cap. Flesh whitish, pale yellow beneath cuticle or towards base of stipe. No particular odour or flavour. Spores blackish, elongated, smooth, 16–22 × 9–15 microns.
Edibility Edibility uncertain.

Habitat On droppings, especially of horses, in grassland and woodland.
Season Spring to autumn. More common in north and west of Britain.
Note A large coprophilous species, easily identifiable because of its ring. *A. phalaenarum* is another large and very similar species, cap whitish tinged with reddish, also on the stipe, with no ring and a smell of burnt sugar.

---

220 LACRYMARIA VELUTINA

Synonyms *Hypholoma velutinum; Psathyrella velutina.*
Common name Weeping widow.
Etymology From Latin, meaning 'velvety'.
Description Cap 5–15 cm, dirty ochre, campanulate then expanded with slight central relief, hygrophanous, for a long period covered with tufts of adpressed fibrils, margin appendiculate with white velar remains. Gills brown then blackish-brown dotted with black, adnexed, easily detachable, not very crowded, white-edged, floccose, producing watery droplets. Stipe 5–13 × 0.4–1.5 cm, dark ochre, cylindrical, fistular, fragile, covered with silky fibrils, downy at top above velar remains. Veil white then black and woolly. Flesh whitish. Insignificant odour and flavour. Spores violet-brown, blackish, elliptical, warty, 8–12 × 5–7 microns.

Edibility Good when young, but see **caution**.
Habitat In woodland and grassland, usually tufted, common by roadsides and in disturbed areas.
Season Late summer to autumn. Common.
Note This is a common urban and suburban mushroom that comes up in large numbers in parks and grassy areas.
Caution Because of its overall similarity to some poisonous species of *Inocybe*, a spore-print should be made to be sure the spores are dark violet-blackish.

221 PSATHYRELLA CONOPILEA

Etymology From Latin, 'conical cap'.
Description Cap 2.5–5 cm, campanulate then expanded, obtuse or almost umbonate, thin, reddish-grey, soot brown, olive brown, turning light reddish when drying out, smooth, slightly striate at the margin. Gills blackish, fairly adnate depending on the state of expansion of the cap, linear or ventricose. Stipe 2.5–20 × 0.2–0.4 cm, quickly becoming whitish, straight, rigid, cylindrical, smooth. Flesh yellowish or dark brown in the cap, whitish in the stipe, thin. Odour undefined, flavour bitter. Spores soot black, elliptical, smooth, 14–17 × 7–9 microns.
Edibility Of no value because of size and bitterness.
Habitat Gregarious, in grassland and woodland, and under bushes.
Season Autumn.
Note *Psathyrella* is a large genus comprising some 200 species. Many grow in the same habitat and are too similar to differentiate without microscopic examination. These are mostly fragile mushrooms with brownish fading caps, black to brownish-black spores, and delicate, brittle white stipes.

222 BOLBITIUS VITELLINUS

Etymology From Latin, 'yolk-like', from its odour.
Description Cap 2–5 cm, oval becoming almost flat, cuticle viscous, yolk yellow tending to fade from the edge, deeply striate-sulcate when mature. Gills ochreous or yellow-brown tinged pinkish, quite distant, semi-free, edge frayed. Stipe 5–8 × 0.3–0.7 cm, almost cylindrical, fragile, hollow, pale yellow and white floccose elements at the base. Flesh thin, almost membranous, pale yellow. No particular odour or flavour. Spores light yellow-ochre, oval, almond-shaped, smooth, 12–14 × 7–8 microns.
Edibility Of no value because slimy, small and fleshless.
Habitat Gregarious on very decomposed dung, on compost, in fertilized land or amongst wood chips.
Season Late summer to autumn. Common.
Note This mushroom is often found in large quantities in the autumn, preferring cooler weather. It is readily identified by its viscid, striate yellow cap and its pinkish-brown gills.

223   COPRINUS ATRAMENTARIUS

Common name Ink cap.
Etymology From Latin, 'inky' or 'pertaining to ink'.
Description Cap 5–8 cm, soot brown, lead grey, adpressed scales, persistently marked, brown or brown-ochre, silky and shiny, ovate, obtuse then campanulate with lengthwise grooves and ribs, soft to touch, minutely pruinose when young, often squamulose at disc, darker, margin recurved when mature. Gills white then blackish brown, deliquescent, free, ventricose, up to 1.5 cm long, edge floccose. Stipe 7–20 × 0.8–1.8 cm, white, initially ventricose, fusiform, narrowing in lower part slightly, more at top, sulcate, with three-ring zone and small brown scales near base, hollow. Flesh grey-brown, fibrous in stipe. No special odour or flavour. Spores black, elliptical, smooth, 7–11 × 5–6.5 microns.

Edibility Good, but avoid alcohol (see **Note**).
Habitat In grassy areas, often tufted, usually associated with buried wood or roots.
Season Spring to early winter. Common.
Note When eaten with or followed by alcohol (up to 24 hours later), some people experience a 'poisoning' characterized by flushing in face and neck, tingling in fingers and toes, headache and sometimes nausea.

224   COPRINUS COMATUS

Common names Shaggy ink cap; lawyer's wig.
Etymology From Latin, 'with dense hair', from its cap.
Description Cap 4–6 cm, white turning pink at margin then black, cylindrical when young, up to 20 cm in height, then campanulate, cuticle initially continuous then quickly breaking up into soft, broad, imbricate scales, often raised, white then ochreous at margin, with top of cap non-squamose, entire, brown-ochre, striate lengthwise, margin often recurved and split when mature. Gills white then pink, finally black and deliquescent, free, straight, crowded, up to 1 cm long. Stipe 12–25 × 1–2 cm, white then dirty white or tinged pale lilac, narrowing towards top, with enlarged rooting base, hollow, with white, movable, thin, fugacious ring. Flesh white, fibrous in stipe, soft in cap where it splits radially. No odour or flavour. Spores blackish, elliptical, smooth, 11–13 × 6–7 microns.

Edibility Very good when young while gills are still white.
Habitat Isolated or gregarious, in woods, grassland, gardens, by roadsides, very common in urban and suburban areas disturbed by man.
Season Autumn. Common.

225 COPRINUS DISSEMINATUS

Synonym *Pseudocoprinus disseminatus.*
Common name Trooping crumble cap.
Etymology From Latin, 'scattered'.
Description Cap 1–2 cm, whitish or yellowish, then ash-coloured, normally grey-brown, with the centre yellowish, at first ovate, then parabolic, finally slightly expanded, furfuraceous, then glabrous and deeply striate-sulcate. Gills whitish then blackish, adnexed. Stipe 2.5–6 × 0.2 cm, white, fragile, sometimes supple, at first slightly furfuraceous owing to a silky white mycelium. Flesh very thin, whitish, faintly yellow at cap centre. No odour or flavour. Spores blackish, elliptical, smooth, 9–10 × 5–6 microns.
Edibility Of no value because of size and difficulty of cleaning.
Habitat In myriads, on or around old broadleaved stumps or in leaves.
Season Spring to late autumn. Common.
Note *C. disseminatus* occurs in groups of hundreds, often with successive generations being added in the span of a few weeks. Although it appears to be a typical *Coprinus* its gills do not become inky as it matures.

226 COPRINUS MICACEUS

Common name Mica ink cap.
Etymology From Latin, 'mica-like', because of the ornamentation of the cap when very young.
Description Cap 3–6 cm, rust yellow, greyish yellow-brown, darker at centre, finally greyish-brown, ochre-rust when dry, oval then campanulate, undulate, split lengthwise, at first striate, entirely sulcate, in early stages covered with small glassy, mica-like, fugacious granules. Gills white or very light brown, then brown, greyish-brown with age, eventually soot brown, adnexed, deliquescent. Stipe 5–10 × 0.3–0.5 cm, white or whitish, cylindrical, silky, often curved, fibrillose then smooth. Flesh thin, pale ochre. Barely detectable odour and flavour. Spores blackish-brown, elliptical, smooth, 7.5–10 × 4.5–6 microns.
Edibility Good when young.
Habitat Tufted, on broadleaved stumps and rotting wood, often on the ground arising from buried wood.
Season Spring to the first winter frost. Common.
Note One of the most common urban and suburban fungi, this mushroom appears in great numbers about stumps or on hidden roots of former street, yard and park trees.

227   COPRINUS NIVEUS

Etymology   From Latin, 'snow white'.
Description   Cap 1.5–5 cm, conical, finally with recurved margin, split and curled over on itself, completely white, floccose and mealy, often squamose. Gills white, then flesh-coloured, finally blackish, adnexed, crowded, deliquescent. Stipe 2.5–7.5 × 0.3–0.6 cm, narrowing towards top, densely covered with fugacious, pointed, floccose elements, finally smooth, always completely white, hollow. Flesh white, thin. Undefined odour and flavour. Spores black, broadly elliptical, smooth, 12–18 × 10–13 × 8–10 microns.
Edibility   Of no value because of its size.
Habitat   On dung, especially horse droppings, sometimes also on wet or fertilized ground.
Season   Summer to winter. Occasional.

228   COPRINUS PICACEUS

Common name   Magpie.
Etymology   From Latin, 'magpie-like', from its colour.
Description   Cap 5–10 cm, soot black, variegated with broad, unequal, superficial scales (originating from the break-up of the universal veil) that are white, fugacious and easily detachable, striate lengthwise, sulcate, shiny, smooth and viscid. Gills white then pink, finally black, deliquescent, free, ventricose, up to 1.2 cm long. Stipe 10–25 × 0.6–1.2 cm, white, narrowing towards the top, starting from the basal bulb, fragile, hollow, smooth. Flesh whitish, brown beneath the cuticle of the cap. Odour either non-existent or nauseous, flavour mucous. Spores blackish and elliptical, 14–18 × 10–12 microns.
Edibility   Not recommended. Probably slightly poisonous and unpleasant to eat.
Habitat   On the humus in broeadleaved woods especially with beech.
Season   Autumn. Occasional.

229 COPRINUS PLICATILIS

Common name Little Japanese umbrella.
Etymology From Latin, 'wrinkled'.
Description Cap 1–3 cm, grey-brown, then ash grey-blue, darker at centre, first oval-cylindrical then campanulate, finally expanded, sulcate-plicate radially, almost diaphanous, glabrous. Gills cream-coloured then grey, eventually blackish-grey, separated from stipe by a collarium. Stipe 2.5–7.5 × 0.1–0.2 cm, pale, sometimes transparent, cylindrical, smooth. Flesh whitish, extremely thin. No odour or flavour. Spores black, broadly elliptical, smooth, 10–12 × 8–9 microns.
Edibility Of no value because of size.
Habitat Solitary in grass, meadows, gardens, roadsides and woodland.
Season Late summer to autumn. Common.
Note This small fungus is easily recognizable by its deeply and radially sulcate cap with no ornamentation and with a conspicuous collarium. Coprophilous *C. miser* is quite distinctive when young with its red-brown or orange-red colouring. *C. auricomus* grows on the ground: the cap is covered with yellowish hairs when seen under the microscope and it lacks a collarium. It is, however, a rare or possibly overlooked species.

230 COPRINUS RADIANS

Etymology From Latin, 'radiating', because of the mycelium at base of stipe.
Description Cap 2–3 cm, ochreous then paler, membranous, ovate then campanulate, finally expanded, with small, mica-like granules at the centre, sulcate, margin striate. Gills white, violet-black when mature, adnexed, straight. Stipe 2–4 × 0.4–0.8 cm, white, slightly narrowing towards the top from the enlarged base, which originates from a dense mass of orange-brown mycelium. Flesh thin, pale ochre. Odour and flavour negligible. Spores black, elliptical-fusiform, smooth, 9–10 × 4–5 microns.
Edibility Of no value because of size.
Habitat Often tufted, on fallen trunks, especially elm, or on stacked timber.
Season All year.
Note This is an easily identifiable lignicolous species, even with no carpophore, because of the bright orange-brown tufts of mycelium. The latter resembles a moss and has been given the name *Ozonium*.

231 COPRINUS SILVATICUS

Etymology From Latin, 'of woods'.
Description Cap 2.5–4.5 cm, ovoid to conical-convex, expanded with recurved margin, leather ochre with centre orange-ochre or cinnamon-coloured, then often greyish from margin, sometimes with ochreous disc, apparently smooth, finely pubescent under a lens, deeply plicate-striate or grooved from centre, quite often incised at margin. Gills whitish then greyish, finally blackish with some deliquescence, free. Stipe 4–8 × 0.2–0.6 cm, white then ochreous especially in lower part, striate with silky fibrils, pruinose and pubescent at top, quite fragile. Flesh thin, almost non-existent in cap, whitish in stipe, ochreous at base. No particular odour or flavour. Spores blackish-brown, almond- or lemon-shaped, warty, 11–15 × 6–10 microns.
Edibility Of no value because of size.
Habitat On the ground or on leaf litter, possibly associated by the mycelium with buried wood, tufted.
Season Autumn. Uncommon.
Note This is one of a large number of *Coprinus* species that look more or less alike in the field.

232 GYROPHRAGMIUM DUNALII

Etymology After the mycologist Dunal.
Description Cap 3–3.5 cm, dry, smooth, ochreous white, greyish, or dusted with blackish-brown spores, fairly irregularly cracked, papery. Gills (pseudo-gills) violet-black. Very irregularly fused and interconnected, at first soft then dry and very fragile. Stipe 8–10.5 × 0.6–1.5 cm, narrowing at both ends, lower part with peridial remains (fragments of varying sizes and shapes), sometimes like one or more rings, sometimes volva-like, with yellow markings at base. Pale straw-coloured flesh, compact but light, suberose. Slight cyanic odour and flavour. Spores blackish-brown, globose to elliptical, smooth, 4.5–6.5 microns.
Edibility Of no value because of size.
Habitat In sandy places, coastal or desert dunes.
Season Autumn to spring. World-wide in the correct habitat, but rare. Not known in Britain.
Note This strange Gasteromycete resembles a dry field mushroom. This is but one of a large variety of desert puffball-like fungi that, unlike gilled mushrooms, do not forcibly discharge their spores. Rather, the spores are retained within the fruit-body and dispersed over a long period.

233 CHROOGOMPHUS RUTILUS

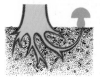

Synonym *Gomphidius viscidus*.
Etymology From Latin, 'yellowish-red'.
Description Cap 3–9 cm, viscid but soon drying, copper- or wine-coloured, often brick red or brown, margin recurved. Gills large, distant, sometimes forked, decurrent, easily detachable, red then blackish. Stipe 4–8 × 0.8–1.5 cm, yellow then cap-coloured, long, enlarged towards top, full, first viscid then with squamose ring-like zones, then with velar remains just beneath gills. Flesh yellowish, darker in stipe, yellower at base, soft. Mild odour, pleasant flavour. Spores blackish-brown, elongated-fusiform, smooth, 16–22 × 6–8 microns.
Edibility Mediocre; remove the cuticle.
Habitat In groups in coniferous woods, especially beneath pines, in moss.
Season Autumn. Occasional.
Note The genus *Chroogomphus* has been separated from the genus *Gomphidius* because it has a fibrillose veil that dries quickly and is not glutinous, and the flesh of the cap is coloured and, along with the basal mycelium, stains violet in Melzer's reagent. All species grow under conifers.

234 GOMPHIDIUS MACULATUS

Etymology From Latin, 'spotted'.
Description Cap 3–5 cm, fleshy, convex then open, fairly depressed, almost invariably obtuse with no umbo, somewhat viscid, often with black spots, margin involute. Gills whitish then grey, finally blackish, distant, decurrent, ventricose, detachable. Stipe 6–7 × 0.8–1 cm, white, speckled with small blackish or pale purple spots or fibrils, yellow at base, not viscous and without a veil. Spores olive black, fusiform, smooth, 20–30 × 7–9 microns.
Edibility Good, but remove the cuticle.
Habitat In groups beneath larch.
Season Autumn. Rare.
Note More slender forms are sometimes distinguished as a separate species, *G. gracilis*. One distinguishing feature is the fact that the flesh darkens to black without turning reddish first. *G. roseus* is easily identifiable by its bright pink-red viscid cap contrasting sharply with stipe and gills, which remain white for a long time. The stipe has a yellowish base and is sheathed, like most other *Gomphidius* members, by a glutinous veil that forms a sort of ring. Like *Chroogomphus*, species of *Gomphidius* grow under conifers.

235   GOMPHIDIUS GLUTINOSUS

Etymology   From Latin, 'viscid' or 'slime-covered'.

Description   Cap 5–12 cm, fleshy, glabrous, very viscous, violet-brown, often with black spots, cuticle completely detachable. Gills whitish then soot-coloured, detachable, distant, decurrent. Stipe 6–12 × 1.2–2.5 cm, white at top, yellow at base, solid, soft, with fugacious viscous veil. Flesh white and soft in cap, pale ash-coloured beneath cuticle, tough in stipe, yellow at base. Spores blackish, elongated-fusiform, smooth, 18–22 × 6–8 microns.

Edibility   Good, but remove the glutinous cuticle.

Habitat   Coniferous woods.

Season   Autumn. Uncommon.

Note   Easily recognized when young by the transparent viscid veil.

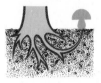

---

236   PAXILLUS INVOLUTUS

Common name   Roll rim fingus.

Etymology   From Latin, 'incurved edge'.

Description   Cap 7–20 cm, rust ochre, fleshy, flat-convex then depressed, pubescent then smooth, sometimes slightly viscid particularly at centre in wet weather, silky when dry, margin obtuse, villose, conspicuously involute for long periods, often ribbed, and acute when completely expanded. Gills pale ochre then rust-coloured, becoming marked with dark brown when touched, decurrent, quite broad, ramified towards stipe where often anastomosed thus forming a reticulum, easily detachable from flesh. Stipe 5–8 × 1–4 cm, dark yellowish, often spotted, enlarged towards top, glabrous or barely pruinose, solid. Flesh reddish-yellow then yellow, soft, juicy. Slightly acid and fruity odour, similar flavour. Spores rust ochre, elliptical, smooth, 8–10 × 5–6 microns.

Edibility   Not recommended, although tasty; it is now known to cause a gradually acquired hypersensitivity that can result in massive haemolysis, which could prove fatal.

Habitat   Heathland, with birch.

Season   Summer to late autumn. Common.

Caution   See **Edibility**.

237 PAXILLUS ATROTOMENTOSUS

Etymology From Latin, 'black and very velvety'.

Description Cap 5–30 cm, convex, slightly irregular and humped then expanded and depressed, quite often spatula- or kidney-shaped, cuticle entirely detachable, thick, reddish-yellow-brown, olive brown, dry, velvety, finally almost glabrous or finely aerolate, margin often curled, whitish-yellow then cap-coloured. Gills crowded, ramified and anastomosed, often alveolate towards stipe, arcuate, decurrent, soft, fragile, easily detachable, cream-coloured then yellow-ochre, yellow tinged with orange, brownish when touched, edge darkening with age. Stipe central, eccentric or lateral, 4–9 × 2.5–5 cm, sturdy, solid, rooting, covered with velvety hairs of a dark brown to blackish-brown. Flesh thick, soft, watery, pale yellow with pale lilac-pink speckling or marbling in cap and brownish towards base. Slightly fetid odour, very bitter flavour. Spores rust brown, elliptical, smooth, 6–7 · 3–4 microns.

Edibility See *P. involutus* (**236**).

Habitat On old stumps and dead roots of conifers.

Season Autumn. Occasional.

Caution See **Edibility**.

238 PHYLLOPORUS RHODOXANTHUS

Synonyms *Paxillus rhodoxanthus; Phylloporus pelletieri*.

Etymology From Latin, 'rose-yellow'.

Description Cap 2–10 cm, orange-brown, olive brown towards margin, hemispherical then flat, sometimes depressed, without umbo, surface uniformly velvety, margin interrupted. Gills bright golden yellow, interconnected by septa, anastomosed, alveolate, distant, large and long, adnate, decurrent, detachable. Stipe 2–6 × 0.5–1.5 cm, first reddish-yellow then brownish, pale green-yellow at base, cylindrical, almost rooting at base, often arcuate, solid, fibrillose. Flesh yellowish, wine red beneath cuticle and in stipe, colour intensifying on exposure to air, thick at centre, soft. Odour pleasant, flavour sweet. Spores olive yellow, elliptical-fusiform, smooth, 10–12.5 × 4–4.5 microns.

Edibility Good.

Habitat In broadleaved woods, usually on acid soil.

Season Autumn. Rare.

Note This is a strange fungus that acts as a link between the Boletaceae with gills (*Paxillus, Gomphidius*) and those with pores (*Boletus*).

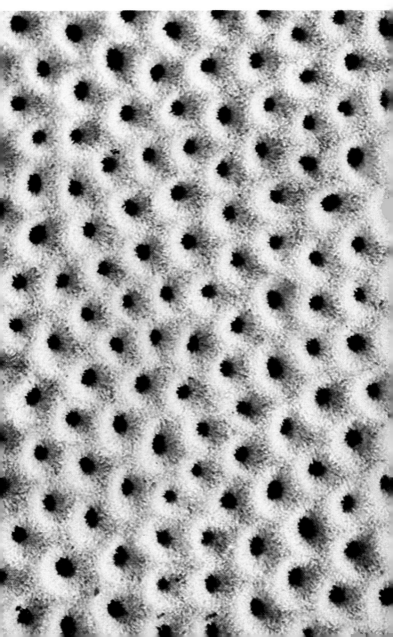

239 BOLETUS AEREUS

Etymology From Latin, 'bronze', from the cap colour.

Description Cap 10–30 cm, hemispherical then convex, cuticle finely velvety, dry, never smooth, dark brown, sometimes almost blackish or brown tinged with rusty colour, edge often lobate. Tubes first whitish, pale green with age, pores initially white covered with fine pruinescence, then tube-coloured. Stipe 7–15 × 3–6 cm, solid, massive, club-shaped when mature, with brownish reticulum that normally does not reach base. Flesh soft, unchanging, white. Pleasant odour and flavour. Spores olive brown, fusiform, smooth, 12–16 × 4–5 microns.

Edibility Excellent, with firm flesh.

Habitat In oak and chestnut woods, in open or sunny places.

Season Summer and autumn, especially in south-east England.

Note Most liable to be confused with *B. edulis* (**240**).

240 BOLETUS EDULIS

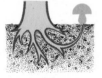

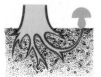

Common names Cep; penny bun bolete.

Etymology From Latin, 'edible'.

Description Cap 5–25 cm, hemispherical, convex then flattened, cuticle smooth, slightly viscous in damp weather, barely detachable, whitish, ochreous, light brown or chestnut, not uniform. Fairly long tubes, almost free from stipe, first whitish then greenish-yellow; pores small, circular, tube-coloured. Stipe 4–18 × 2–5 cm, solid, bulging or cylindrical, white or light ochre, covered by a reticulum first white then slightly darker than background. Flesh white, unchanging, soft then softening further. Odour pleasant, flavour sweetish and tasty, like hazelnuts. Spores olive brown, fusiform, smooth, 14–17 × 4.5–6.5 microns.

Edibility Excellent.

Habitat Beneath conifers and broadleaved trees.

Season Late summer until first cold spell. Common.

Note There are many recognized varieties of this species; key characteristics are the slightly viscid cap, the white reticulation on the young stipe and its pleasing odour and taste. It is sold dried in some delicatessens.

241   TYLOPILUS FELLEUS

Synonym *Boletus felleus*.
Etymology From Latin, 'of gall', from its bitterness.
Description Cap 5–15 cm, hemispherical then convex, finally flat, cuticle dry, finely velvety, difficult to detach, light brown. Tubes long, semi-free, increasing in size towards stipe and margin, longer at centre, whitish or cream-coloured then pinkish; pores round, quite small, tube-coloured. Stipe 4–12 × 1–4 cm, solid, slightly club-shaped, almost cap-coloured, slightly lighter tinged with olive, marked dark brown reticulum, surface velvety towards base. Flesh soft, white, faintly pinkish when exposed to air, slightly brown beneath cuticle. Odour insignificant, flavour very bitter. Spores pinkish, elliptical or fusiform, smooth, 9–18 × 4–6 microns.
Edibility Much too bitter to eat.
Habitat On acid or acidified soil, beneath broadleaved trees.
Season Autumn. Rare.
Note This is not infrequently mistaken for *Boletus edulis* (**240**) because of its shape, but it is bitter, reticulation on the stipe is dark and the pores turn pinkish.

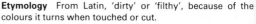

242   BOLETUS LURIDUS

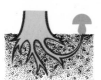

Etymology From Latin, 'dirty' or 'filthy', because of the colours it turns when touched or cut.
Description Cap 5–12 cm, hemispherical then convex, cuticle dry, velvety in young specimens, smooth with age, colour variable from leather to olive brown, or chamois to rust brown, even on the same carpophore; darkens when touched; pores small, roundish, reddish to orange, bruising greenish-blue. Stipe 4–20 × 1.5–5 cm, soft, solid, bulging then club-shaped or cylindrical, reddish-yellow, largely covered by a conspicuous, elongated red reticulum, with bright red pruinescence in upper part, surface turning blue-green when exposed, with a distinctive orange-red coloration at tube attachment. Odour fruity, flavour sweetish. Spores olive brown, ovoid or almond-shaped, smooth, 11–15 × 5–8 microns.
Edibility Sometimes eaten but not recommended. See Caution.
Habitat Beneath broadleaved trees, especially oak.
Season Autumn. Occasional.
Caution Can cause vomiting and diarrhoea.

243   BOLETUS PARASITICUS

Etymology From Greek, 'parasitic', from its habitat.

Description Cap 3–8 cm, hemispherical then convex, final-ly flattened, cuticle downy, tending to crack in dry weather, not detachable, colour light ochre, sometimes tinged olive. Tubes short, slightly decurrent, yellow, slightly olive brown when mature; pores large, round to polygonal, tube-coloured and also spotted with rust brown. Stipe 2.5–7 × 0.5–1.5 cm, solid, slender, tapering and curved at base, yellowish, fibrillose, speckled with brown floccose element at top. Flesh soft, quite leathery, rarely rots but dries ou naturally, yellow, sometimes turning blue at tube attach ments and at edges of stipe. Odour insignificant, flavour sweetish. Spores olive yellow, cylindrical or fusiform smooth, 10–17 × 4–6 microns.

Edibility Good.

Habitat Isolated or in groups, parasitic on carpophores of *Scleroderma*.

Season Summer and early autumn. Occasional.

Note A unique bolete that grows only on *Scleroderma* particularly *S. citrinum* (**376**). The size of the host car pophore effects the size and the number of specimens of the bolete that it can support.

244   BOLETUS QUELETII

Etymology After the French mycologist Quélet.

Description Cap 5–20 cm, hemispherical then convex, cuti cle slightly velvety, orange to rust- or brick-coloured. Tube semi-free, yellow to pale green-yellow turning blue; pore small, round, orange, tinged with pale purple-red, lighter in colour than tubes, yellow towards edge, turning blue. Stipe 5–18 × 1.5–4 cm, solid, soft, fairly club-shaped or fusiform with base slightly rooting, beet red at base, tinged with yellow towards top, sometimes with light green coloration half-way up. Flesh soft, yellow, red at base of stipe, blue when exposed to air then back to slightly greyer origina colours. Odour fruity, slightly acid, flavour sweet with slight ly bitter aftertaste. Spores olive brown, fusiform, smooth 8–17 × 5–7 microns.

Edibility Edible but not particularly good. See **Note**.

Habitat Under broadleaved species in open areas.

Season Autumn. Uncommon.

Note Liable to be confused with *B. erythropus*, which has a minutely red-dotted stem, orange-red pores and flesh that is not beet-root red at the base of the stem.

245 BOLETUS SATANAS

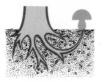

Common name Devil's bolete.
Etymology From Hebrew, 'evil'.
Description Cap 6–40 cm, subglobose then fairly convex, margin undulate, cuticle finely velvety, then smooth and, in dry weather, cracked, whitish tinged ash grey or greenish, then light brown. Tubes shorter toward stipe and edge, longer in centre, yellowish, pale blue when touched; pores small, slightly irregular, red to orange-red at margin, turning blue when bruised. Stipe 4–20 × 3–10 cm, solid, squat, sturdy, fat, reticulum with polygonal elements varying in colour from bottom to top; brown at bottom, then reddish in middle, pink-red or white in upper part, on a yellow background at top, red lower down, turning blue. Flesh soft, then softening further, quick to rot, white, pale yellow at tube attachments, becoming slowly sky blue on exposure. Strong odour of cabbage or dung when mature, flavour initially mild, walnut-like then nauseous. Spores olive brown, ovoid, smooth, 11–15 × 5–7 microns.
Edibility Poisonous, as are some other red-pored boletes.
Habitat In small groups beneath beech on calcareous soil.
Season Autumn. Rare. In Britain found mostly in southeast England. Widespread in Europe.
Note Boletes that stain blue and have reddish pores are best avoided because of possible confusion with *B. satanas*.

246 BOLETUS PRUINATUS

Etymology From Latin, 'frosty', alluding to the whitish pruinescence on young caps.
Description Cap 5–10 cm, convex to flat with dry cuticle, with white pruinescence when young, then downy, sometimes aerolate, dark purple-brown, margin often reddish. Tubes quite long, adnate, initially olive yellow then deep yellow, slowly turning blue when touched; pores polygonal, tube-coloured. Stipe 5–8 × 0.7–1.3 cm, solid, cylindrical or tapering towards the top, with apricot mycelium at the base, fairly finely spotted or uniformly coloured with red, on yellow background towards the base. Flesh in stipe of young specimens yellow, in adult specimens reddish, pale yellow in cap in some parts, turning blue in some parts. Odour insignificant, flavour slightly acidic. Spores olive brown, ellipsoid, smooth, 12–15 × 4–5 microns.
Edibility Good when young.
Habitat Solitary or in small groups. Common.
Season Autumn. Common.
Note This species is quite similar to *B. chrysenteron* (**248**), differing mainly in its darker-coloured pruinose cap and in the microscopic structure of the cuticle.

247 GYROPORUS CASTANEUS

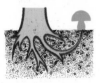

Synonym *Boletus castaneus*.
Etymology From Byzantine Greek, 'chestnut'.
Description Cap 3–10 cm, hemispherical to convex, sometimes depressed, sometimes irregular, cuticle detachable from edge, thin, dry, at first felt-like velvety then almost smooth, reddish-brown, fairly deeply coloured. Tubes free and always shorter towards stipe, whitish and detachable, pores roundish, white then lemon yellow, darkening when bruised. Stipe 4–7 × 1–3 cm, easily detachable from cap, sinuate towards top and base, hollow, fragile, cap-coloured. Flesh fragile, white, sometimes slightly pinkish when exposed, brownish beneath cuticle and on sides of stipe. Pleasant odour, flavour like hazelnut. Spores light lemon yellow, elliptical, smooth, 8.5–12.5 × 5.5–6.5 microns.
Edibility Very good when young.
Habitat Singly and in small groups, beneath broadleaved trees, especially oak, almost world-wide.
Season Autumn. Occasional.
Note This mushroom is best eaten while the pores are still white. *Gyroporus* is distinguished as a genus by its yellowish spores and the stipe, which is hollow.

248 BOLETUS CHRYSENTERON

Etymology From Latin, 'with a golden interior'.
Description Cap 3–12 cm, hemispherical then convex, finally flat, various shades of brown, cuticle dry, velvety, easily cracking revealing slight purple-pink subcuticle stratum. Tubes yellow then pale green, turning blue when touched; fairly large, polygonal, tube-coloured pores. Stipe 3–10 × 0.5–2 cm, solid, cylindrical, tapering at base, slightly curved, with striations in upper part that extend into hymenium, yellowish tinged with brown or pale red, turning blue and then pinkish, purple-pink under cuticle. Odour and flavour pleasant. Spores olive brown, fusiform, smooth, 11.5–15.5 × 4–7 microns.
Edibility Fair to good.
Habitat Beneath broadleaved or coniferous trees.
Season Autumn. Common.
Note There is a complex of closely related species that often can be reliably differentiated only by microscopic examination. The tendency to turn blue or green on bruising is sometimes delayed or partial.

249 PORPHYRELLUS PSEUDOSCABER

Synonyms *Tylopilus pseudoscaber; Boletus pseudosca* ber.

Etymology From Greek, 'resembling *scaber*', from its re semblance to that species.

Description Cap 5–16 cm, hemispherical then convex finally flat, cuticle velvety in dry weather, smooth when wet very dark brown bruising blue then purplish-brown. Tube long, semi-free, dark brown to purple-brown, bruising blue pores small, angular, tube-coloured, blue then blackish when touched. Stipe cylindrical, 4–16 × 1–3 cm, slightly club-shaped, solid, hard, almost cap-coloured, outer surfac pubescent, sometimes with striations that may resemble false reticulum. Flesh firm when young, then soft, fibrous in stipe, whitish, turning pink and then grey when exposed becoming pale blue at tube attachments. Faint, thoug slightly acrid odour and flavour. Spores purple-red-brown in mass, fusiform, elliptical, smooth, 10–20 × 6–10 microns.

Edibility Mediocre.

Habitat Solitary or in small groups under broadleave trees.

Season Autumn. Rare.

250 BOLETINUS CAVIPES

Synonyms *Suillus cavipes; Boletus cavipes.*

Etymology From Latin, 'hollow-legged'.

Description Cap 5–20 cm, hemispherical or conical, finall slightly concave, chestnut-coloured, reddish-brown, initially with white margin, partial velar remains, cuticle with tufts o brown hairs, dry. Tubes short, very adherent to flesh, yellow to pale green; pores elongated, rhomboid, polygonal, from yellow to pale green. Stipe 5–8 × 0.5–2.5 cm, hollow cylindrical, slightly club-shaped, slightly curved, cap coloured but lighter, ring whitish, floccose. Flesh quite tender, pale yellow, unchanging. Odour insignificant, fla vour sweet. Spores olive yellow, fusiform, smooth, 7–15 × 3–4 microns.

Edibility Mediocre.

Habitat In small groups beneath larch.

Season Autumn. Rare.

Note The dry scaly cap, hollow stipe and occurrence unde larch make this species easy to recognize.

251 SUILLUS GREVILLEI

Synonym *Boletus elegans.*
Etymology After the Scottish mycologist Greville.
Description Cap 5–12 cm, lemon yellow or golden yellow then reddish-orange, conical-obtuse then convex-flattened, sometimes obtuse and umbonate, cuticle detachable, viscid in wet weather, fleshy, soft, margin incurved, regular, lighter than disc. Tubes yellow then rose grey, adnate, decurrent, fine, detachable, short; pores round then polygonal, tube-coloured, sometimes marked with reddish-purple, thin. Stipe 5–10 × 1.5–2.5 cm, yellow, orange-red, with brownish reticulation above ring, brownish striations or speckling below ring, blackish-brown or olive-coloured at base, fleshy, solid; ring yellowish-white, quite viscid, ascending. Flesh yellow in cap, slightly greenish at base of stipe, soft but soon limp, fibrous in stipe. Odour of geraniums, flavour sweet. Spores olive yellow, ellipsoid-fusoid, smooth, 7–11 × 2–4 microns.
Edibility Fair if the cuticle and ring are removed.
Habitat In groups under larch, in sunny, grassy areas.
Season Autumn. Common.
Note Also growing only under larch is *B. cavipes* (**250**).

252 SUILLUS GRANULATUS

Synonym *Boletus granulatus.*
Etymology From Latin, 'dotted'.
Description Cap 4–18 cm, hemispherical, convex then flattened, cuticle viscous in damp weather, smooth and shiny when dry, entirely detachable, yellow tinged with brown or reddish. Tubes first short, lengthening with age, adherent to stipe, pale yellow then yellow with pale green shades; pores small, angular, emitting droplets of opalescent latex when young, first markedly yellow then pale green-yellow. Stipe 4–10 × 1–2 cm, cylindrical, often curved, solid, light yellow then marked with brown, upper part with small reddish-brown markings caused by dried drops of latex, present as such in young specimens. Flesh tender, soft and spongy when old, pale yellow or white, unchanging. Pleasant, slightly acid, fruity odour, flavour sweetish. Spores brown-ochre, fusiform, smooth, 8–10 × 3–4.5 microns.
Edibility Good without cuticle, or dried.
Habitat In groups, beneath conifers, especially pine.
Season Late summer to Autumn. Common.

253 SUILLUS LUTEUS

Synonym *Boletus luteus.*
Common name Slippery Jack.
Etymology From Latin, 'yellow'.
Description Cap 4–18 cm, hemispherical or somewhat conical then convex with a slight umbo at times, margin regular with some partial velar remains, various shades of brown, violet highlights in damp weather, tending to fade with age and dry weather, cuticle viscous and detachable. Tubes adherent or briefly decurrent on stipe, sulphur yellow then slightly pale green; pores tiny even when mature, round, tending to become polygonal, tube-coloured but darkening slightly with age. Stipe 3–13 × 1–3 cm, cylindrical, solid and soft, whitish or pale yellow, with pale yellow dots that turn reddish-brown, brownish at base, ring membranous, sleeve-like, whitish, pale purple beneath. Flesh tender, soft, pale yellow, whitish, unchanging. Slight odour and sweet flavour. Spores brown-ochre, fusiform, smooth, 7–10 × 3–3.5 microns.

Edibility Good after removing cuticle and drying, although some people experience diarrhoea.
Habitat Gregarious beneath conifers, preferably pine.
Season Autumn. Common.

254 SUILLUS PLACIDUS

Synonyms *Boletus placidus.*
Etymology From Latin, 'peaceful' or 'placid'.
Description Cap 3–13 cm, hemispherical, convex, finally flattened, sometimes depressed, cuticle viscous, detachable, white to yellow tinged with pink, darkening with age to brown from the centre. Tubes slightly decurrent, not easily detachable in young specimens, whitish to yellow tinged with greenish; pores small, irregular, with drops of opalescent latex that on drying produce small spots varying from orange-yellow to reddish-brown, at first tube-coloured, then speckled reddish-brown or violet. Stipe 5–15 × 0.5–3 cm, cylindrical, sinuate, sometimes slightly eccentric, solid, with no ring, pale yellow at top, brown or pinkish lower down where the droplets of dried latex form a purple ornamentation. Flesh soft, white, pale yellow at edges, violet-grey when exposed to air. Odour insignificant, flavour sweetish. Spores dark ochre, elliptical or fusiform, smooth, 7–9 × 3–3.5 microns.

Edibility Fair after removing cuticle.
Habitat Gregarious, under exotic, five-needle pines.
Season Autumn.

Note The smooth slimy white cap, mild taste, lack of stipe ring and occurrence under exotic pines make this an easy bolete to identify. Only one British collection is known, from Bedgebury Pinetum, but the species is found in central and southern Europe.

255　BOLETUS PULVERULENTUS

Etymology From Latin, 'dusty'.
Description Cap 3–15 cm, hemispherical, convex, rarely flat, cuticle velvety when young, when mature quite smooth or viscid in wet weather, not easily detachable, Havana brown, olive-ochre-grey or brownish, quickly turning dark blue when touched, then blackish. Tubes long, fine, adnate yellow to greenish, turning blue; pores quite large when mature, polygonal, tube-coloured. Stipe 4–10 × 1–2 cm solid, tapering, rooting towards base, reddish-brown, pale purple on ochre background, darker at base, yellow at top, fairly uniformly brown when mature, turning dark blue then blackish, initially velvety. Flesh tender then soft, bright yellow, when exposed to air immediately dark blue then sky blue-grey. Odour fruity, flavour slightly acid, sweetish. Spores olive-coloured, fusiform, smooth, 11–15 × 4–6 microns.
Edibility Fair when cooked.
Habitat Beneath broadleaved trees.
Season Autumn. Occasional.
Note Its typically dark brownish cap, large pores and very quick colour change to blue-black make this a distinctive species.

256　SUILLUS VARIEGATUS

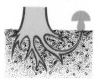

Synonym *Boletus variegatus*.
Etymology From Latin, 'variegated' or 'many-coloured'.
Description Cap 5–15 cm, hemispherical then convex, finally flattened, cuticle only slightly viscid in wet weather, covered with brown hairy tufts that may wash off with age, standing out against pale straw yellow or ochreous background. Tubes adnate or slightly decurrent, pale yellow then olive brown, blue when touched; pores roundish to angular, tube-coloured. Stipe 3–13 × 1.5–3 cm, solid, cylindrical, sometimes slightly enlarged at base, slightly velvety in lower part, cap-coloured. Flesh tender, soft, watery in wet weather, pale yellow, slightly orange, reddish-brown at base, turning slightly blue. Odour slightly acid, flavour quite pleasant, sweetish. Spores olive brown, elliptical or fusiform, smooth, 7.5–10.5 × 3–4 microns.
Edibility Mediocre; the flesh turns grey when cooked.
Habitat Gregarious in pinewoods.
Season Autumn. Common.

257 LECCINUM AURANTIACUM

Synonym *Boletus aurantiacus.*
Etymology From Latin, 'golden orange'.
Description Cap 4–25 cm, subspherical to fairly convex, cuticle with margin that for a short section sheaths the stipe in yet-unopened specimens, orange-red, various shading, tending to discolour, finely velvety. Tubes long, thin, free, easily detachable, white or cream then greyish; pores small, round, tube-coloured. Stipe 8–25 × 1.5–5 cm, solid, soft, elongatedly club-shaped, with small raised scales, whitish then brown to black, clearly standing out against whitish background. Flesh quite soft in cap, fibrous in stipe, white turning reddish-brown then blackish-grey when exposed. Odour pleasant, flavour sweetish. Spores light Havana brown, fusiform, smooth, 12–20 × 4.5–5 microns.
Edibility Good; darkens when cooked.
Habitat Scattered beneath aspen.
Season Autumn. Rare.
Note *L. quercinum,* found under oak, is very similar and much more frequent, differing in its dark brick- or chestnut-coloured cap and stem with white scales, which soon turn rusty brown or amber-coloured.

258 LECCINUM CARPINI

Synonyms *Leccinum griseum.*
Etymology From Latin, from its association with the hornbeam *Carpinus.*
Description Cap 4–15 cm, hemispherical then campanulate, grey to ochreous to dark brown, cuticle wrinkled, finely pruinose when young, then glabrous, tending to split or crack, slightly viscid when wet. Tubes very long, free, straw-coloured when young, greyish when mature; pores small, round, tube-coloured. Stipe 5–20 × 1–3 cm, slender, cylindrical or club-shaped, solid, fibrous, surface rough, covered with whitish scales that blacken, standing out against the greyish-white background. Flesh tender then soft in cap, fibrous in stipe, white, pale yellow at tube attachments, turning violet-grey on exposure to air, gradually darkening. Faint, pleasant odour and flavour. Spores olive brown, fusiform, smooth, 11–20 × 5–7 microns.
Edibility Mediocre, best in sauces; black when dried.
Habitat Fairly gregarious, beneath hornbeam.
Season Autumn. Rare.
Note *L. scabrum* is somewhat similar, with a dark hazel- or clay-buff-coloured, fibrous cap and flesh that is usually unchanging or faintly pink. It occurs under birch.

259 BOLETOPSIS SUBSQUAMOSA

Synonyms *Polyporus leucomelas; Polyporus griseus.*
Etymology From Latin, 'somewhat scaly'.
Description Cap 4–17 cm, hemispherical to convex, irregularly humped and lobate, grey to olive-grey to blackish grey where damaged, fibrillose, tending to crack. Tubes short, decurrent, whitish then brown; pores quite broad, irregular, concolorous. Stipe 2–8 × 1–3 cm, sturdy, solid, cap-coloured, shape variable. Flesh white, when exposed to air rose then grey, firm. Odour insignificant, flavour bitterish. Spores whitish to pale brownish, oval and irregularly angular, with protruding nodes, 6–4 × 3.5–4.5 microns.

Edibility Palatable if soaked, parboiled, and then cooked.
Habitat On acid ground beneath coniferous trees.
Season Autumn. Rare. In Britain found mostly in Scotland; more widespread in Europe.
Note This looks like a bolete but has very short tubes and tuberculate spores. Although several species are sometimes recognized based on cap colour, there are no significant microscopic differences and this is now seen as a monotypic species with lighter and darker forms.

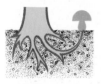

260 POLYPORUS TUBERASTER

Etymology From Latin, 'tuberous'.
Description Cap 5–20 cm, flat to funnel-shaped, yellowish-ochre, covered with hairy scales, brown, adpressed, margin at first involte then expanded, fleshy, soft. Tubes white, decurrent; pores polygonal, not broad, white. Stipe 5–20 × 2.5–4 cm, sturdy, solid, quite elastic, full, glabrous, ochreous, brown at base that emerges from large hypogeal sclerotium. Flesh whitish, soft but elastic. Odour and flavour resemble cheese. Spores white, ovoid or elliptical, 12–14 × 3.5–4 microns.

Edibility Good and tender while young, but needs lengthy cooking when mature.
Habitat On the ground in broadleaved woods, especially under oak and beech.
Season Spring to late autumn. Not known in Britain; occasional in Europe.
Note The mycelium of this fungus forms large, fairly compact sclerotia with the consistency of porous rock. When cut, the blackish-brown mass is marbled with white clumps of hyphae. This is sold for consumption in continental Europe and, if well watered, will produce carpophores at home.

261 ALBATRELLUS OVINUS

Synonym *Polyporus ovinus*.
Etymology From Latin, 'pertaining to sheep'.
Description Cap 6–10 cm, convex then flat or depressed, irregularly humped, margin sinuate, sometimes lobate, cuticle detachable, dry, thick, whitish turning yellow, faintly brown with age, often cracked, aerolate. Tubes short, 1–2 mm, decurrent, white; pores very small, fairly round, whitish then pale yellow. Stipe 3–6 × 1–2 cm, central or eccentric, irregular, solid, hard, whitish sometimes marked with brown, pruinose, often concrescent. Flesh white, slightly yellow at base, thick, firm but fragile. Odour somewhat acid, fruity, flavour sweet, of almonds, sometimes a little bitter. Spores white, ovoid, smooth, 3.5–4.5 × 3 microns.
Edibility Good, especially when preserved in oil.

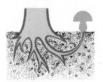

Habitat In large groups often joined together by cap or stipe, in mountainous regions beneath conifers.
Season Summer and autumn. Not yet found in Britain; occasional in Europe.
Note *A. confluens*, cap pinkish to orange-brown, grows in the same locale. The carpophores have a greater tendency to grow with cap and stipe joined. *A. cristatus* has a greenish-yellow cap soon aerolate and often concrescent. Neither is known in Britain.

---

262 ALBATRELLUS PES-CAPRAE

Synonym *Polyporus pes-caprae*.
Etymology From Latin, 'like a goat's foot'.
Description Cap 6–12 cm or more, semi-circular or kidney-shaped, sometimes irregularly lobate, convex then flat or depressed toward stipe, cuticle dry, not detachable, felt-like and squamose, covered with scales at first adpressed then raised, often delimited by cracks, reddish-brown, margin initially incurved. Pores not detachable, short, decurrent, white or light lemon yellow, finally beige, wide, polygonal. Stipe 3–5 × 1–2 cm or more, eccentric or lateral, whitish, pale yellow at base, irregular, with brownish reticulum at top, squamose like cap. Flesh white tending to lemon-coloured, reddish at base, firm, thick. Faint pleasant odour, flavour of hazelnuts. Spores white, elliptical or oval, smooth, 8–11 × 5.5–7.5 microns.

Edibility Excellent.
Habitat On acid ground, solitary or in small concrescent groups, in broadleaved and coniferous woods.
Season Summer and autumn. Widespread in Europe, but not known in Britain.

263 POLYPORUS ARCULARIUS

Synonym *Polyporellus arcularius.*
Etymology From Latin, 'vaulted', from pore shape.
Description Cap 2–5 cm, convex then umbilicate when mature, not zoned, brown, greyish-brown, tending to ochreous when drying, first covered with small darker scales, abundant towards margin, which normally appears ciliate. Tubes white, adnate-decurrent, not removable; pores white then light brownish-ochre, broad, oblong, rhomboid. Stipe 1–2.5 × 0.1–0.2 cm, brownish-grey or blackish-brown, at first barely squamulose, then glabrous. Flesh white, leathery. Mushroomy odour. Spores white, cylindrical, smooth, 6–9 × 2–3.5 microns.
Edibility Inedible.
Habitat On dead branches and sticks in woodland or on the ground growing from buried wood, especially beech, birch, elm, maple, oak and poplar.
Season Especially in the spring, but into summer. Widespread in Europe but not known in Britain.
Note *P. brumalis* is similar, with dark greyish-brown, hairy or squamulose cap, margin at most velvety, pores at first round, and stipe velvety or squamulose, not glabrous. The *P. badius* complex is a group of similar species distinguished by the stipe, which is partially or entirely black.

---

264 GANODERMA LUCIDUM

Etymology From Latin, 'shiny' or 'brilliant'.
Description Carpophore 5–28 cm, cap circular or kidney-shaped, covered with a shiny crust, cap zoned from yellow to dark red, margin white or yellow. Stipe, when present, 5–18 × 1–5 cm, usually eccentric-lateral, surface like that of the cap. Tubes white then cinnamon-coloured, small and round. Flesh whitish and spongy, then reddish and ligneous, zoned. Spores brown, elliptical, finely warty, 10–12 × 6–8 microns.
Edibility Inedible once encrusted, but soft and tasty when young.
Habitat Typically at the base of oaks but also on stumps and roots of these and other broadleaved trees.
Season Late spring to late autumn. Occasional.
Note An attractive species when fresh, easy to dry and preserve as a decorative object. In the Orient it is called *ling chi* and is cultivated and sold commercially, and used for many of the same reasons that people use ginseng: to alleviate minor disorders, increase vitality and ensure long life.

265 POLYPORUS MORI

Synonyms *Favolus alveolaris; Favolus canadensis; Favolus europeus.*

Description Cap 2–8 cm, roughly kidney-shaped, thin, ochreous to cream-coloured, cuticle not detachable, marked by radial fibrils, sometimes joined to form small adpressed scales, smooth, tending to fade, margin curved then expanded. Tubes short, decurrent, whitish; pores broad, alveolate, polygonal, often with fine hairs. Stipe 0.4–1 × 0.5–0.8 cm, lateral, very short, rudimentary, often reticulate down to the base, whitish, faintly pubescent, leathery then rigid and fragile. No special odour or flavour. Spores white, elliptical-elongated, smooth, 7–12 × 3–4 microns.

Edibility Usually too tough; of no value.

Habitat Saprophytic and, more rarely, parasitic on various broadleaved species.

Season Most commonly seen in the spring. Not known in Britain but widespread in warmer parts of Europe.

Note The honeycomb-shaped pores are the most distinctive feature of this mushroom. Sometimes it lacks any stipe development and what stipe there is is mostly covered with pores.

---

266 COLTRICIA PERENNIS

Synonym *Polyporus perennis.*

Etymology From Latin, 'long-lasting', because the carpophores may live for one or more years.

Description Cap 2–8 cm, flattened or funnel-shaped, thin, finely velvety, then zoned and glabrous, rust-coloured and brown. Tubes cinnamon-coloured, slightly decurrent; pores quite broad, roundish or polygonal, initially whitish then cinnamon brown, velvety. Stipe 1–3 × 0.5 cm, cylindrical, reddish-brown, velvety. Flesh cinnamon-coloured, leathery, thin. Odour mushroomy, flavour astringent. Spores from yellow to ochreous, elliptical, smooth, 5–10 × 3.5–6 microns.

Edibility Inedible because of consistency.

Habitat Frequent on burnt ground and heaths, with caps often concrescent.

Season New growths summer to autumn; present all year.

Note *C. cinnamomea* is very similar but has a zoned, shiny, cinnamon-coloured cap. Both species have cinnamon-coloured to orange-brown flesh that blackens when touched with a drop of potassium hydroxide. *C. cinnamomea* does not occur in Britain.

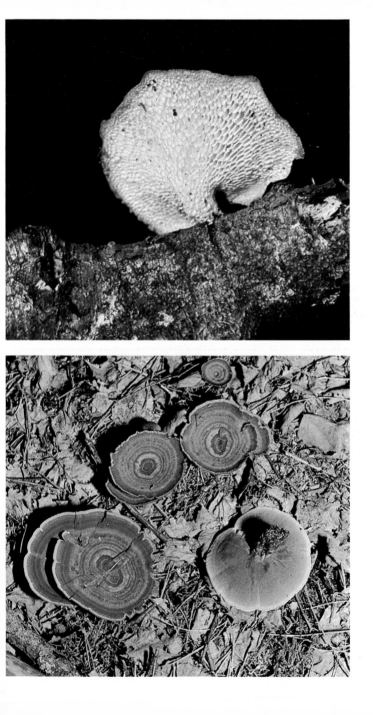

267 ONNIA TOMENTOSA

Synonym *Polyporus tomentosus.*
Etymology From Latin, 'downy' or 'velvety'.
Description Cap 5–10 cm, convex, flat or umbilicate, rust
brown, rust red or cinnamon-coloured to yellow, not radially
zoned, rugose, velvety, lighter at margin, which is entire or
lobate, fading to yellowish with age, sometimes with confluent
crescent or fairly imbricate caps. Tubes decurrent, reddish
brown; pores angular, irregular, often maze-like, tube-
coloured or more often greyish. Stipe 1–3 × 0.7–1.5 cm,
central or otherwise, irregular, solid, spongy, soft, felt-like,
downy, dark brown or blackish, sometimes almost absent.
Flesh in two ochreous-brown layers, the upper layer spongy,
the lower firm, fibrous and shiny when cut. Spores pale
yellow in mass, elliptical, smooth, 4–5 × 3–3.5 microns.
Edibility Too leathery to eat.
Habitat On the ground or on roots of conifers, often seem-
ing terrestrial but in fact growing from buried wood.
Season Summer and autumn. Not known in Britain but
widespread in Europe.
Note An otherwise identical fungus, *O. circinata*, lacks a
stipe and grows directly out of wood; it also differs somewhat microscopically.

268 PSEUDOHYDNUM GELATINOSUM

Synonym *Tremellodon gelatinosum.*
Etymology From Latin, 'like gelatin'.
Description Cap 3–6 cm, fan-shaped, sessile or with a short
stipe, surface papillose, brown to white. Hymenium with
white translucent spines, conical, straight, 2–4 mm long.
Stipe, when present, is short, squat and whitish. Flesh
transparent, thick, gelatinous. Odour insignificant, flavour
distinctive. Spores white, globose, smooth, 14–18 × 10–12
microns.
Edibility Good, especially when candied in sugar water,
dried and dusted with confectioner's sugar.
Habitat On coniferous wood.
Season Autumn. Uncommon.
Note This fungus is easy to recognize because of its
distinctive aculeate hymenium. It is a member of the jelly
fungi.

269   AURISCALPIUM VULGARE

Etymology From Latin, 'common'.

Description Cap 1–2 cm, kidney-shaped to almost circular, convex, with the stipe attached laterally, villose, dark brown, sometimes zoned, edge cliate, initially lighter. Fairly sparse aculei, at first violet-brown then whitish from the spores. Stipe 3–10 × 0.1–0.2 cm, cylindrical, with greyish hairs on a dark brown background. The base extends into a mycelial thread, surrounded by brown filaments. Flesh leathery, white, delimited by a black line from the hairy layer. Odour insignificant, flavour slightly acrid. Spores white, ovoid, finely warty, 4–6 × 3–4 microns, amyloid.

Edibility Of no value because of size.

Habitat On buried pinecones, widely distributed in Britain and Europe but only occasional.

Season All year, but particularly autumn.

Note Very often grows out of moss, beneath which there is a host cone.

270   SARCODON IMBRICATUM

Synonym *Hydnum imbricatum.*

Etymology From Latin, 'covered with tiles', because of the appearance of the cap.

Description Cap 6–30 cm or more, convex then flat, often slightly umbilicate, eventually funnel-shaped, floccose, tessellated and squamose with large grey-brown scales, persistent or slightly caducous. Teeth decurrent, ash white then brown, 1–1.2 cm long. Stipe 2.5–7.5 × 2.5–5 cm, short, thick, smooth, whitish or cap-coloured. Flesh whitish then light grey-brown, thick, consistent, sometimes zoned. Odour slightly iodized, sometimes horse-like, flavour astringent or slightly bitter. Spores reddish-brown, oval or subglobose, warty, 5–6 × 5 microns.

Edibility Fair to good, best when reduced to powder and used for flavouring.

Habitat In conifer woods; often in groups.

Season Autumn. Rare in southern England, less so in Scotland; more widespread in Europe.

Note *S. scabrosum* is intensely bitter, has a less coarsely scaly cap and a stipe that becomes dark greenish-black at the base. It occurs in both coniferous and broadleaved woods.

271 HYDNELLUM SCROBICULATUM

Etymology From Latin, 'pitted'.

Description Cap 3–8 cm, first hemispherical-convex, soon expanding, irregular, humped, markedly downy and felt-like, roughening with protruding knobs and bumps, first white, exuding drops of red, then brownish-yellow or brownish-red with an oblong margin, whitish then cap-coloured. Teeth up to 5 mm long, unequal, decurrent, crowded, white then pinkish with brown spots, finally entirely rust brown, fragile. Stipe 2–3 × 1–2 cm, irregular, cap-coloured, downy, enlarged at spongy base. Flesh spongy then suberose, pinkish-brown in cap with faint concentric zonation, pale purple-brown in stipe. Faint mealy odour, flavour sweetish. Spores light brown, subglobose or broadly elliptical, sometimes polyhedral, 4.8–5.6 × 3.5–4.5 microns.

Edibility Inedible because of consistency.

Habitat Gregarious, often concrescent, on the litter in coniferous and broadleaved woods.

Season Autumn. Occasional.

Note The flesh reacts violet then olive green with potash (potassium hydroxide).

---

272 HYDNUM REPANDUM

Synonym *Dentinum repandum; Sarcodon repandus.*

Etymology From Latin, 'bent backwards'.

Description Cap 5–15 cm, convex then open, irregular, often depressed, margin incurved, lobate, undulate, surface dry, adherent, typically orange but sometimes pale yellow to whitish. Teeth up to 6 mm long, fragile and easily detachable, cream-coloured or reddish-ochre. Stipe 3–8 × 0.5–3 cm, fairly slender, solid, quite irregular, flared at top, whitish, sometimes with brown markings, downy at base. Flesh thick, consistent, white turning pinkish-yellow, fragile. Odour slightly fruity, flavour sweet to slightly bitter. Spores white, subglobose, smooth, 6–7 × 5–6 microns.

Edibility Fair to very good.

Habitat Gregarious, sometimes concrescent, beneath broadleaved trees and conifers.

Season Autumn. Occasional.

Note *H. rufescens* is similar but smaller and has orange-yellow to vivid orange-brown caps.

273 LEOTIA LUBRICA

Common name Jelly-baby fungus.

Etymology From Latin, 'viscid' or 'slippery'.

Description Carpophore 5–20 mm wide, irregularly rounded, fairly lobate, separated from stipe by a fairly deep groove, greenish-orange, darker with age, smooth, slightly viscous in wet weather. Stipe 1–5 × 0.2–0.5 cm, cylindrical or slightly enlarged at the base, hollow when mature, ochreous-yellow or orange tending to become greenish, viscous. Flesh soft, almost gelatinous in the head, waxy in the stipe. No particular odour or flavour. Spores colourless under microscope, elliptical, slightly curved, smooth, 20–25 × 5–7 microns.

Edibility Of no value because of size and texture.

Habitat In small groups in woods, on the ground, amid ferns or moss.

Season Autumn. Occasional.

Note *L. viscosa* has a dark green head and buff- to orange-coloured stipe; *L. atrovirens* has both a green head and stipe, although often of different hues.

---

274 HELVELLA ELASTICA

Synonym *Leptopodia elastica*.

Etymology From Greek, 'pushing' or 'elastic', referring to the texture of the flesh.

Description Carpophore 4–8 cm high, two-lobed head, undulate, free, at most 4 cm wide, whitish turning brown with age and dry weather, greyish-ochre when mature. Stipe 2.5–7.5 cm × 2–10 mm, slightly supple, pruinose when young, white, sometimes with reddish marking at base when mature, fairly compressed. Flesh whitish, elastic. No particular odour or flavour. Spores whitish, elliptical, smooth, 21–27 × 13–16 microns.

Edibility Fair when cooked; do not eat raw. See **Note**.

Habitat In cool shady parts of woods, among leaves.

Season Autumn. Occasional.

Note This is one of the more common species in the genus. Many are small and most are difficult to identify without a microscope. Although many are well known and eaten in Europe and North America, **none should ever be eaten raw**.

Caution Be very careful with this group because of its close relationship to some seriously poisonous species of *Gyromitra*, or false morels.

275 HELVELLA LACUNOSA

Etymology From Latin, 'with holes', because of the structure of the stipe.

Description Carpophore 5–12 cm high, head 2–4 cm wide, normally three-lobed, blackish, fairly undulate, margins sometimes partly joined at stipe. Stipe 4–10 × 1–2 cm, dark grey to blackish, deeply sulcate lengthwise, fistular at the centre of the flesh. Flesh quite thin and elastic. Pleasant mushroomy odour and flavour. Spores whitish, elliptical, smooth, 18–20 × 12–13 microns.

Edibility Good when cooked. See **Note**.

Habitat On fine, sandy ground, especially in open woodland near paths.

Season Autumn. Occasional.

Note Although large and common *H. lacunosa* is easily overlooked. As with other species of *Helvella*, **great caution should be exercised** in identifying or sampling this mushroom.

276 HELVELLA MONACHELLA

Etymology From Greek, 'small nun', from its resemblance to a nun's habit.

Description Carpophore not wider than 4 cm, head with two or, more frequently, three lobes, partly joined together to form a typical mitre shape, brown, blackish-brown uppermost, faintly brownish or finely pubescent below. Stipe 4–12 × 0.8–2 cm, slightly club-shaped, whitish or later faintly ochreous, from pubescent to glabrous, fistular, enlarged at the base. Flesh whitish, slightly elastic. No special odour or flavour. Spores whitish, elliptical, smooth, 21–22 × 14–15 microns.

Edibility Quite good when cooked.

Habitat Gregarious on sandy ground, preferably beneath poplars.

Season Spring. Occasional.

277 HELVELLA CRISPA

Etymology From Latin, 'curled', from its shape.
Description Carpophore 5–15 cm high, head 3–5 cm wide, kidney- or saddle-shaped, irregularly lobed, undulating and curled, edge free, white or whitish, glabrous, ochreous and pale beneath, venose and villose. Stipe 5–12.5 × 2–3 cm deeply sulcate lengthwise, lacunose, whitish, barely pubescent when young, then glabrous. Flesh whitish, quite elastic. Mushroomy odour and flavour. Spores whitish, elliptical smooth, 20–22 × 12–13 microns.
Edibility Good when cooked, although somewhat chewy. See **Note**.
Habitat On ground by paths and in open woodland.
Season Autumn. Common.
Note This somewhat resembles *H. lacunosa* (**275**) except for its colour and that its head is more saddle-shaped than lobed. **Caution is recommended** because some saddle-shaped mushrooms are believed to be poisonous, and are closely related to the dangerous false morels, species of *Gyromitra*.

278 GYROMITRA INFULA

Synonym *Helvella infula*.
Etymology From Latin term describing a turban-like headdress worn by Roman priests and vestal virgins.
Description Carpophore with saddle-shaped head with two, three or four lobes, 6–10 × 8–12 cm, enlarged, rugose, irregular, ending in a point, external surface fertile, plicate, pinkish-brown in wet weather, brownish-yellow when dry, darker and brown with age. Stipe 6–10 × 1.5–3 cm, cylindrical then compressed and deeply sulcate, hollow, pruinose, pale brown then reddish-pink or lilac-grey, yellow at the base. Flesh soft, wax-like. Faint mushroomy odour and flavour. Spores pale yellow, elliptical, smooth, 19–24 × 7–8 microns.
Edibility Although eaten in parts of Europe, and reportedly good, *Gyromitra* can be dangerously poisonous to some people and should be avoided. See **Caution**.
Habitat Under pine, among remains of wood, in charcoal kilns or burnt areas, also on sawdust.
Season Autumn. Rare, mostly found in Scotland.
Note Although saddle-shaped, this is placed with the brain-shaped mushrooms in the genus *Gyromitra*. *G. ambigua* is shorter, its stipe is tinged with violet and is more common in colder regions of Europe.
Caution No *Gyromitra* should be eaten in any form.

279 GYROMITRA ESCULENTA

Synonym *Helvella esculenta.*
Etymology From Latin, 'edible'.
Description Carpophore up to 10–12 cm high, head 5–10 cm, subglobose, irregularly lobate and brain-like, brownish Stipe 2–5 × 2–4 cm, compressed or irregularly plicate whitish or tinged with pink or violet, glabrous or pruinose the whole length. Flesh whitish, waxy, fragile. Strong mushroomy odour, flavour sweetish. Spores whitish, elliptical, smooth, 17–21 × 9–11 microns.

Edibility Rated by some as an excellent edible species especially in eastern Europe, this fungus can prove fatal if toxins are not thoroughly removed by cooking. Some ways of preparation will reduce or eliminate the chances of an acute poisoning, but this mushroom is also known to contain a potent carcinogen. Best avoided. See **Note**.
Habitat In pinewoods on sandy soil.
Season Spring and early summer. Occasional.
Note Acute poisoning from this mushroom usually occurs about six hours after ingestion, and symptoms include a bloated feeling, cramps, vomiting, diarrhoea, convulsions and coma. Death can occur.

280 VERPA CONICA

Synonym *Verpa digitaliformis.*
Etymology From Latin, 'conical'.
Description Head 2–3 × 1.5–2.5 cm, campanulate, obtuse and slightly depressed at top, slightly sulcate, brownish or fertile surface, whitish or yellowish in sterile part, margin white, fairly adherent to stipe, but always free, hollow. Stipe 5–7 × 0.8–1 cm, cylindrical, slightly narrowing at top, almost hollow, whitish or tinged with pink-ochre, with small, slightly darker, adpressed scales. Flesh white, watery, waxy fragile. Odour and flavour slight. Spores white, elliptical smooth, 23–30 × 13–17 microns.

Edibility Fair.
Habitat At the edge of woods or in hedges, especially under hawthorn, or other members of the Rosaceae (rose family).
Season Early spring. Occasional in southern England.
Note This is one of the first terrestrial mushrooms to appear in the early spring. It is rarely found in quantity and is easily overlooked; it appears before most mushroom hunters are out looking for morels.

281 VERPA BOHEMICA

Synonym *Ptychoverpa bohemica*.
Etymology From Latin, 'Bohemia'.
Description Head 2–5 × 3–4 cm, campanulate or conica ovoid, free, yellowish-brown covered with lengthwise rib ramified, undulate in specimens growing in wet condition straight when dry, forming irregular alveoli, elongated straight, hollow. Stipe 6–8 × 0.8–1 cm, coarsely cylindrica narrowing toward top, smooth, white, fistular, solid. Fles white, waxy, watery, fragile. Odour slightly acidic, flavou slightly bitter but not unpleasant. Spores white, elliptica sometimes slightly curved, smooth, 60–80 × 18–20 micron
Edibility Fair, though slightly watery. Caution is advise however, because immoderate ingestion of this species ca cause some temporary but uncomfortable loss of muscula co-ordination.
Habitat In the leaf litter beneath broadleaved trees, espe cially poplars.
Season In very wet spring periods. Occurs in Europe but not known in Britain.
Note This mushroom can be differentiated from morels k examining the attachment of the head to the stipe; i morels, the attachment is at the base of the head and no pa is free from the stalk. In *Verpa* it is at the apex of the hea and the cap is free except at this point.

282 MITROPHORA SEMILIBERA CRASSIPES

Synonym *Mitrophora crassipes*.
Etymology From Latin, 'swollen-footed'.
Description Carpophore up to 20 cm high, head conica dark olive brown, pointed at top, with long primary ribbin angular, with a few irregular secondary alveoli, margin fre quite undulate. Stipe 5–12.5 × 1–2 cm, with fairly enlarge base, sulcate, hollow, attached half-way up head, surface first markedly furfuraceous-squamose, then slightly orange ochre. Flesh thin, whitish. No particular odour or flavou Spores whitish to cream-coloured, elliptical, smooth, 22–3 × 14–18 microns.
Edibility Good.
Habitat Gregarious, on humus-rich ground with deciduou trees and hedges with elm.
Season Spring. Occasional.
Note This is a variety or only a variant form of *M. sem libera* (**283**). The size and shape of morels are affected k habitat, rainfall and whether they appear at the beginning c end of their season: later morels are often larger and thicke

283 MITROPHORA SEMILIBERA

Synonyms *Morchella hybrida*; *Morchella semilibera*.
Etymology From Latin, 'half-free', because the lower part of the head does not touch the stipe.
Description Carpophore 5–15 cm high, head conical, pointed or obtuse at top, free in lower half, olive brown, ochreous in dry weather, with lengthwise ribbing, sinuate then symmetrical, often anastomosed, with secondary four-sided alveoli, hollow. Stipe 5–12.5 × 1–2 cm, white or light ochre, slightly enlarged at base, furfuraceous, hollow. Flesh thin, firm. No particular odour or flavour. Spores whitish, elliptical, smooth, 22–30 × 13–17 microns.
Edibility Good.
Habitat Single to several in leaf litter under broadleaved trees.
Season Spring. Occasional.
Note This fungus is distinguished from other morels by the free margin of its head; it is attached to the stipe about half-way up the head. It usually follows the appearance of the *Verpas* and precedes and overlaps the appearance of the various true morels.

284 MORCHELLA ELATA

Etymology From Latin, 'slender'.
Description Carpophore 6–12 cm high, head conical or cylindrical, blackish, divided by lengthwise blackish ribbing connected by blackish ribs, thus forming fairly large alveoli, fairly rectangular, hollow. Stipe 5–7.5 × 1–2 cm, almost cylindrical, ochreous-grey, sometimes sulcate, conspicuously furfuraceous, hollow. Flesh quite thin and tough, whitish or greyish. No particular odour or flavour. Spores white, elliptical, smooth, 25–27 × 16–18 microns.
Edibility Good.
Habitat Beneath conifers.
Season Spring. Rare. In Britain occurs in Scotland and northern England.
Note This is a blackish mushroom easily recognized by its radially arranged longitudinal ribbing. Because of unusual variation in colour, shape and size, morels are difficult to identify to species. But all species of *Morchella*, true morels, are edible and very good when cooked and eaten in moderate amounts. The photograph represents *Morchella elata* var. *purpurascens*, a variant more common in Europe, but in Britain known only in Dunbartonshire. It is said to differ from the typical form only in its pale purple colour.

285 MORCHELLA CONICA

Etymology From Latin, 'cone-shaped'.
Description Carpophore 5–10 cm high, head pointed, conical, olive ochre to greyish-black, varying in colour with age and moisture, with elongated alveoli and lengthwise ribs often as long as the head, which soon become blackish; crosswise ribs divide the primary alveoli into secondary, almost quadrangular alveoli, hollow. Stipe 5–7.5 × 1–2 cm, pale yellowish, furfuraceous, almost cylindrical, hollow. Flesh quite thin and tough, whitish. No particular odour or flavour. Spores whitish, elliptical, smooth, 22–24 × 12–15 microns.
Edibility Good.
Habitat On acid or burnt ground, beneath conifers.
Season Spring.
Note Like all the species of *Morchella*, in addition to the typical form there are a great many varieties, each with distinctive colour and appearance. The specimen in the photograph belongs to the variety *distans*.

286 MORCHELLA ESCULENTA

Synonym *Morchella rotunda*.
Etymology From Latin, 'edible'.
Description Carpophore 10–20 cm high or more, head normally rounded, sometimes slightly conical, ochreous-yellow, with large alveoli, irregularly rounded, slightly venose, separated by sterile paler ribs, hollow. Stipe 5–14 × 1–2 cm, sometimes up to 5 cm at base, strong, hollow, pale, barely furfuraceous, enlarged and sulcate at base. Flesh thick, tender, whitish. Strong mushroomy odour, sweetish flavour. Spores white, elliptical, smooth, 20–23 × 12–13 microns.
Edibility Excellent; also good for drying.
Habitat On sandy or clayey-sandy ground, in open places, under broadleaved trees.
Season Spring. Occasional.
Note Morels are especially variable in shape, size and colour, and many species described in the literature, such as *M. deliciosa*, may prove to be only variants of this one very common polymorphic species.

287 MORCHELLA UMBRINA

Etymology From Latin, 'dark'.

Description Carpophore 3–7 cm high, head globose, up 3 cm in diameter, blackish-grey, initially with prima adpressed ribs, fairly sinuate, then dilated, with numerou deep alveoli, first roundish then irregular. Stipe 2–2.5 × 1 c at top, conspicuously enlarged at base, where it is als sulcate and cavernous, almost glabrous, whitish, sometime with ochreous markings, hollow like the fertile part. Fles quite thick, white to brownish. No particular odour or fla vour. Spores whitish, elliptical, smooth, 18–23 × 9–12 mi rons.

Edibility Excellent.

Habitat On sandy ground, in sunny places, near poplars other broadleaved species.

Season Spring. Occurs in Europe but is not known Britain.

Note The clear contrast between the blackish head and th white stipe make this one of the most easily identifiab morels. The fungi belonging to the genus *Morchella* have wide variety of carpophores, which often look as if the belong to more than one species.

---

288 MORCHELLA VULGARIS

Etymology From Latin, 'common'.

Description Carpophore up to 10–15 cm high, head elon gated, rarely roundish, blackish-grey, with elongated alveo quite irregular, with thick lengthwise ribbing, sometime with reddish markings, hollow. Stipe 7.5–10 × 1–2 cm whitish, almost glabrous, enlarged and sulcate at the bas hollow. Flesh tender, whitish. Mushroomy odour and swee ish flavour. Spores whitish, elliptical, smooth, 18–20 10–12 microns.

Edibility Excellent.

Habitat On fine ground, in open places, frequent beneat elms.

Season Spring. Occasional.

Note This morel differs from *M. esculenta* (**286**) by it darker colour and more elongated shape, and from suc black morels as *M. conica* (**285**) and *M. elata* (**284**) by th flush attachment of its head to the stipe; the others have slight overhang or depression between the margin of th head and the stipe.

BRACKET OR CRUST MUSHROOMS

289 PANUS TORULOSUS

Synonym *Panus conchatus.*
Etymology From Latin, 'a tuft of hair'.
Description Cap 5–10 cm, fairly funnel-shaped, eccentric or fan-shaped, irregularly undulating, first entirely amethyst violet, or only at edge, with centre then completely ochreous-yellow, first glabrous, with radial fibrils, innate or finely pubescent, downy at margin, squamulose when mature. Gills whitish, finally ochreous, tinged with amethyst or or towards edge, very decurrent in parallel rows, with some ramifications, edge curling as it dries. Stipe 1–3 × 0.5–1 cm eccentric or lateral, light ochre, irregular, compressed with downy base. Flesh white, limp but leathery, especially when mature. Sometimes a slight anise-like odour and faint earthy flavour. Spores white, elliptical, smooth, 4–7.5 × 2–3.5 microns.
Edibility Can be eaten but of poor quality.
Habitat On trunks and stumps of broadleaved trees.
Season Autumn. Occasional.
Note Widely distributed but not very common.

290 CREPIDOTUS MOLLIS

Etymology From Latin 'soft'.
Description Cap 3–7 cm, almost sessile, bracket- or kidney-shaped with rudimentary tiny lateral stipe, glabrous, sometimes with large, sparse, adpressed scales, pale olive grey at the water-soaked striate margin, then whitish, pale yellow, undulate and lobate when mature. Gills whitish-grey then light brown, convergent and decurrent at base, often ramified. Stipe, when there is one, up to 1.5 cm long, villose. Flesh whitish, soft, gelatinous beneath cuticle. No odour, flavour sweet. Spores ochreous-brown, elliptical, smooth, 7–9 × 5–6 microns.
Edibility Fair. See **Note**.
Habitat In groups, often imbricate, or isolated on trunks.
Season Autumn. Occasional.
Note *Crepidotus* is a genus of mostly sessile brown-spored mushrooms that resemble small, fragile species of *Pleurotus*. There are a great many species; most are small, a few are common. Because their identification to species is difficult without a microscope, and because little is known about the edibility of the various species of *Crepidotus*, none should be gathered casually for the table.

291 MERULIUS TREMELLOSUS

Etymology From Latin, 'trembling', because of its gelatinous appearance.

Description Carpophore with encrusting basal part extending to free brackets, connate and also imbricate, sterile surface free and downy, whitish, with a pinkish-orange sinuate, denticulate margin. Hymenium from pinkish-white to bright orange, with alveolar folds 1–3 mm wide, or linear supple, anastomosed. Flesh gelatinous, elastic-leathery, cartilaginous when dry. Spores white, cylindrical-arcuate smooth, 3.5–4.5 × 1–1.2 microns.

Edibility Too leathery to eat.

Habitat On rotted broadleaved wood.

Season Autumn. Common.

Note This is the most common and most widely distributed species of *Merulius*, a genus of fungi that are shelving and fleshy, or sometimes crust-like.

292 SCHIZOPHYLLUM COMMUNE

Common name The split gill.

Etymology From Latin, 'common', or 'widespread'.

Description Cap 1–3 cm, grey or flesh-coloured, tending to become white, fan- or kidney-shaped, fairly lobate, sessile, dry, inclined downwards or horizontal, covered with felty greyish-white hairs, sometimes zoned concentrically. Gills greyish-white or pink-tinged, split lengthwise into two parts that tend to curve away from each other, converging radially towards base, where they are attached. Flesh brownish, becoming whitish and sometimes malodorous as it dries. Spores white, straight or curved, smooth, 3–4 × 1–1.5 microns.

Edibility Of no value because of texture.

Habitat On wood, stumps, dead trunks or living trees in poor health.

Season All year. Occasional, chiefly found in southern England. Common in Europe.

Note This is probably the most widely distributed mushroom in the world; there seems to be no place where it is not found, except in areas where the climate is very cold. Besides growing on wood, it has also been found on animal matter (saprophytic on whalebone or, in mycelial form with no fruit-body, on scar tissue in human mouth).

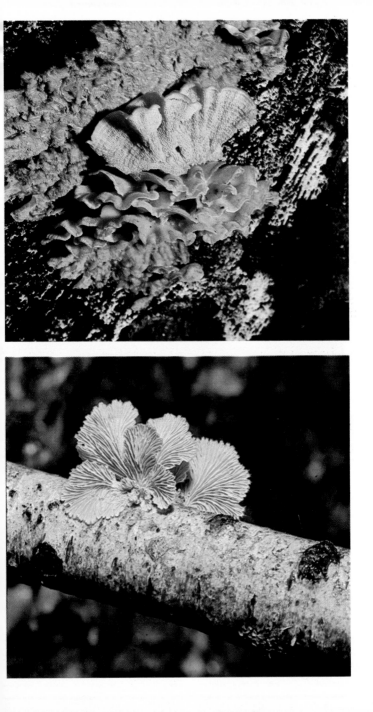

293 DAEDALEA QUERCINA

Common name Maze gill.

Etymology From Latin, 'pertaining to oak', because of it[s] habitat.

Description Carpophore bracket-shaped, 9–50 cm, sessile, light brown, smooth or rough, quite rugose, unequal, marked by alternate concentric zones, raised and depressed. Pores 6–50 mm long, sinuate, gill-like, ramified and maze-like, thick, ligneous, brown-grey or leather-coloured. Flesh pale reddish-brown or light brown, woody, thick, quite light. Mushroomy odour. Spores white, elliptic, smooth, 6–7 × 2.5–3 microns.

Edibility Too leathery to eat.

Habitat Saprophytic, on oak.

Season All year. Common.

Note A perennial, varying somewhat in the formation of the hymenium and in the presentation of the carpophore.

294 LENZITES BETULINA

Etymology From Latin, 'of birch', because of its preferred habitat.

Description Carpophore 2.5–10 cm, bracket-shaped, usually flat, sessile, upper surface felty, with not very conspicuous zonation, but sometimes with concentric zones, basic colour greyish-white, with a tendency to turn paler and become uniform. Hymenium with dirty white, radiating, gill-like plates, which may be unbranched or ramified, often anastomosed, sharp-edged. Flesh white, suberose, leathery. Spores white, cylindrical, smooth, 4–7 × 2–3 microns.

Edibility Inedible because of the leathery texture.

Habitat Frequently on birch, but also on a wide variety of dead broadleaved wood, even construction timbers and telegraph poles.

Season All year. Occasional.

Note Similar species include *Gloeophyllum sepiarium* (**295**) and *G. abietinum*, which grow on firs and other conifers, and have dark brown flesh, brownish or black felty surface, and reddish-grey-brown pruinose gill-like plates.

295   GLOEOPHYLLUM SEPIARIUM

Synonym *Lenzites sepiaria.*

Etymology From Latin, 'of fences', because of its habitat.

Description Carpophores bracket-shaped, very broad, 2–10 cm, sessile, isolated, superposed or joined laterally to each other, coarsely tomentose, with radial wrinkles and concentric grooves, brownish-yellow then dark red, finally blackish-brown, margin regular or slightly undulating, downy, orange-yellow. Hymenium maze-like with gill-like plates radially arranged, crowded, anastomosed, ligneous, not separable, brownish-ochre, edge at first pruinose, whitish then reddish-brown. Flesh thin, suberose, tobacco-coloured. No particular odour or flavour. Spores white, smooth, cylindrical, 7.5–8.5 × 2.5–3 microns.

Edibility Inedible because of texture.

Habitat On coniferous wood in open, sunny places.

Season All year. Occasional in Scotland but otherwise rare in Britain. More common and widespread in Europe.

Note It often attacks wood put to human use, such as telegraph poles and fences, causing the wood to rot and turn red.

296   PHAEOLUS SCHWEINITZII

Synonym *Polyporus schweinitzii.*

Etymology After the mycologist Schweinitz.

Description Carpophore 10–40 cm, typically bracket-shaped and imbricate, initially leather-coloured, then darkening towards the edge, rust brown in central part, remaining yellow at margin, surface rugose, felt-like, downy. Tubes decurrent, yellow to rust brown; pores irregular, polygonal, sometimes maze-like. Stipe, when present often central, 3–12 × 5–6 cm, rust brown, solid, rugose, sometimes covered with tubes to the base. Flesh rhubarb-coloured, tending to darken, spongy then fibrillose, finally dry and fragile. Spores white, elliptical, smooth, 7–8 × 4 microns.

Edibility Inedible because of texture.

Habitat On coniferous stumps and roots, rarely on trunks.

Season Summer and autumn. Occasional.

Note This fungus is commonly found with grasses and other debris such as twigs and branches apparently pushing through the fruit-body but in fact having been encircled and engulfed by the fungus during growth.

297 PIPTOPORUS BETULINUS

Synonym *Polyporus betulinus.*
Common names Razor strap fungus; birch bracket.
Etymology From the Latin, 'of birch', because of its habitat.
Description Carpophore 4–20 cm or more, up to 6 cm thick, bell- or hoof-shaped, sometimes with a short peduncle, pale tending to darken with age, often dappled, covered with a thin, smooth, separable crust, margin rounded, obtuse and sterile. Tubes white, 2–8 mm, sometimes detachable; pores white, darkening, small and round. Flesh white, soft, rubbery. No odour, flavour bitterish. Spores white, cylindrical, often curved, smooth, 5–7 × 2 microns.
Edibility Mediocre, can only be eaten when very young; tough and unpalatable when mature.
Habitat Parasitic on birch.
Season Grows in summer and autumn, but present all year. Common.
Note This is a very common, conspicuous mushroom in winter throughout northern birch woodlands; sometimes many fruit-bodies occur up a single trunk.

298 PYCNOPORUS CINNABARINUS

Synonym *Polyporus cinnabarinus.*
Etymology From Greek, 'like cinnabar' or 'dragon's blood', because of its colour.
Description Carpophore 3–6 cm or more, bracket-shaped, sessile, deep orange-red, tending to darken, at first slightly pubescent then glabrous, fairly rugose with faint zonation towards margin. Tubes 1–3 mm long, blood red; pores small, round, pubescent, vermilion. Flesh red, leathery, first spongy then suberose. Odour and flavour negligible. Spores white, cylindrical, smooth, 5–6 × 2–2.5 microns.
Edibility Inedible because of toughness.
Habitat On dead broadleaved branches and trunks.
Season Summer and autumn. Rare.
Note This is an easily indentifiable polypore, readily seen at a distance because of its bright cinnabar red colour. It occurs in Europe, espcially in central, southern and eastern parts, less common in western regions; known in Britain from a very few reports, which may have been introductions. It is certainly not of regular occurrence in this country.

299　PHELLINUS PUNCTATUS

Etymology From Latin, 'spotted' or 'dotted'.

Description Carpophores crustaceous, up to 20 cm long and 0.5–2.5 cm thick, stratified, cinnamon-coloured or brownish; pores up to 0.7 cm long, fine, roundish, cinnamon- or tobacco-coloured, with a greyish hazel pruina, mycelium pale or sulphur yellow. No particular odour or flavour. Spores white then pale yellow, oval, subglobose, smooth, 6.5–9 × 5–8 microns.

Edibility Inedible because of texture.

Habitat On all types of broadleaved wood or bushy shrubs.

Season All year.

Note *Phellinus* is a genus of corky polypores in which the species can be crust-like or bracket-like. The flesh is reddish-brown, and many species have setae (microscopic, darkly pigmented, awl-shaped, sterile cells in the hymenium lining the tubes). *P. igniarius* is a perennial bracket found on old willow trees, with orange-brown flesh and tubes stuffed with an abundant, thread-like white mycelium. *P. panacens* is similar and forms small woody brackets on branches of domestic plum trees.

300　TRAMETES VERSICOLOR

Synonyms *Polyporus versicolor; Coricolus versicolor.*

Common name Many-zoned bracket fungus.

Etymology From Latin 'varying in colour'.

Description Carpophores 3–8 cm wide, flattened or slightly depressed at the attachment, thin, in superposed brackets or joined together to form a rosette structure, sessile, smooth or velvety, with variously coloured zonation, separated by satin-like shiny zones. Tubes short, whitish, darkening to brownish on maturity; spores small, round, initially white then light brown. Flesh thin, leathery, whitish. No odour or flavour. Spores white, cylindrical or slightly arcuate, smooth, 4.5–8 × 1.5–3 microns.

Edibility Inedible because of texture.

Habitat On dead and living trunks and wood, both coniferous and broadleaved.

Season All year.

Note This is a common species, quite variable in colour, but with the upper surface invariably velvety and conspicuously zoned with different colours.

301 FOMES FOMENTARIUS

Synonym *Ungulina fomentaria.*
Etymology From Latin, 'producing tinder for fire', because of its use.
Description Carpophore 10–60 cm, hoof-shaped, sessile, very pale greyish to grey-brown with faint semi-circular markings, the most conspicuous of which is growing; margin cream-coloured, hazel or light brown. Tubes 1–3 cm long, rust-coloured, many-layered; pores small, round, pruinose, grey or light hazel. Flesh brown, suberose, soft, 7–20 cm thick, with annual series of stratified tubes, beneath a hard thick crust, shiny blackish-grey in cross-section. Spores white, elliptical, smooth, 14–22 × 5–7 microns.
Edibility Inedible because it is too wood-like.
Habitat Parasitic on birch, beech and sycamore.
Season This species is perennial. Common on birch in Scotland, rare in southern Britain on beech. Widespread and common in Europe.
Note The flesh of the pulverized carpophore was used in ancient surgery as a styptic agent; when mixed with salt-petre it produced amadou, the best tinder for lighting fires. This mixture is also used for drying fishermen's flies.

302 FOMITOPSIS PINICOLA

Synonym *Ungulina marginata.*
Etymology From Latin, 'pine'.
Description Carpophore 10–30 cm, hoof-shaped, sessile, thick or flattened, yellowish then red, finally black, with small semi-circular concentric markings, covered in the older parts by a resinous, blackish crust, shiny or pruinose; margin yellow or red. Tubes ochreous, stratified, 3–6 mm long; pores round, small, cream or very light brown, sometimes reddish when rubbed. Flesh white or pale yellow, suberose, hard with stratified tubes. Odour of tobacco, flavour slightly acid and bitter. Spores pale yellow-white, elliptical, smooth, 6–10 × 3–4.5 microns.
Edibility Inedible because it is too wood-like.
Habitat Parasitic on broadleaved and coniferous species, also saprophytic on dead tree trunks.
Season Perennial. Only one British record, but common and widespread in Europe.
Note This species is easy to identify because of the bright red obtuse margin, and also because the pallid flesh changes to cherry red when KOH is applied. The resinous crust is so heavily impregnated with wax that it will melt and boil from the heat of a lighted match.

303 GANODERMA APPLANATUM

Etymology From Latin, 'flattened'.

Description Carpophore 10–40 cm, flat bracket-shaped, often imbricate, sessile, sometimes first white, soon covered by a smooth, horny crust, becoming reddish-brown and knobbly or grooved, margin sharp white or greyish. Tubes rust-coloured, stratified, 1–4 cm long; pores white, turning brown when touched, small, round or irregular. Flesh cinnamon brown and felt-like. Spores rust brown, elliptical or ovate and finely warty, 6.5–8.5 (9.5) × 5–6.5 (7) microns.

Edibility Inedible because it is too wood-like.

Habitat Parasitic, persisting after death of the host as a saprophyte, especially on broadleaved trees such as beech.

Season All year, perennial. Common.

Note This fungus is easily identified by its flat brackets, somewhat crusty surface and white, readily discolouring surface. It is often called artist's conk because a picture can be etched on the whitish pore surface; wherever touched it turns brown and, if left to dry, will retain a drawing. *G. adspersum* is very similar but thicker with rounded margin, dark brown flesh and larger spores (9–11.5 × 6–8 microns). It is more common than *G. applanatum*.

304 GANODERMA TSUGAE

Etymology From the Japanese for hemlock, *Tsuga*, the preferred host.

Description Carpophore 4–20 cm, fan- or kidney-shaped, surface glabrous, unequal, concentrically sulcate, appears varnished, vermilion yellow-red to red-black or blackish with margin acute, bright yellow, finally cap-coloured and radially sulcate, often undulate or fairly lobate. Tubes 0.5–0.7 cm long, brown, not detachable; pores circular or polygonal, from white to light cinnamon-coloured. Stipe 2–20 × 1–4 cm, sometimes very small, lateral, cylindrical, often forked, similar in colour and surface formation to cap. Flesh soft, rubbery, white or whitish beneath the surface crust. Spores ochreous-brown, ovoid, warty, 9–11 × 6–8 microns.

Edibility Edible and tender when it first forms in the spring, but becomes too tough when mature.

Habitat On trunks and stumps of eastern hemlock (*Tsuga canadensis*) and other conifers.

Season An annual species, which grows in summer and autumn, fairly persistent. An American fungus not known in Britain or Europe.

Note The stipe may be fairly well developed and may be either on the same level as the cap or perpendicular to it and erect. *G. lucidum* occurs on broadleaved trees in Britain and Europe.

305 HETEROBASIDION ANNOSUM

Synonym *Fomes annosus*.
Etymology From Latin, 'with many years'.
Description Carpophore 7–45 cm, bracket-shaped, sessile, brown then blackish, convex or almost flat, sometimes barely imbricate, often resupinate or with a false stipe; surface uneven, rugose, sulcate, developing a crust, margin thin, first white. Tubes yellowish, stratified; pores roundish, slightly angular, white then whitish or yellowish. Flesh whitish, suberose, then ligneous. No particular odour or flavour. Spores white, subglobose, minutely spiny, 4.5–6 × 3.5–4.5 microns.
Edibility Inedible because it is too wood-like.
Habitat Parasitic on conifers, rarely on broadleaved trees.
Season A perennial species that grows in summer and early autumn but is present all year round. Common.
Note The mycelium parasitizes the root system of many conifers, causing serious damage. The fruit-bodies may also form on the ground in association with roots or at the foot of trunks and stumps. The trees attacked by this fungus are easily blown down by wind.

306 INONOTUS HISPIDUS

Synonym *Polyporus hispidus*.
Etymology From Latin, 'hirsute' or 'hairy'.
Description Carpophore 10–30 cm or more, bracket-shaped, sessile, rust yellow turning brown, then finally blackish and very bristly. Tubes 2–3 cm, rust-coloured; pores small, round, brown, glancing in the sun, often with brown watery droplets. Flesh up to 10 cm thick, rust-coloured, spongy, fibrous, becoming fragile when dry. Aromatic mushroom odour when young, flavour quite astringent. Spores ochreous-brown, subglobose, smooth, 9–10 × 7–8 microns.
Edibility Inedible because astringent and too fibrous.
Habitat Parasitic on various broadleaved species, especially ash, but also apple and walnut.
Season Summer and autumn, but present all year. Common.
Note *I. cuticularis* is similar but smaller, has a fibrillose-tomentose rather than bristly surface, smaller, elliptical spores and anchor-like setae on cap surface.

307 FISTULINA HEPATICA

Common name Beefsteak fungus.
Etymology From Greek, 'liver-like'.
Description Carpophore 5–30 cm or more, bracket-shaped, spatula-shaped or roundish, sessile or with a short lateral stipe, blood red or liver red, surface thick and gelatinous, quite viscous; as it ages it becomes blackish-brown and dries out. Tubes fine, pale, reddening, separate; spores round, cream-coloured then reddish. Flesh reddish, marbled like raw meat, thick, fibrous, succulent. Slightly acid odour and flavour. Spores pink, subglobose, smooth, 4.5–6 × 3–4 microns.
Edibility Good, cooked and raw.
Habitat On oak trunks and stumps, but very occasionally on sweet chestnut.
Season Autumn. Occasional.
Note Unlike most polypores, whose tubes are fused, this fungus has individually separate tubes. It is a good, unmistakable, edible mushroom, especially raw: it has a lemony tart flavour and pleasing texture.

308 TYROMYCES CAESIUS

Synonym *Polyporus caesius*.
Etymology From Latin, 'blue-grey'.
Description Carpophore 1–8 cm, bracket-shaped, often imbricate, white then blue-grey, surface villose, silky in old specimens. Tubes 3–9 mm long, white, not stratified; pores white, turning blue when touched, small, unequal, maze-like or aculeiform. Flesh white, blue when broken, soft, watery then brittle. Sweet odour and flavour. Spores light blue, elongated, often curved, smooth, 4–5 × 1–1.5 microns.
Edibility Inedible because it is too tough.
Habitat Solitary or imbricate on dead wood of both conifers and broadleaved trees, widely distributed.
Season All year. Common.
Note *T. chioneus (T. albellus)* is similar but whitish and very common on dead broadleaved wood.

309 POLYPORUS SQUAMOSUS

Common name Dryad's saddle.
Etymology From Latin, 'scaled'.
Description Cap 10–60 cm, ochreous, variegated with adpressed brown scales, fan-shaped or hemispherical, convex, flat then concave, often umbilicate when young, margin thin, cuticle dry. Tubes 0.2–1 cm long, decurrent, not detachable, cream-coloured; pores quite large, whitish then pale yellow, angular. Stipe 3–8 × 1–5 cm, central or more usually lateral, solid, sturdy, squat, ochreous, reticulate uppermost, blackish at base. Flesh white, soft, thick, then leathery-suberose. Strong odour, cheese-like then mealy, with flavour of watermelon rind. Spores white, elliptical, smooth, 10–12 × 4–5 microns.
Edibility While edible, this is not to everyone's liking because of its flavour. Some people deep-fry the tender edges, some pickle them and others boil the mushroom to add flavour to a soup stock, discarding the boiled mushroom.
Habitat Parasitic on various broadleaved trees.
Season Spring through autumn. Common.
Note This fungus is fairly abundant, especially on elms and beech.

310 ISCHNODERMA BENZOINUM

Synonym *Polyporus resinosus*.
Etymology After its odour which is like benzoin.
Description Carpophore 8–20 cm wide, 1–2.5 cm thick, bracket- or oyster-shaped, sessile, but attached with a tuberculate base, surface blackish-brown with bright blackish-blue highlights, rugose, downy, often with resinous droplets; margin thin in mature specimens, often lobate, brown. Tubes thin, whitish then brown; pores roundish, whitish tinged with rust brown, yellowish, finally tobacco brown. Flesh fibrous then suberose-ligneous, first whitish then rust brown. Changeable, sometimes anise-like odour. Spores white, cylindrical-arcuate, smooth, 4–7 × 1.5–2.5 microns.
Edibility Inedible because it is too fibrous.
Habitat On dead broadleaved and coniferous trunks and stumps; sometimes a very inactive parasite.
Season Spring to late autumn, with carpophores persisting on wood. Occasional.
Note Some mycologists recognize a distinct species, *I. resinosum*, which lacks bluish tones and grows on broadleaved trees; others consider it only a variant.

311 OSMOPORUS ODORATUS

Synonym *Trametes odorata.*
Etymology From Latin, 'scented'.
Description Carpophore 5–6 × 2–8 cm, bracket-shaped, sessile; turbinate-circular when growing on a horizontal surface, yellowish-brown or reddish, or older parts at back blackish; quite irregular with conspicuous nodular outgrowths, divided into broad zones by deep, close grooves, very downy, rugose, margin thick, obtuse, lobate, whitish or more often bright yellow or orange, finally rust brown. Tubes yellowish, not perfectly stratified; pores roundish, distant, felt-like, yellowish then ochreous-rust-coloured. Flesh orange-brown, suberose, first soft then hardening. Strong smell of anise or vanilla tending to disappear with age. Spores white then darkening, elliptical, smooth, 6–9 × 3–5 microns.
Edibility Inedible.
Habitat On coniferous wood, especially Norway spruce stumps, also on worked wood where it forms aberrant carpophores.
Season All year. Widespread in Europe, but not known in Britain.
Note The strong odour of the carpophores is also present in wood invaded by the hyphae, causing a breakdown of the tissue ('rot'), which turns red.

---

312 ECHINODONTIUM TINCTORIUM

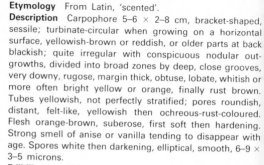

Common name Indian paint fungus.
Etymology From Latin 'used for dyeing'.
Description Carpophores 5–30 cm, bracket-shaped or hoof-shaped, sessile, upper surface black and cracked. Hymenium towards edge in early stages with pores or maze-like tubes, gradually changing into teeth 1–2 cm long, varying in colour, eventually greyish then black. Flesh ligneous, leathery, brick red. Spores whitish, oval, minutely spiny, 6–8 × 3–5 microns.
Edibility Inedible because it is too wood-like.
Habitat Parasitic on mature conifers in western North America.
Season All year, growing from spring to autumn. Not known in Britain or Europe.
Note This is a common and widespread parasite on conifers, causing tremendous damage to the forests of North America. It is in fact a living fossil of the fungus kingdom, the only species that forms ligneous and perennial carpophores with hymenium of teeth. When ground up and reduced to fine powder the flesh of this fungus was used by the indigenous American Indians to paint war signs on their bodies, as well as for other purposes. The same powder was also used by shamans as medicine; in fact it contains various alkaloids and tannin.

313 SPONGIPELLIS PACHYODON

Synonym *Irpex pachyodon; Irpex mollis.*
Etymology From Greek, 'large-toothed', because of th‹ shape of the hymenium.
Description Carpophore 3–8 cm, bracket-shaped or fair‹ crustaceous, sessile, glabrous uppermost, white the‹ cream-coloured with darker striations. Hymenium ca‹ coloured tinged with pink, variable, formed by teeth 1–1 cm long, somewhat fused together forming sinuate plates ‹ false gills, especially at the margin. Flesh rather leather‹ white, unchanging. Spores white, subglobose or broadl‹ elliptical, smooth, 5–8 × 4.5–6.5 microns.
Edibility Inedible because of its leathery texture.
Habitat Parasitic on various broadleaved trees.
Season All year. Widespread in Europe but does not occu‹ in Britain.
Note Many species of *Trametes*, thin bracket-shaped fung with a poroid hymenium, may form carpophores with tube‹ that become split and spine-like. A similar but mor‹ crust-like white polypore is *Irpex lacteus*, also unknown i‹ Britain.

314 HERICIUM ERINACEUS

Synonyms *Dryodon erinaceus; Hydnum erinaceum.*
Etymology From Latin, 'porcupine', from its appearance‹
Description Carpophore 5–30 cm, cushion-shaped, forme‹ by thick, interwoven branches, often partly joined together‹ with a rudimentary stipe, white tending to yellow, covere‹ by teeth 3–6 cm long, slender, pendant, supple, pruinose‹ Flesh white, unchanging, thick and cavernous, soft bu‹ slightly elastic. Odour slightly acid, flavour sweetish. Spore‹ white, subglobose, smooth, 6–7 microns, amyloid.
Edibility Good.
Habitat Parasitic on various broadleaved trees, especiall‹ beech trees.
Season Autumn. Rare.
Note The dried and ground flesh is sometimes used as ‹ styptic agent. *H. coralloides*, which may also grow o‹ conifers, has a more coralloid appearance with distinct‹ clusters of shorter teeth (2 cm at most), and its flesh turn‹ blue in Melzer's reagent.

315 STECCHERINUM OCHRACEUM

Etymology From Latin, 'ochre-coloured'.
Description Carpophore 2–7.5 cm, bracket-shaped, often encrusting the substrate behind, membranous, but the brackets, when formed, are zonate, pubescent, whitish or pale yellow-ochre. Hymenium with crowded ochreous teeth, tinged with bright yellow-pinkish, small, shorter at the margin. Flesh thin, membranous, leathery, white. Odour and flavour negligible. Spores white, ovoid, smooth, 3–4 × 2–2.5 microns.
Edibility Of no value because of texture.
Habitat On dead branches, especially of gorse.
Season All year. Occasional.
Note The carpophore of many lignicolous species, depending on the substratum and its structure, may grow either as small brackets or as crusts (resupinate carpophores).

316 STEREUM HIRSUTUM

Etymology From Latin, 'covered with hair'.
Description Carpophore 2–10 cm, yellowish or grey with yellow margin, broadly adherent to the substratum, sometimes encrusting, sessile, usually bracket-shaped, covered with felty hairs, slightly zonate. Hymenium smooth, yellow-ochreous when old, leather-coloured or greyish. Flesh thin, membranous, leathery. No odour or flavour. Spores white, elliptical, curved, smooth, 5–8 × 2–4 microns, amyloid.
Edibility Inedible because it is too tough.
Habitat On the wood of dead broadleaved trees.
Season All year. Common.
Note This is a fairly common lignicolous species, easy to spot because of the colour of the hymenial surface. *Stereum* is a genus of bracket-shaped fungi growing on wood and resembling several thin-fleshed polypores except that the hymenium is smooth instead of poroid.

317 STEREUM INSIGNITUM

Etymology From Latin, 'friezed' or 'ornate'.
Description Carpophores 2–10 cm, bracket-shaped and semi-circular or concrescent-lobate, sessile, normally imbricate, with rust brown velvety zonations uppermost, then glabrous, fibrous, wine brown with age, alternating with lighter, concentric, yellowish-brown, downy zones, sometimes greenish because of algae, margin undulate and lobate, ochreous-yellow. Hymenium smooth, pale ochre sometimes tinged with pink, finally pale grey. Flesh thin leathery with a lower whitish stratum and a shiny reddish-brown crust. No particular odour or flavour. Spores whitish elliptical, smooth, 5.6–6.5 × 2.5–3 microns, amyloid.
Edibility Inedible because it is too tough.
Habitat On beech.
Season All year, growing from spring to autumn. Widespread in central and southern Europe, but not known in Britain.
Note *S. subtomentosum*, though quite similar, is easily identifiable by its hymenium, which turns chrome yellow when touched. It grows on various broadleaved species, mainly beech and willow.

318 CHONDROSTEREUM PURPUREUM

Synonym *Stereum purpureum*.
Etymology From Latin, 'purple'.
Description Carpophore 2–6 cm, encrusting or adpressed to substratum, sessile, commonly bracket-shaped, connate and imbricate, sterile surface felt-like and downy, greyish-white to brownish, with slight zonations, margin acute, undulate, sinuate. Hymenium smooth, waxy in damp weather, initially whitish then purple-violet or pale lilac-brown, finally dark brown or violet, tending to fade. Flesh thin, leathery-soft, horny when dry, with various distinct strata, whitish. Spores white, elliptical and ovoid, smooth, 6–8 × 3–4 microns.
Edibility Of no value because it is thin and leathery.
Habitat Almost cosmopolitan, on broadleaved trees, rarely on conifers.
Season All year. Common.
Note The parasitism of this fungus causes a withering of the upper part of the leaf lamina, resulting in silver leaf disease in plum trees. Other hosts may not show this symptom.

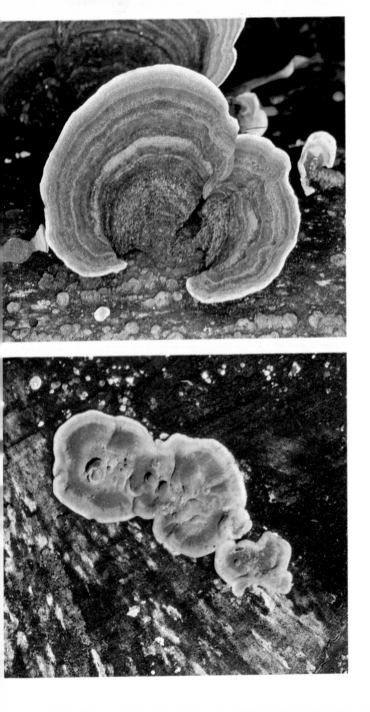

319 PULCHERRICIUM CAERULEUM

Synonym *Corticium caeruleum*.
Etymology From Latin, 'blue'.
Description Carpophore 2–5 cm, prone, sessile, at first rounded, dark blue, downy with edges normally lighter, then merging with others in sheets. Hymenium faintly rugose or tuberculate. Flesh thin, membranous, soft, fairly detachable when fresh, more adherent to substratum when dry, bluish. No odour or flavour. Spores white, oval, smooth, 7–11 × 5–7 microns.
Edibility Of no value because of texture.
Habitat On dead wood, especially ash.
Season All year. Occasional.
Note This is a species of no gastronomic interest but conspicuous because of its beautiful colour.

320 TREMELLA MESENTERICA

Common name Jelly brain fungus.
Etymology From Greek, 'like the middle intestine'.
Description Carpophore 1–8 cm, orange-yellow, variously contorted, plicate, undulate, circumvolute, cerebriform, pruinose becasue of the spores. Flesh gelatinous, yellow, becoming elastic when drying, then horny. Insignificant odour and flavour. Spores white, ovate, smooth, 13–14 × 7–8 microns.
Edibility Of no value because of texture.
Habitat On dead wood, especially small branches.
Season All year. Common.
Note This fungus can be very common in the spring and autumn. *T. foliacea* is similar but reddish-brown and can be quite large. The closest look-alike is *Dacrymyces palmatus*, which is brain-like and orange-yellow, but has a white point of attachment to the wood (conifers) and is very different microscopically. Many species of *Tremella* will dry to an insignificant horny structure in drought only to revive again on return of rain.

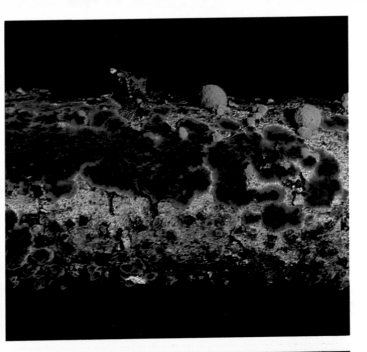

321   **AURICULARIA AURICULA-JUDAE**

Common name   Judas's ear.

Etymology   From Latin, 'ear'.

Description   Carpophore 6–10 cm, ear-shaped, sessile or with a short attaching peduncle, outer surface sterile, pubescent, with slight venations; inner surface fertile, reddish-brown, at first almost smooth then venose, pruinose because of the spores. When drying out it tends to turn violet and become increasingly circumvolute. Flesh soft, gelatinous, slightly elastic, translucent, horny when dry, reviviscent. No particular odour or flavour. Spores white, cylindrical, smooth, 12–17 × 4–7 microns.

Edibility   Good, although its value is more in its texture than its flavour.

Habitat   On broadleaved wood, especially elder.

Season   All year, more conspicuous in rainy periods, in winter and spring. Common.

Note   A very similar species, *A. polytricha*, is grown commercially in the Orient. It is called *Mu ehr*, 'small ear'. Besides being eaten in soups and vegetable dishes, it is used in folk medicine to soothe coughs and generally improve the physical condition. *A. auricula-judae*, however, is not known to confer any medical benefits.

322   **AURICULARIA MESENTERICA**

Etymology   From Greek, 'intestine-like', from its shape.

Description   Carpophore 5–12 cm, bracket-shaped, sessile, edge lobate, grey-brown, outer surface sterile with whitish zonations, quite villose, pale blue-grey, slightly velvety; lower surface fertile, very pleated, purple-brown, pruinose because of the spores. Flesh gelatinous, quite thick and elastic, leathery when dry. No particular odour or flavour. Spores white, slightly incurved, smooth, 15–18 × 7–8 microns.

Edibility   Inedible because of elastic texture.

Habitat   On broadleaved wood in great quantity, especially on elm.

Season   All year, especially in winter and spring. Common.

Note   This fungus has become more frequent in Britain following the advent of Dutch elm disease and the consequent abundance of elm stumps suitable for colonization.

323   DACRYMYCES STILLATUS

Synonym   *Dacrymyces deliquescens*.
Etymology   From Latin, 'in drops'.
Description   Carpophore 0.2–1 cm, pustular, sometimes roundish, yellow or orange-yellow, with no margin, finally contorted, usually sessile, sometimes with a very small stipe. Flesh pale yellow, transparent, gelatinous. No odour or flavour. Spores white, cylindrical, incurved, septate, smooth, 8–22 × 4–7 microns.
Edibility   Of no value because of its texture.
Habitat   Gregarious on dead wood and fallen branches of broadleaved trees and conifers.
Season   All year. Common.
Note   This belongs to a small group of gelatinous fungi that grow parasitically and saprophytically on wood. *D. palmatus* is brain-shaped and reddish-orange. Other cup-like to cushion-shaped jelly fungi, also some shade of yellow, include species of *Ditiola* and *Guepiniopsis*.

---

324   EXIDIA GLANDULOSA

Common name   Witches' butter.
Etymology   From Latin, 'full of glands', because of the warty surface of the hymenium.
Description   Carpophore 5–10 cm wide, blackish, globose or lenticular, attached by a tiny peduncle, sometimes flat, undulate, gelatinous, becoming ash-coloured or faintly downy; when drying out it forms a black crust on the substratum. The fertile downward-facing part is covered with lower small conical papillae. Flesh blackish, gelatinous, transparent, soft. No odour or flavour. Spores white, cylindrical, sometimes incurved, smooth, 12–15 × 4–5 microns.
Edibility   Not known.
Habitat   On dead, but often still attached, broadleaved branches.
Season   All year. Common.
Note   Other members of this genus also grow on dead wood. *E. truncata*, brownish, hemispherical with a short peduncle; *E. nucleata*, milky, tinged with lilac, with central white nucleus; *E. thuretiana*, opal or pinkish, discs drying to a varnished crust; and *E. viscosa*, white, greyish or violet, completely smooth and quite viscid.

CORAL, BUSH OR CLUB MUSHROOMS

325 GRIFOLA FRONDOSA

Synonym *Polyporus fondosus.*
Common name Hen-of-the-woods.
Etymology From Latin, 'leafy'.
Description Carpophore 20–40 cm in diameter, rosette-like, hemispherical, made up of many imbricate caps, very crowded in young specimens, spatula-shaped, up to 10 cm wide, undulate, brown, darker with faint zonation towards margin, velvety, covered with small clusters of radial fibrils; stipes connate and merging into a main trunk. Tubes decurrent to branch attachments, difficult to detach, up to 3 mm long, whitish; pores round or maze-like, white. Flesh whitish, quite fibrous, slightly watery. Odour mushroomy with a hint of meal, flavour sweet. Spores white, subelliptical, smooth, 5–7 × 3.5–4.5 microns.
Edibility Choice, very sought after in some areas.
Habitat Parasitic on the roots of broadleaved trees, particularly oak.
Season Throughout the autumn. Occasional.
Note This is one of the largest fungi (it can weigh more than 11 kg (25 lb) and one of the most popular autumn edible varieties. It somewhat resembles a small hen, is often found covered with leaves, and grows at the base of living oaks.

---

326 MERIPILUS GIGANTEUS

Synonyms *Polyporus giganteus.*
Etymology From Latin, 'gigantic'.
Description Carpophore rosette-like with fan-shaped caps, imbricate or superposed, 10–30 cm wide, brown, pale then yellowish-brown at margin, blackish-brown at rear and cream or chamois-coloured at margin, velvety or granulose, with faint zonation, radially sulcate, depressed at rear towards base. Hymenium with whitish, decurrent tubes, soot brown then blackish when touched, 1–2 mm long; pores small, round or polygonal, whitish, turning blackish when touched. Flesh white, darkening, tough, quite leathery, fibrous. Odour and flavour acidic. Spores white, globose, smooth, 4–5 microns.
Edibility Good when young, but slightly leathery.
Habitat In crowded groups at the base of stumps, usually beech or oak, but sometimes arising from the roots some distance from the trunk.
Season Autumn. Common.
Note Has a marked degrading effect on wood; sometimes produces an extensive collection of carpophores. Up to 82 kg (180 lb) of fungi have been gathered from old chestnut trunks.

327 POLYPORUS UMBRELLATUS

Etymology From Latin, 'with umbrellas'.

Description Carpophore rosette-like (up to 50 cm in diameter), consisting of caps of 1–4 cm, convex then umbilicate with undulate and sinuate margin, fairly light brown, radially fibrillose, pruinose or slightly squamose, each on a branch. Stipe white or reddish-brown, often originating from a large hypogeal sclerotium, divided into numerous pruinose, cylindrical ramifications. Tubes very short, decurrent on branches, reduced sometimes to mere alveoli; pores wide, irregular, white. Flesh white, soft and juicy, slightly fibrous. Odour slightly mealy, flavour sweet. Spores white, elliptical, smooth, 7–10 × 3–4 microns.

Edibility Choice.

Habitat At the foot of old broadleaved species, probably also parasitic on them.

Season Autumn. Very rare. Found in Essex.

Note Although uncommon, where this fungus does occur it will often appear year after year and its clusters are usually large, providing many meals. This is one of very few polypores that are both tender enough to eat and that taste good. It seemed to have become extinct in Britain but was recently found in Essex.

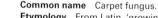

328 THELEPHORA TERRESTRIS

Common name Carpet fungus.

Etymology From Latin, 'growing on the ground'.

Description Carpophore rosette-like, consisting of several pilei, 3–5 cm high, encrusting the substratum at base and merging laterally, upper surface felty with rust brown radiating fibrils, blackish-brown with age, frayed with white at margin then same colour as the rest. Hymenium rugose or papillate, chocolate brown and pruinose. Flesh dark brown, leathery but soft, fibrillose. Odour of damp loam, flavour quite astringent. Spores dark brown, globose-angular, warty, 8–9 × 6–8 microns.

Edibility Inedible because of acrid taste and leathery texture.

Habitat On the ground in sandy pine woods, on roots and twigs.

Season All year, usually in autumn. Common.

Note The species belonging to this genus usually grow in bush-like formations of varying shapes. *T. palmata* has laminae divided at the margin into compressed branches; *T. anthocephala* has wedge-shaped segments; *T. clavularis* has pointed, subcylindrical branches; and *T. caryophylea* often has finely incised lobate pilei.

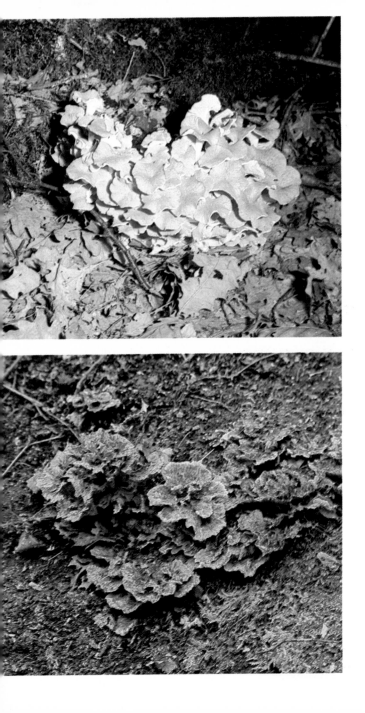

329 SPARASSIS CRISPA

Common name Cauliflower fungus.
Etymology From Latin, 'curled'.
Description Carpophores 10–60 cm, like a cauliflower
whitish or slightly ochreous, with flattened, curled, broad
ribbon-like and intricate branches. Stipe white, darkening
with age, squat, rooting. Flesh whitish or faintly pale yellow
fragile. Odour quite pleasant, faintly of anise, flavour
pleasant, of walnut. Spores whitish to light ochre, ovoid
smooth, 6–7 × 4–5 microns.
Edibility Choice.
Habitat In coniferous woods, at the foot of trees or on
roots.
Season Autumn.
Note *S. laminosa* occurs in deciduous as well as conifer
ous woods, and differs in having broad strap-like lobe
forming an altogether more lax fruit-body. It is far les
common than *S. crispa*.

330 RAMARIA FORMOSA

Synonym *Clavaria formosa.*
Etymology From Latin, 'handsome'.
Description Carpophore up to 30 cm high and 15 cm wide
bush-shaped, with a thick, solid, rooting stipe, sometimes
already divided into several branches from the base, white
faintly pinkish; branches crowded, cylindrical, rugose
lengthwise, pinkish-buff to salmon-coloured, with yellowish
tips, ochreous and powdery because of the spores when
mature. Flesh white, darkening slowly when exposed to air,
thin, pinkish-grey, exuding aniline water. Odour insignificant, flavour slightly bitter. Spores ochreous, elliptical
rugose, 12–15 × 4–5 microns.
Edibility Inedible, a powerful purgative.
Habitat On humus-rich ground beneath broadleaved trees.
Season Autumn. Rare.
Note There are a great many species of branched coral
fungi and they are very difficult to tell apart. Because *R.
formosa* is known to cause gastro-intestinal distress, and
because some others are somewhat indigestible, it is best to
proceed with great caution when experimenting with any
species of *Ramaria*.

331 RAMARIA FLAVA

Synonym *Clavaria flava.*
Etymology From Latin, 'yellow'.
Description Carpophore at most 20 cm high and 15 cm wide, bush-like. Stipe thick, short, narrowing at the base, solid and white; branches straight, quite distant, cylindrical or often compressed, divided several times at the bottom, dichotomous at the top, sulphur yellow or lemon yellow, ochreous when mature, tips concolorous, denticulate. Flesh white, marbled, tender. Light odour, flavour sweet and pleasant. Spores ochre, elliptical, rugose, 9.5–15.5 × 3.2–6.5 microns.
Edibility Good, but avoid older specimens.
Habitat In broadleaved and coniferous woodland.
Season Autumn. Rare.
Note There is a complex of related yellowish coral fungi. The species differ somewhat in colour, branching and microscopic characters. None is known to be poisonous but caution is recommended because of the somewhat similar, inedible *R. formosa* (**330**).

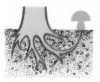

332 CLAVICORONA PYXIDATA

Synonym *Clavaria pyxidata.*
Etymology From Latin, 'with small vases', because of the form of the apical branchlets.
Description Carpophore 5–12 cm, whitish or faintly hazel, sometimes darkening when mature. Stipe thin, smooth, quickly ramifying; branchlets like tiny cups from the edge of which proliferation may occur. Flesh white, solid. Faint odour, flavour slightly peppery. Spores whitish, elliptical, smooth, 4 × 3 microns, amyloid.
Edibility Can be eaten, but is a mild laxative.
Habitat On rotting wood.
Season Autumn. Widespread in Europe and many other parts of the world but not known in Britain.
Note This is one of the few coral fungi that grow on wood. It is further distinguished by the candelabra-like clusters of branching tips.

333   RAMARIA BOTRYTIS

Synonym *Clavaria botrytis.*
Etymology From Greek, 'like a bunch of grapes'.
Description Carpophore up to 15 cm high and 20 cm wide, bush-shaped. Stipe stout, narrowing at the base, white, pale yellow when mature, divided into short cylindrical branches, white then ochreous, surmounted by short, denticulate coral red or brick red tips, ochreous when mature. Flesh firm, brittle, white, unchanging. Odour slightly fruity, flavour sweetish. Spores ochre, fusiform, longitudinally striate, 12–17 × 4–6 microns.
Edibility Good.
Habitat On the ground in broadleaved woods.
Season Autumn. Rare.
Note Species of *Ramaria* are generally recognized by spore size and shape or other microscopic or chemical characteristics. Field identification is rarely reliable for species of this genus.

334   RAMARIA INVALII

Synonym *Clavaria invalii.*
Etymology After the estate of Inval, Surrey.
Description Carpophore 4–5 cm high, golden yellow, bush-like, compact and dense. Stipe fairly evident, short, often with white or yellowish root-like filaments at the base, pointed; numerous branchlets, thin, short, unequal, straight, cylindrical, smooth, with tipped apex. Flesh white. Odour slightly sharp, flavour slightly bitter. Spores ochreous yellow, echinulate, 7–9 × 4 microns.
Edibility Unknown.
Habitat In coniferous litter.
Season Autumn. Rare.
Note Other small species of *Ramaria* grow in the humus in coniferous woodland, such as *R. ochraceovirens*, olive yellow turning green when rubbed; *R. palmata*, very pale ochre with compressed branchlets; and *R. gracilis*, pale orange with whitish upper branches and sometimes smelling strongly of anise.

335 RAMARIA MAIREI

Synonym *Clavaria pallida*.
Etymology From Latin, 'discoloured'.
Description Carpophore 6–18 cm high, bush-like. Stipe thick, short, very light brown, whitish at base, with crowded, dichotomous branchlets, rugose lengthwise, first whitish then tinged with pink, then ochreous as well; tips obtuse with short teeth, pale purple when young. Flesh white, not hygrophanous. Slight soap-like odour, slightly bitter after-taste. Spores ochreous, elliptical, finely rough, 9–12 × 5–6 microns.
Edibility Causes violent and painful intestinal disorders; becomes bitter when cooked.
Habitat In coniferous or broadleaved woodlands.
Season Autumn. Rare.
Note *R. testaceoflava*, found under conifers in central and southern Europe, is at most 5 cm high, stipe reddish, branchlets cinnamon red, tips yellow. The flesh is wine red when exposed to the air. *R. fennica* is also purple or violet when young. *R. fennica violaceibrunnea*, which grows under conifers, turns brownish when mature.

---

336 CLAVARIA INAEQUALIS

Etymology From Latin, 'unequal'.
Description Carpophore 2.5–6 cm, golden yellow, pale sulphur yellow at the base, usually single, cylindrical, tip pointed, sometimes forked, solid. Flesh pale yellow. No particular odour or flavour. Spores white, globose or ovoid, smooth, 7–9 × 6–8 microns.
Edibility Of no value because of small size.
Habitat In woodland, open places and heathland.
Season Autumn.
Note *C. inaequalis* is an ambiguous name. Different mycologists have described different entities as *C. inaequalis*, and the diagnostic differences among these otherwise identical species are microscopic. The very common *C. fusiformis* is similar, with typically unbranched, yellow, tubular to compressed clubs that are more or less joined at the base. *C. vermicularis* is similar but white, and *C. purpurea* is purplish brown. None is known to be poisonous and *C. fusiformis*, when found in quantity, is worth gathering to add to a cooked vegetable dish.

337 CLAVULINA RUGOSA

Synonym *Clavaria rugosa*.
Etymology From Latin, 'wrinkled'.
Description Carpophores 5–12 cm high, white, single or slightly ramified, enlarged at the top, up to 1 cm wide, irregular and rugose, tuberculate, sulcate. Ramifications few in number, irregular, obtuse but rarely cristate. Flesh white, abundant, firm. No particular odour or flavour. Spores white, subglobose, smooth, 8–9 × 6–8 microns.
Edibility Can be eaten.
Habitat Gregarious in woodland and adjacent grassy areas.
Season Autumn. Common.
Note Although quite variable, this fungus is typically only slightly branched, whitish and wrinkled. In addition, it has only two-spored basidia with strongly incurved sterigmata; these characteristics, while microscopic, are useful for precise identification. Other species with similar microscopic characteristics include the more densely branched, whitish *C. cristata* and the ash grey *C. cinerea*, both of which are very common.

338 CLAVARIADELPHUS PISTILLARIS

Synonyms *Clavaria pistillaris*.
Etymology From Latin, 'pestle-shaped'.
Description Carpophore 8–25 cm high with a maximum diameter of 6 cm, club-shaped, slender or stout, surface at first smooth then sulcate lengthwise, light yellow tending to become greyish-brown. Flesh white, bruising brownish, solid, soft then spongy-fibrous. Odour pleasant, flavour somewhat bitter. Spores cream-coloured, elliptical, smooth, 9–16 × 5–7 microns.
Edibility Edible but poor in flavour.
Habitat Beneath broadleaved trees, particularly beech, on calcareous ground.
Season Autumn. Rare. In Britain, found only in south-eastern England.
Note This is a gregarious species. The genus includes other club-shaped fungi such as *C. truncatus* (**339**); *C. ligula*, up to 10 cm high, with a hairy base, light ochre then reddish, grows beneath conifers; *C. fistulosus*, up to 20 cm high, very thin, yellowish, hollow, with a white and downy base that grows on fallen branches, including the stems of leguminous plants; and *C. junceus*, up to 15 cm high, very thin, at most 2 mm in diameter, ochreous and growing on the litter in broadleaved woods.

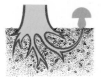

339 CLAVARIADELPHUS TRUNCATUS

Synonym *Clavaria truncata*.
Etymology From Latin, 'cut or broken off'.
Description Carpophore 5–15 cm high, conical, turbinate, with the upper part convex then flattened, slightly depressed, irregular, rugose, light yellow then bright yellow or orange, margin sulcate and lobate, very fragile, sterile like the whole upper surface, 3–8 cm wide. Lower part is like a stipe, tapering conspicuously towards base, mainly fertile, at first smooth then sulcate lengthwise or with small ramified veins at top, dirty pale lilac, tending to turn yellow with the spores, yellowish at edge. Stipe felt-like and white. Flesh whitish, reddish when rubbed, thick and cottony. Faint odour and a sweet, distinctly sugary flavour. Spores pale yellow, ellipsoid, smooth, 10–11 × 6–7 microns.
Edibility Edible, but acts as a mild laxative in quantity.
Habitat Gregarious in mountains in coniferous woods.
Season Autumn. Widespread in Europe but not known in Britain.
Note The sugary flavour is due to the large amount of mannitol, a sweet-tasting higher alcohol found in the liquid exuded by certain plants. It is produced commercially from certain species of maple and ash, and is used as a mild purgative for infants, in the production of alcoholic beverages and in the pharmaceutical industry.

340 CALOCERA CORNEA

Etymology From Latin, 'horn-like', because of its appearance.
Description Carpophore up to 1 cm high, cylindrical, pale yellow, white and hairy at the base, tapering at the top, pointed, gregarious or in small clusters. Flesh virtually non-existent, yellow, and elastic. Spores ochreous, elliptical, depressed laterally, smooth, 7–9 × 4–4.5 microns.
Edibility Of no value because of size.
Habitat On fallen broadleaved trees.
Season Autumn. Common.
Note Although this may resemble some kind of small unbranched coral or tooth fungus, its texture is gelatinous, horny and it is related to those jelly fungi that possess tuning-fork-shaped basidia.

341   CALOCERA VISCOSA

Etymology From Latin, 'sticky'.

Description Carpophore 3–6 cm high, ramified, bright yellow, orange-yellow, each branchlet ending with two or three obtuse tips, very short; surface barely viscid. Stipe dry, hairy, extending into a white mycelial thread. Flesh yellow, tough, elastic. Spores bright yellow-ochre, elliptical, smooth, 7–12 × 4–4.5 microns.

Edibility Of no value because of texture.

Habitat From rotting coniferous wood or roots.

Season Autumn. Common.

Note This species resembles a branched coral mushroom but, while corals are brittle, this is somewhat rubbery and will not snap. Jelly fungi are usually found on wood and vary in texture from soft and jelly-like to rubbery-tough. In appearance they resemble fungi in several distinct orders including cup fungi, corals and tooth fungi.

342   GYMNOSPORANGIUM CLAVARIAE-FORME

Etymology From Latin, 'knot-like'.

Description Carpophore 1–2 × 0.2–0.3 cm, shaped like small clubs, cylindrical, compressed, sometimes divided in the top part, orange-yellow, gelatinous. Spores variable, from thick to thin-walled, ochreous, elliptical, smooth, with one septum and a long peduncle; from 76–86 × 13–17 microns in the first instance to 80–105 × 13–15 microns in the second.

Edibility Undetermined.

Habitat On juniper branches, mainly *Juniperus communis* (common juniper).

Season Spring. Occasional.

Note This is a 'rust' that lives as a parasite on two different host plants. In the spring it lives on juniper, where it forms leafy swellings like tumours; in summer, on the lower surface of various Rosaceae, particularly the service tree and hawthorn, where it forms yellow reproductive structures that are enlarged with thimble-shaped extensions, known as *Roestelia lacerata*. Later, the infection is transmitted back and forth from juniper and service tree.

343 MICROGLOSSUM VIRIDE

Common name Green earth tongue.

Etymology From Latin, 'green', from its colour.

Description Carpophore 3–9 cm high, club-shaped, dark green, olive, compressed or sulcate lengthwise, glabrous, but slightly viscous in damp weather. Stipe shorter than the upper fertile part, cylindrical, finely squamulose. Odour and flavour negligible. Spores whitish, fusiform, smooth, 12–17 × 5 microns.

Edibility Of no value because of size and rarity.

Habitat On the ground in grass or woods.

Season Autumn. Occasional.

Note *M. olivaceum* is olive green to olive brown. The genus *Microglossum* resembles an unbranched coral fungus but it is an Ascomycete, producing its spores in asci rather than on the basidia as do Basidiomycetes. Other earth tongues include the blackish genera *Trichoglossum* and *Geoglossum*.

344 XYLARIA HYPOXYLON

Common name Candle snuff fungus.

Etymology From Greek, 'almost ligneous or wooden', because of the texture.

Description Stromata (the club-shaped body in which spores are produced) up to 8 cm high, often branched. Stipe cylindrical, black, the upper part white, powdered because of the asexual conidiospores; or enlarged and unbranched as a tapering, pointed cylinder, without conidiospores, but papillate because of the immersed perithecia. Spores black, bean-shaped, smooth, 11–14 × 5–6 microns.

Edibility Of no value because of texture.

Habitat On dead wood.

Season Can appear at any time of the year. Common.

Note While this species typically occurs on rotten wood, variants or similar species can be found on beechmast, hawthorn berries and leaves.

345 XYLARIA POLYMORPHA

Common name Dead man's fingers.
Etymology From Greek, 'of many shapes', because of its variability.
Description Stromata up to 9 × 2.5 cm, quite club-like, with a short cylindrical stipe, often slightly lobate in the upper fertile part, pointed at the tip, solitary or in small groups, blackish, opaque, minutely cracked around the papillae corresponding to the perithecia. Flesh hard, tough, white with a blackish layer of ovoid perithecia beneath the black superficial crust. Odour and flavour negligible. Spores dark brown or blackish, fusiform, smooth, 20–34 × 5–9 microns.
Edibility Of no value because of its texture.
Habitat On rotting wood, especially beech, with stromata emerging at ground level.
Season Present all year. Common.
Note As they form, the young stromata are covered with ochre-brown conidia (asexual spores). The fungus gets its common name from the appearance of the generally clustered club-like structures that rise out of the ground or from rotting wood at about ground level.

---

346 CLAVICEPS PURPUREA

Common names Ergot; spurred rye.
Etymology From Latin, 'purple'.
Description Sclerotium elongated, fairly cylindrical, with rounded ends, slightly grooved, growing on the ovary of graminaceous flowers and eventually replacing it. It varies in shape and size in relation to the plant infected. Outwardly blackish, internally white and hard. The stromata emerge, either isolated or in small groups, from the sclerotium when it drops to the ground; they consist of a globose head, about 2 mm in diameter, ochreous-brown or pale purple, spotted with immersed perithecia and a long, thin, smooth concolorous stipe. Spores colourless, filiform, septate, smooth, 100 × 1 micron.
Edibility Extremely poisonous.
Habitat Sclerotia parasitic on the inflorescences of Gramineae, including wheat and barley but especially rye.
Season The sclerotium grows in the summer in the grass flower, falls, overwinters and produces small drumstick-like fruit-bodies the following spring; the spores from these fruit-bodies infect the grass flowers and form that summer's sclerotia. Common.
Note A dangerous fungus if ingested in foodstuffs, causing ergotism or St Anthony's fire.

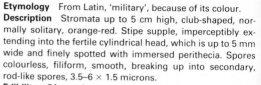

347 CORDYCEPS MILITARIS

Etymology From Latin, 'military', because of its colour.

Description Stromata up to 5 cm high, club-shaped, normally solitary, orange-red. Stipe supple, imperceptibly extending into the fertile cylindrical head, which is up to 5 mm wide and finely spotted with immersed perithecia. Spores colourless, filiform, smooth, breaking up into secondary, rod-like spores, 3.5–6 × 1.5 microns.

Edibility Of no value.

Habitat On lightly buried lepidopterous (butterfly or moth) larvae and pupae.

Season Autumn. Occasional.

Note The stromata of this species contain a powerful antibiotic that stops their alteration by bacterial degradation. Another species parasitic on insects, *C. sinensis*, used as an anti-typhoid agent in Chinese folk medicine, has also shown itself to be rich in antibiotic compounds.

348 CORDYCEPS MEMORABILIS

Etymology From Latin, 'memorable'.

Description Stromata up to 1.5 cm long and 0.1–0.3 mm wide, supple, depressed, sulcate lengthwise, orange, rust-coloured, minutely furfuraceous, occuring singly, some concrescent at the base and sometimes joined lengthwise with ovoid, bare, completely free perithecia, at most 0.5 mm high, variously positioned, grouped in rows or scattered, smooth, rust-coloured, apex sepia brown. Spores colourless, filiform, smooth, breaking up into secondary elliptical spores, 1.7–2 × 1.3 microns.

Edibility Of no value.

Habitat On larvae and adult members of Coleoptera (beetles and weevils).

Season Midsummer. Occurs in Italy, but not in Britain.

Note This species has been said to represent the sexual and fairly rare form of a common mould that parasitizes insects, *Paecilomyces farinosus*, although this connection does not seem to have been as yet definitely proven. *P. farinosus* may also form whitish, elongated, sporigenic structures called coremia. The formation of the coremia is stimulated by sunlight.

349 CORDYCEPS CAPITATA

Etymology From Latin, 'with a head'.
Description Stromata up to 10 cm high, solitary or in small groups. Stipe quite stout, about 1 cm wide at the base, yellow, smooth or sulcate, suddenly enlarging into an ovoid or subglobose head, dark brown or blackish, densely roughened by the perithecial ostioles, which are immersed, particularly when the stroma dries out. Spores colourless, filiform, smooth, breaking up into secondary cylindrical spores, 7–20 × 2–3 microns.
Edibility Of no value.
Habitat Parasitic on the hypogeal fruit-bodies of *Elaphomyces* in broadleaved woodland.
Season Autumn. Occasional.
Note The false truffle, upon which this fungus grows, was once thought to be an aphrodisiac and was sold by apothecaries. Because of the phallic shape of the *Cordyceps* attached to the globular false truffle the two associated fungi have been used as a fertility symbol.

350 CORDYCEPS OPHIOGLOSSOIDES

Etymology From Greek, 'like a snake's tongue'.
Description Stromata up to 10 cm high, club-shaped, mainly solitary. Stipe yellowish, smooth, solid, gradually enlarging into a fertile, cylindrical-ovoid head, at most 2.5 cm high and about half as wide, at first yellowish and smooth, becoming blackish and densely scabrous because of the emergence of immersed perithecia. Spores colourless, filiform, smooth, breaking up into secondary rod-like spores, 2.5–5 × 2 microns.
Edibility Of no value.
Habitat On the hypogeal fruit-bodies of *Elaphomyces*.
Season Autumn. Occasional.
Note This species is best identified when dug up because it is attached to the false truffle indirectly by long, yellowish cord-like strands, rather than directly, like *C. capitata* (**249**).

351 TAPHRINA ALNI-INCANAE

Synonym *Taphrina amentorum*.
Etymology After its host, *Alnus incana* (grey alder).
Description This Ascomycete attacks various species of alder, causing a deformation on the floral cones with consequent enlargement of the squamae and flowers, which leads to the formation of tongue-like outgrowths from the cones. These galls reach a length of 1–3 cm, initially rose-brown, first curling in upon themselves, then drying out and becoming light green, often tinged with red, and finally greyish-brown and becoming brittle and easily detached. Each outgrowth represents a separate fungal infection. The spores are produced in asci on the surface of these outgrowths. Spores colourless, subglobose, smooth, 3–5 × 4–5 microns.
Edibility Of no value.
Habitat Parasitic on alder inflorescences.
Season Autumn. Rare.
Note A similar species, *T. deformans*, is more common and causes peach 'leaf curl'.

352 PILOBOLUS KLEINII

Etymology After the mycologist Klein.
Description Very small clubs called sporangiophores, 5–7 mm high, transparent, erect, not ramified, enlarged in a small bladder-like formation towards the top, at the tip of which there is a black, lenticular formation (the sporangium) containing the spores. There is a small swelling immersed in the substratum at the base.
Edibility Of no value because of size.
Habitat In very dense groups on the droppings of various herbivores, especially cattle.
Season All year. Common but overlooked because of size.
Note In sunlight a strong pressure is manifested in the sporangiophore, first by the emission of droplets of water and then by the explosion of the vesicle or bladder. Thrown some distance in the direction of the light, the sporangium turns upside down in the air so that the lower, viscous part is at the bottom. This enables the sporangium to cling to the first object it touches. Normally the sporangia end up on blades of grass. The grass is then eaten by herbivorous animals (horses, cattle, etc.) along with the sporangia. The spores pass through the gut and out with the faeces whereupon they generate rapidly, enabling the fungus to be one of the earliest colonizers of freshly excreted dung.

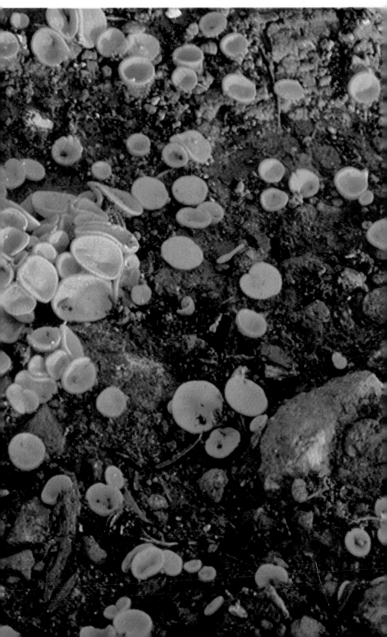

353 ANTHURUS ARCHERI

Common-name Stinkhorn.
Etymology After the Irishman Archer, who collected fungi in Tasmania.
Description Egg 4–6 × 3–4 cm, slightly buried in the ground, peridium pinkish-white tinged with brown; when cut a gelatinous layer can be seen and at the centre is the pinkish-white unexpanded carpophore. Carpophore with 4–7 arms, alveolate, fragile, red, 12 cm long, tapering pinkish-white as soon as they have emerged. Gleba on the inner surface of the arms, dark greenish, mucilaginous, fetid. Odour of radishes. Spores greyish, elliptical, smooth, 5–7 × 2–2.5 microns.

Edibility Can be eaten at the egg stage without the peridium and the gelatinous layer.
Habitat In warm regions of the world on ground with plenty of rotting ligneous fragments, in broadleaved woods.
Season Autumn. A rare introduction in Britain but widely established in various European countries.
Note Stinkhorns resemble puffballs when they first appear, although a cross-section of their egg reveals the characteristic gelatinous layer and true nature. Most are easily discovered by their odour before they are actually seen. They are disseminated by flies who feed on the slimy, fetid spore mass.

354 ASERÖE RUBRA

Common name Stinkhorn.
Etymology From Latin, 'red', from arm colour.
Description Egg up to 3 cm in diameter, whitish with pale yellow coloration; inside, a gelatinous stratum and, at centre, the unexpanded carpophore. Carpophore up to 6 cm high, when mature has a white then pinkish base emerging from volva, with 5–9 arms conspicuously bifurcating, up to 7.5 cm long and less than 0.5 cm wide at base, red. Gleba in central part of carpophore and slightly on base of arms, mucilaginous, fetid, dark olive green. Spores within mucilage, greyish, elliptical, smooth, 4–5.5 × 1.5–2 microns.

Edibility Not known.
Habitat On humus-rich ground, with wood residue, in tropical and subtropical regions, but not Britain or Europe, although it has been found in greenhouses in temperate regions.
Note The fruit-body is attractive to flies on account of the unpleasant smell and floral appearance.

355 CLATHRUS RUBER

Synonym *Clathrus cancellatus*.
Common name Basket fungus.
Etymology From Latin, 'red'.
Description Egg spheroidal, diameter up to 5 cm, white, with rhizomorphs at the base; in section after the white, membranous, leathery peridium, a gelatinous stratum is present and, inside, the unexpanded red carpophore with the greenish immature gleba. Carpophore globose, 5–10 cm high and 5 cm wide, red, with net-like lacunose arms delimiting polygonal mesh. Gleba, when mature, is mucous, greenish-black. Spores greyish, elliptical, smooth, 5–6 × 1.8–2 microns.

Edibility Reportedly poisonous when eaten raw.
Habitat Isolated or in small groups in gardens.
Season Autumn. Rare in southern England. Widespread in Europe.
Note *Ileodictyon cibarium* is a similar but pure white basket fungus with tubular arms. It is an introduction from Australasia that has become established in one or two places near London.

---

356 DICTYOPHORA INDUSIATA

Etymology From Latin, 'shift', referring to the veil.
Description Egg up to 4 cm in diameter, globose, ovoidal, white or greyish. Carpophore 15–20 × 2.5–3.5 cm, fusiform or cylindrical, white, porous, hollow, head conical for a short time, then bell-shaped, yellowish under the gleba, white if stripped of spore mass, with rugose surface, reticulate with apex perforated and delimited by a raised and distinct collar. Veil white, hanging almost to the ground, with wide polygonal mesh-work. Gleba olive green, mucilaginous, not very fetid. Spores colourless, elliptical, smooth, 3.5–4.5 × 1.5–2 microns.

Edibility Reportedly eaten at the egg stage but not recommended.
Habitat Found only in tropical forests, and therefore not in Britain or Europe.
Season During the rainy season.
Note A form of *Phallus impudicus* (**358**) is sometimes found in Britain and Europe with a very short rudimentary pendulous veil. This is sometimes called var. *togatus*.

357 MUTINUS CANINUS

Common name Dog stinkhorn.
Etymology From Latin, 'canine'.
Description Egg 2–4 × 1–2.5 cm, ovoid-elongated or pear-shaped, white or pale yellow with a mycelial root at base, broken at apex into 2–3 lobes, from which the carpophore emerges. Carpophore 6–15 × 1 cm, cylindrical, hollow, first whitish then tinged with orange or faintly pinkish, when mature orange at perforate, pointed apex, fertile part bright red but covered by olive gleba, conical, mucilaginous, 2 cm high, reticulate. Gleba green and sponge-like, slightly fetid. Flesh fragile. Spores colourless, elliptical, smooth, 3–5 × 1.5–2 microns.
Edibility Of no value.
Habitat In humus-rich ground amongst fragments of wood, in damp parts of broadleaved woodland.
Season Autumn. Occasional.

---

358 PHALLUS IMPUDICUS

Common name Stinkhorn.
Etymology From Latin, 'shameless'.
Description Egg 4–6 × 3–5 cm, spheroidal or ovate, white, with a white mycelial thread at the base, peridium white outside, tough, translucent inside, gelatinous. Carpophore up to 20 × 3 cm, tapering towards the conical cap at the top, hollow, lacunose, porous, fragile and white, with a thick volva at the base, free at margin, covered with an alveolar reticulum, white with perforated disc at apex. Gleba olive green, mucilaginous, fetid, covering the cap from which it quickly disappears, carried off by flies. Spores colourless, elliptical, smooth, 5–7 × 2–2.5 microns.
Edibility Sometimes eaten at the egg stage but not recommended.
Habitat In humus-rich ground, mainly beneath broad-leaved trees, sometimes under conifers and often in gardens.
Season Autumn. Common.
Note *P. hadriani* grows in sand dunes. It is smaller, the peridium is conspicuously pale lilac-purple and the smell is not as unpleasant.

359 ASTRAEUS HYGROMETRICUS

Etymology From Greek, 'which measures humidity', be
cause of the behaviour of the exoperidium.
Description Carpophore 2–4 cm, at first slightly hypogeal
globose, slightly viscous, star-shaped, open, epigeal, 6–10
cm wide. Exoperidium brown, opening in damp weather
into 6–10 or more arms, closing inwards when dry, made up
of four strata, the innermost one tending to be deeply
cracked. Endoperidium sessile, globose, 2–3 cm in diameter
brownish, with irregular apical pore. Odour and flavour
negligible. Spores chocolate brown, round, warty, 9–11.5
microns.
Edibility Of no value because of texture.
Habitat In woods and heaths.
Season Autumn, but old carpophores remain for about a
year, with the exoperidium becoming increasingly thin. Rare
in Britain, chiefly in the south. Widespread in Europe, espe
cially in warmer regions.

360 GEASTRUM FORNICATUM

Common name Earthstar.
Etymology From Latin, 'arched'.
Description Carpophore 6–7 × 5–6 cm, light brown. Ex
operidium opening in four triangular arms, the tips of which
are supported on the tips of four similar upward-pointing
lobes of an otherwise cup-shaped structure, covered on the
outside with vegetable debris and earth. Endoperidium
subglobose, up to 2.5 cm in diameter, on a peduncle 2–3 mm
high, with an apical, radiate peristome. Gleba powdery
when mature. Odour and flavour negligible. Spores cocoa
brown, round, warty, 3.5–4 microns.
Edibility Inedible because of texture.
Habitat On sandy soils, in coniferous and broadleaved
litter.
Season Autumn. Rare.
Note There are many species of *Geastrum*, all collectively
known by the popular name earthstars.

361 GEASTRUM PECTINATUM

Common name Earthstar.
Etymology From Latin, 'with comb-like teeth'.
Description Carpophore first oval then exoperidium opens into 5–10 triangular lobes up to 6 cm wide, white then ochreous overall, with a fleshy inner stratum that breaks up and disappears with age. Endoperidium subglobose, 1–2.5 cm, brown or lead-coloured, mealy, striate at base, which extends into a thin peduncle, whitish to grey-brown, cylindrical, 6–8 × 2–3 mm, with raised fluted peristome. Gleba powdery and dark brown when mature. Spores brown, globose, distinctly warty, 4–7.5 microns.
Edibility Of no value because of leathery texture.
Habitat In coniferous woodland and among bushes.
Season Autumn, old carpophores remaining unchanged for long periods. Rare.
Note *G. minimum*, which forms small carpophores up to 3 cm in stony grassland, has the peristome clearly delimited by a ring-like groove.

362 GEASTRUM SESSILE

Synonym *Geastrum fimbriatum*
Common name Earthstar.
Etymology From Latin, 'without a stalk'.
Description Carpophore up to 7 cm in diameter. Exoperidium opens into 6–9 triangular lobes, chamois-coloured, with an outer mycelial stratum which is thin, membranous, separable and whitish. Endoperidium globose, sessile, same colour as exoperidium, with fairly salient apical pore, edge fibrous. Gleba powdery when mature, cocoa brown. Spores cocoa brown, round, finely warty, 3–4 microns.
Edibility Inedible because of leathery texture.
Habitat Under broadleaved trees.
Season Autumn, although old carpophores remain unchanged for some time on the ground. Occasional.
Note This fungus is easily identifiable because the endoperidium rests directly on the exoperidium without any peduncle, and because the peristome (the area surrounding the apical pore through which the spores are dispersed) is unevenly fringed.

363 GEASTRUM TRIPLEX

Common name Earthstar.

Etymology From Latin, 'triple', from the peridium.

Description Carpophore first subglobose, shaped like tulip bulb. Exoperidium opening into 4–7 triangular lobes up to 7 cm wide overall, the lobes curling under the spore sac; olive-brown outside, light brownish inside, with a thick fleshy stratum that breaks up and disappears except for the central part where a cup forms at base of endoperidium which is globose, 1.5–3.5 cm in diameter, light brown, sessile, membranous, with lighter apical ostiole, conical, fibrillose-fringed, with base not delimited. Gleba whitish at first, soon olive ochre, powdery. Spores brown, globose, warty, 4–5 microns.

Edibility Of no value because of texture.

Habitat In broadleaved woods.

Season Autumn. Occasional.

Note The distinctive tulip-bulb shape hallmarks the large unexpanded carpophores of *G. melanocephalum* as well which can reach a diameter of 22 cm when fully opened. This is a rare species, not known in Britain, easily recognized by the fact that the blackish-brown gleba is not enclosed in membranous endoperidium, so that it becomes totally dispersed.

364 MYRIOSTOMA COLIFORME

Etymology From Latin, 'like a colander'.

Description Carpophore 4–9 cm, at first hypogeal or semi-hypogeal, fairly globose, ochreous, often covered with fibrillose scales, brown or tinged reddish. Exoperidium opens up into a star, with 4–14 (usually 8) triangular arms, extending to 25 cm, felt-like outside, smooth inside, whitish then reddish-brown, with transverse wrinkles. Endoperidium 1.5–7.5 cm, unevenly globose, surface shiny grey, tuberculate, then perforated with 30–50 ostioles, 1–2 mm wide, prominent; it is supported by one or more peduncles up to 5 mm high. Gleba white then cocoa brown, divided into loculi each of which opens into an ostiole. Spores reddish-brown, globose, strongly warty, 4–6 microns.

Edibility Inedible because of leathery texture.

Habitat World-wide in sunny, dry woodlands, less frequent in open, sandy places.

Season Autumn; carpophore remains can be found all year. Not known in Britain for many years, possibly extinct. Last found in Norfolk.

365 BOVISTA NIGRESCENS

Etymology From Latin, 'blackening', from the colour of the endoperidium.

Description Carpophore 1.5–5 cm, globose, with a mycelial tuft at the base. Exoperidium at first white, slightly pubescent, then with very faint aerolations, flaking away from the endoperidium, which is shiny, grey turning dark brown and finally black, opening at top into an irregular ostiole. Gleba white in immature specimens, cocoa brown and powdery when mature. Odour and flavour slightly acrid in young specimens. Spores brown, globose, warty, 5–6 microns, pedicellate.

Edibility Mediocre while gleba remains white, then inedible.

Habitat Fields, pastures and similar grassy places.

Season Autumn. More common westwards and northwards in Britain; widespread in Europe.

366 BOVISTA PLUMBEA

Etymology From Latin, 'lead-like', from the colour of the endoperidium.

Description Carpophore 2–4 cm, subglobose, with no sterile base, attached to the soil by a small mycelial tuft. Exoperidium pure white, barely areolate, thin, fragile, soon flaking away from the endoperidium, opening via an apical ostiole, which is grey or lead grey. Gleba white, yellowish olive brown and powdery when mature, with no sterile base. Flavour slightly acid. Spores brown, oval, finely warty, 5–7 4–6 microns, pedicellate.

Edibility Mediocre while gleba remains white, then inedible.

Habitat Short grass in fields, on acid and basic ground, also in coastal dunes.

Season Late summer to autumn. Occasional.

Note The dry carpophore persists for many months and is blown about by the wind; as it rolls around the spores are gradually dispersed.

367 CALVATIA UTRIFORMIS

Synonym *Lycoperdon caelatum; Calvatia caelata.*
Etymology From Latin, 'like a wineskin'.
Description Carpophore 7–15 cm or more in diameter subspherical, globose or pear-shaped. Exoperidium fragile pure white, breaking up into polygonal aerolae, pyramidal which then disappear, leaving the surface of the endoperidium areolate. The brown endoperidium, quite shiny when mature, opens unevenly, and up to half the carpophore disappears. Gleba white, then greenish-ochre, finally dark olive brown, at first compact then watery, finally powdery, subgleba with large cells, separated from the gleba by a pseudodiaphragm. Spores brownish, subglobose, smooth 3.5–5 microns.
Edibility Very good while the gleba is immature (white).
Habitat In fields and meadows.
Season Summer and autumn. More common northwards and westwards in Britain.
Note When the spores have been released the rest of the carpophore – the subgleba with part of the endoperidium, a brown leathery cup – remains in the field and is rolled here and there by the wind. *C. craniformis* is very similar and differs only microscopically; *C. cyathiformis* produces lilac spores.

368 CALVATIA GIGANTEA

Synonyms *Lycoperdon maximum; Langermannia gigantea.*
Common name Giant puffball.
Etymology From Latin, 'gigantic'.
Description Carpophore 10–65 cm in diameter, globose Exoperidium white, thin, slightly mealy, pale ochreous when mature, minutely fragmented. Endoperidium thin, fragile becoming fragmented and distintegrating. Gleba white, floccose, elastic when mature, olive brown; subgleba almost absent. Thick, cord-like root. Spores olive yellow, globose smooth or barely warty, 3–5 microns.
Edibility Excellent when young, but see **Caution**.
Habitat World-wide, in meadows, fields and gardens.
Season Summer and autumn. Occasional.
Note This fungus can become very large indeed; weight of up to 25 kg (56 lb), diameters of 160 cm and heights of 24 cm have been mentioned.
Caution Some people find this fungus indigestible.

369 CALVATIA EXCIPULIFORMIS

Synonym *Lycoperdon saccatum*.
Etymology From Latin, 'vase-shaped'.
Description Carpophore higher than it is wide, of variable size up to 15 cm high, with a maximum diameter in the head of 10 cm and in the stipe of 6 cm. Stipe always well defined. Exoperidium white, cream-coloured or ochreous, with bristle-like spines converging at the apex. Endoperidium smooth, ochreous-yellow, opening wide. Gleba initially white, when mature powdery and dark brown or cocoa coloured, globose; subgleba (interior of stalk) cellular, brown when mature. Spores cocoa brown, globose, warty, 4–5.5 microns.
Edibility Can be eaten when immature.
Habitat In woods and roadside verges.
Season Autumn. Occasional.

Note A fairly variable species, hence the numerous varieties that have been described on the basis of size, ornamentation, form, habitat and colour. The genus *Calvatia* is separated from *Lycoperdon* on the basis that at maturity the entire apex of the fruit-body flakes away, exposing the glebal spore mass, whereas in the latter genus the fruit-body becomes perforate with an apical pore through which the spores are liberated.

370 LYCOPERDON PERLATUM

Synonym *Lycoperdon gemmatum*.
Etymology From Latin, 'widespread'.
Description Carpophore 1.5–8 cm high, pear- or club-shaped, densely covered with pyramidal warts, 1–2 mm high, each surrounded by a ring of smaller granular warts. When the pyramidal warts fall off, the endoperidium is left with a reticulate pattern. The endoperidium becomes perforate at the apex. Gleba at first white, ochre-brown when mature; subgleba (stalk) well developed, with interior of large cells. Spores yellowish-brown, globose, warty, 3.5–4 microns.
Edibility Mediocre when immature.
Habitat Ubiquitous, on the ground, in woods and often tufted.
Season Autumn. Common.

371 LYCOPERDON UMBRINUM

Etymology From Latin, 'dark-coloured'.

Description Carpophore 1–4 cm in diameter and up to 5 cm high, pear-shaped or subglobose. The exoperidium has scattered brown spines that reveal glimpses of the shiny yellowish-brown endoperidium; initially the spines are arranged in groups that converge at the apex and then usually separate. The endoperidium opens at the apex into a small pore. Gleba from white to cocoa brown when mature; subgleba has large cells. Spores cocoa brown, globose, warty, 4–5 microns.

Edibility Fairly mediocre.

Habitat Very widespread in the northern hemisphere, mainly in dry parts of coniferous and broadleaved woods.

Season Autumn.

Note In dry, sunny grassland, especially in the Mediterranean countries, we find *L. decipiens*, with thin, soft, white spines, fairly convergent, which, as they drop off, reveal the shiny white endoperidium. *L. mammiforme* is an impressive species found in calcareous woodland, covered with a white veil that breaks up into thick caducous warts and leaves a ring-like zone on the upper part of the stem.

372 LYCOPERDON ECHINATUM

Etymology From Latin, 'covered with spines'.

Description Carpophore 2–7 cm in diameter, up to 5 cm high, pear-shaped or subglobose, brown, covered with spines joined together in threes, thus forming pyramidal warts up to 5 mm high, caducous, leaving behind them a continuous polygonal mosaic on the endoperidium, which opens by an apical pore. Gleba white then ochre, soft then powdery and purple-brown; small subgleba with small, irregular cells. Spores chocolate brown, globose, warty, 4–5 microns, pedicellate.

Edibility Edible when immature after removing exoperidium (warts).

Habitat In broadleaved woodland.

Season Autumn. Occasional.

Note Unmistakable on account of the very long spines that cover the endoperidium.

373 LYCOPERDON PYRIFORME

Etymology From Latin, 'pear-shaped'.
Description Carpophore 1–5 cm in diameter, up to 8 cm high, pear-shaped or subglobose. Exoperidium consists of fine warts or is broken up into small scales, rarely smooth, ochreous or hazel, darker at the apex. Endoperidium ochreous, tending to yellowish, opening at the apex by a pore. At the base the fruit-body has a conspicuous white mycelial thread. Gleba white, then greenish-yellow, olive or brown; subgleba with small cells. Spores brownish-yellow, globose, smooth, 3–4 microns.
Edibility Mediocre when young.
Habitat On stumps, often in large compact groups, rarely on ground rich in woody fragments.
Season All year. Common.
Note *L. pyriforme* is an extremely variable species, easily identified by its habit of growing in large numbers on rotting stumps, to which the fruit-bodies are attached by conspicuous white rhyzomorphic strands.

374 VASCELLUM PRATENSE

Synonyms *Lycoperdon hiemale; Vascellum depressum.*
Etymology From Latin, 'of fields', from its habitat.
Description Carpophore 2–4 cm high, subglobose or tuberate, typically white but more rarely yellowish-brown; peridium covered with fragile, mealy ornamentation, either floccose granules or thin, fairly connate spines. At maturity opens by a pore, but gradually the entire upper part of the fruit-body flakes away. Gleba, when mature, is powdery and dark brown, separated from the sterile part quite distinctly by a diaphragm; subgleba cellular, dark when mature. Immature flesh white. Spores light brown, subglobose or ovoid, spiny, 3–4.5 microns.
Edibility Mediocre while immature.
Habitat Widespread in temperate climates, often gregarious, in grassland, often with *Bovista plumbea* (**366**).
Season Late summer to autumn. Common.
Note This mushroom is most commonly found on lawns and grassy areas. When growing on golf courses it can cause golfers problems when searching for lost balls.

375 CALOSTOMA CINNABARINA

Etymology From Greek, 'cinnabar'.

Description Carpophore 5–9 cm high, 1.5–2.5 cm in diameter in the fertile part, globose, peridium orange-yellow, supported by a stipe, partly underground, venose-lacunose, whitish, gelatinous. A gelatinous peridium, like a transparent cap, covers the other two strata of the peridium; when mature it separates *en bloc* allowing the release of the spores from a crown-like peristome, orange-red in colour. Gleba when mature is powdery and ochreous. Spores light ochre, elliptical, pitted, 10–15 × 8–10 microns.

Edibility Of no value because of texture.

Habitat Partly buried in the ground (especially along road banks) in southeastern North America, but extending up to New England.

Season Late summer and autumn. A North American species not found in Britain or Europe.

Note Two other American species with southern distribution, *C. lutescens* and *C. ravenelii*, differ from this mushroom by their lack of reddish colour except at peristome; and they differ from one another in that the latter lacks a gelatinous exoperidium.

---

376 SCLERODERMA CITRINUM

Synonyms *Scleroderma aurantium; Scleroderma vulgare.*

Common name Common earthball.

Etymology From Latin, 'lemon yellow'.

Description Carpophore diameter up to 12 cm, subglobose, peridium very thick, bright yellow, sometimes pale or cream-white because the pigment is water-soluble, split into polygonal scales, coarse in texture, especially at the top where it opens out irregularly. Gleba soon violet-black, blackish, finely marbled, pale greenish-grey when mature, powdery. Odour and flavour strong and acrid. Spores brownish-black, globose, spiny with faint reticulum that is chain-like, 7–15 microns.

Edibility When eaten raw and sometimes even when cooked, this mushroom causes gastric disorders or acute indigestion; very thin cooked slices occasionally are used as pseudo-truffles, but **not recommended**.

Habitat Widespread, in woods and heaths, in acid or acidified soil.

Season Late summer and autumn. Common.

Note This mushroom is often seen parasitized by *Boletus parasiticus* (**243**). Several other species of *Scleroderma* prefer sandy soil, such as *S. geaster*, which resembles a large earthstar when open, but without a spore-sac.

377 TULOSTOMA BRUMALE

Synonym *Tylostoma mammosum.*
Etymology From Latin, 'wintery'.
Description Carpophore 0.5–1 cm, spheroidal or sometimes depressed, whitish then pale yellow, outer peridium fragile, inner one smooth, thin, membranous, papyraceous, peristome small, slightly prominent, entire, brownish when mature. Stipe 2–5 × 0.2–0.3 cm, brownish, cylindrical, slightly tapering at top where attached to peridium, base enlarged, bulb-like because of the mycelial mass, smooth or fairly fibrillose, brownish towards top. Gleba powdery when mature, ochreous. Spores pinkish-yellow, globose, finely aculeate, 4–6 microns.
Edibility Of no value because of leathery texture.
Habitat Gregarious, with the stipe usually buried in moss in sand dunes with high calcareous content.
Season Autumn and winter. Rare.
Note *Tulostoma* is a genus of stalked puffballs that develop underground and emerge at maturity. Often the stipe remains imbedded in the substrate.

378 HYDNANGIUM CARNEUM

Etymology From Latin, 'flesh-coloured'.
Description Carpophore 1–3 cm in diameter, globose, surface pinkish to rose, then tending to yellow, ochreous in dry specimens, base sterile, like a small stipe, evident only in younger specimens. Gleba lacunose, fragile, marbled, with no particular odour or flavour. Spores pale yellow, globose, densely spiny, 10–18 microns.
Edibility Fair, although small.
Habitat Widespread in all warm temperate areas or in greenhouses beneath various broadleaved species, particularly eucalyptus.
Note This species is associated essentially with eucalyptus trees, which are world-wide as a result of reafforestation using these Australian trees. In warm climates the fungus can be found in winter and spring under the leaf litter.

379 GAUTIERIA MORCHELLAEFORMIS

Etymology From Latin, '*Morchella*-like' (morel-like).

Description Carpophore 1–3 cm, sometimes 5 cm, g
bose, spheroidal; no peridium in the adult state and w
open hymenial cells and a tiny stipe. Gleba ochreous-ru
coloured, consisting of broad cells 1.5–8 × 1–4 mm, po
dery because of the spores. Flesh ochre-rust-coloure
lacunose, fairly firm. Very strong odour of bouillon cub
and a sweetish flavour. Spores rust-coloured, broadly ell
tical, with 8–10 lengthwise ribs, 12–24 × 8–12 microns.

Edibility Sometimes eaten but **not recommended**.

Habitat In beechwoods, quite deeply buried and norma
beneath leaves.

Season Summer and autumn. In Britain, known only fro
Gloucestershire.

Note This is one of a large number of fungi that gro
underground. It is rare in Europe and not easily identified

Caution Because very little is known about the edibility
this or similar species, it cannot be recommended.

---

380 MELANOGASTER VARIEGATUS

Etymology From Latin, 'speckled', because of the appea
ance of the gleba.

Description Carpophore 1.5–4 cm in diameter, spheroid
elongated or humped, peridium at first yellow, ochre-rus
coloured, downy, turning to blackish-brown when touche
then yellowish-brown, eventually dirty greenish-brown. Gl
ba brown-violet, blackish, marbled with yellowish venatio
that emit a blackish mucous fluid. Odour at first of chick
liver then becoming more pleasant, like liqueur chocolate
flavour sweetish, slightly sulphurous. Spores blackis
brown, elliptical, smooth, 6–10 × 3.5–5.5 microns.

Edibility Sometimes eaten when young but **not recor
mended**.

Habitat Hypogeal, symbiotic with broadleaved trees.

Season All year. In Britain, occasional in southern Englan

Note If exposed to the sun this fungus develops a ve
strong smell. The fluid that comes from the gleba originat
from the hymenium, which, when mature, is deliquescen
and the colour is produced by the spores.

Caution Although edible, this fungus is not well known ar
is best avoided.

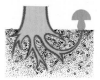

381 PISOLITHUS TINCTORIUS

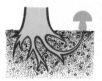

Synonym *Pisolithus arhizus.*
Etymology From Latin, 'used for dyeing'.
Description Carpophore up to 30 cm high, at most 20 cm wide, subglobose or pear-shaped with a fairly long stipe, peridium dry, thin, smooth or faintly rugose or tuberculate, initially ochreous then dark brown, fragile and dehiscent when mature, cracking open at top into small polygonal scales. Base buried, sterile and solid, sturdy, 3–10 cm in diameter, often irregular with, originally, a tuft of brown mycelial threads. Upper portion of the gleba formed by crowded, pea-sized, violet-black peridioles with yellow or sulphur yellow outline, which mature from top, becoming finally ochreous-brown and powdery. The sterile lower part has, initially, a marbled appearance, brown, white or deep yellow, with minute areolas, ochreous-brown when mature. Strong and pleasant mushroomy odour, flavour sweetish. Spores ochreous-brown, globose, spiny, 9–12 microns.
Edibility Edible when immature, but unappealing.
Habitat World-wide, in acid, sandy, thin soils, in dry pine-woods, remains of charcoal kilns or slag heaps.
Season Autumn. In Britain, very rare in southern England. Widespread in Europe.
Note The mature fungus, in section, appears as if filled with small pea-sized stones or gravel.

382 RHIZOPOGON VULGARIS

Etymology From Latin, 'common'.
Description Carpophores 1.5–5 cm, globose, slightly lobate, at first white, then yellowish tinged with reddish, finally greenish-brown, covered with ramified mycelial threads, adpressed, on the surface; peridium not detachable. Gleba soft, white at first, with narrow, maze-like cells, becoming greenish and finally olive brown. Odour slightly acid and fruity, then acrid and penetrating, flavour initially sweet. Spores whitish, elliptical, smooth, 5–8 × 2–3 microns.
Edibility Can be eaten while immature, but difficult to identify to species in a genus where few species are known in terms of their edibility.
Habitat Semi-hypogeal beneath conifers, often gregarious.
Season Spring to late autumn. Very rare in Britain, where it is found in Hampshire.
Note *Rhizopogon* is a large genus of mushrooms that grow on or below the surface of the ground, are typically covered with rhizomorphs, and may at first be thought to be truffles, though truffles lack rhizomorphs and are very different microscopically. *Rhizopogon* is a Gasteromycete, producing its spores on basidia, whereas truffles are Ascomycetes, producing spores inside mostly globose asci.
Caution Difficult to identify. See **Edibility**.

383 CYATHUS OLLA

Etymology From Latin, 'a pot', from its shape.
Description Carpophore 10–15 mm, with a maximum diameter of 8–15 mm, funnel-shaped, grey or ochreous and faintly pubescent; smooth outside, initially closed by a leathery diaphragm, whitish, fugacious, then open with an undulating margin erect or turned back, inner surface lead grey or ochreous, smooth with peridioles (up to 10), circular in shape, compressed and almost seed-like, umbilicate, grey or blackish, shiny, up to 3–4 mm wide, attached with a white funiculus (cord) or peduncle. Spores white, broadly elliptical, smooth, 10–14 × 8–10 microns.
Edibility Of no value because of size.
Habitat On thin soil, roots or rotting sticks, in flower pots.
Season Summer and autumn. Occasional.
Note This is one of the most widespread bird's nest fungi.

384 CYATHUS STRIATUS

Common name Splash cup.
Etymology From Latin, 'with stripes'.
Description Carpophore 10–15 mm high with a maximum diameter of 8–10 mm, shaped like a funnel, dark reddish-brown, covered externally with evident hairs, initially with the upper part closed by whitish diaphragm, fugacious, then open, the interior a shiny, lead-coloured cavity, fluted lengthwise, containing the whitish-grey peridioles, circular, compressed, umbilicate and about 2 mm in diameter, attached by a white, elastic funiculus. Spores white, elliptical, smooth, 18–22 × 8–12 microns.
Edibility Of no value because of size.
Habitat Isolated or in large groups, on dead wood or on the ground.
Season Autumn. Occasional.
Note The spores are contained inside the peridioles, which are expelled by drops of rain that fall into the carpophore and splash them out. In the air the funiculus, when completely extended, acts like a whip, trailing behind the peridiole and coiling around blades of grass to which it becomes attached.

385 CRUCIBULUM LAEVE

Synonyms *Crucibulum levis; Crucibulum vulgare.*
Etymology From Latin, 'smooth'.
Description Carpophore 5–8 mm high, with a maximum diameter of 6 mm, at first subglobose then campanulate or cup-shaped, greyish, ochreous-brown or ochre, initially closed by a fugacious diaphragm then opening wide, finely downy on the outside then glabrous, whitish, smooth on the inside with whitish, circular, biconvex peridioles, 1.5–2 mm wide, attached to a papilla by a funiculus or peduncle. Spores white, elliptical, smooth, 5–10 × 4–6 microns.
Edibility Of no value because of size.
Habitat Gregarious on sticks, wood and stems of herbaceous plants.
Season Autumn. Occasional.
Note The carpophore consists of two distinct layers that can be separated. The peridioles develop and for some time remain in gelatinous liquid. This is one of the commonest bird's nest fungi.

386 SPHAEROBOLUS STELLATUS

Etymology From Latin, 'star-shaped'.
Description Carpophores 2 mm wide, whitish or pale yellow, downy then smooth, globose then oval and opening to form a star, splitting into 6–8 triangular, yellowish lobes allowing the expulsion of the gleba in a single gelatinous spheroidal mass, at first whitish and transparent then brown. Outer surface covered by a sparse mycelial layer. Spores white, elliptical, smooth, 8–11 × 4–6 microns.
Edibility Of no value because of size.
Habitat Typically gregarious on rotting brambles, sticks, leaves or sawdust.
Season Autumn. Occasional.
Note The multi-stratified peridium that splits open like a star allows for the active expulsion of the spores gathered in a gelatinous globule. On the basis of size and habitat various similar species have been described.

387 ELAPHOMYCES GRANULATUS

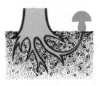

Etymology From Latin, 'granular', because of the appearance of the peridium.

Description Carpophores up to 4 cm in diameter, globose or ovoid, outer surface of the peridium ochreous, covered with small, sometimes pyramidal, warts. When cut it reveals a thick peridial 'bark' formed by two layers, the outer one thin and yellowish, comprising the warts, the inner one whitish and thicker. Gleba violet-black, at first divided by whitish veins of sterile tissue, then powdery. Spores blackish-brown, spherical, covered with low warts, 24–32 microns.

Edibility Undetermined.

Habitat Hypogeal in acid soils, beneath pine, also under broadleaved species.

Season Autumn. Occasional.

Note This Ascomycete is the commonest of the hypogeal or semi-hypogeal fungi that resemble truffles in appearance, but that are not reliably known to be edible. This mushroom is best found by finding one or two conspicuous parasites on it: *Cordyceps capitata* (**349**) or *C. ophioglossoides* (**350**).

388 TUBER AESTIVUM

Common name Summer truffle.

Etymology From Latin, 'of summer'.

Description Carpophore normally 2–10 cm, sometimes larger, globose or irregularly lobate or deformed, with or without a small basal cavity, brownish-black, with a thin peridium and large pyramidal warts with 5–7 facets up to 12 mm wide and 3 mm high, thinly striate concentrically and grooved lengthwise. Gleba at first whitish, light ochreous-brown, then brownish, marbled by numerous white veins, ramified and anastomosed, at first firm then rather soft. Odour increasingly strong and aromatic with age, flavour distinctive and pleasant. Spores brownish-yellow, subglobose, alveolate-reticulate, with spines in the nodal points of the reticulum, 18–41 × 14–32 microns.

Edibility Very good, even though tougher than the most prized truffles.

Habitat Semi-hypogeal in calcareous ground, under broadleaved trees, prefers beech, but may occur under conifers.

Season Late summer and autumn. Uncommon but widespread in Britain and Europe, and north Africa.

389　TUBER MELANOSPORUM

Common name　French truffle; Perigord truffle.
Etymology　From Greek, 'black-spored'.
Description　Carpophores variable in size, normally 2–7 cr
globose or irregular, peridium at first reddish then blac
warty with quite small pyramidal warts with 4–6 facet
Gleba tender, faintly watery, first greyish then violet, blac
ish when mature, marbled with whitish veins, quite ramifie
Very strong odour of garlic and acetylene, flavour uniqu
and highly regarded. Spores blackish, elliptical, spiny, 30–5
× 20–30 microns.
Edibility　Excellent, raw or cooked.
Habitat　Hypogeal in red calcareous ground containing irc
salts, symbiotic with broadleaved trees (especially oak)
southern Europe and in the Perigord region of France.
Season　The carpophores start to form in late summer, b
mature between November and March. Not known in Br
tain.
Note　This famous truffle is extremely highly prized gastre
nomically. Related species are *T. aestivum* (**388**), *T. brumal*
T. moschatum, *T. macrosporum* and *T. mesentericum*, a
black truffles, less sought after although all good to eat; the
have a wider distribution than *T. melanosporum* itself.

390　TUBER EXCAVATUM

Etymology　From Latin, 'hollow'.
Description　Carpophore 2–5 cm, globose, often lobate
perforated at base with an internal cavity; peridium yellow
ochreous, olive, reddish-orange or brown, with tiny papilla
or almost smooth, hard, woody. Gleba at first ochreou
reddish or orange, brownish when mature, with a fe
whitish or yellowish veins, tough, horny. Strong garlick
odour, pleasant flavour. Spores brownish-ochre, elliptica
reticulate-alveolate, 22–55 × 16–40 microns.
Edibility　Although tough it can be eaten grated.
Habitat　On dry, sunny, calcareous ground, usually unde
broadleaved species, especially beech.
Season　Not mature until autumn. In Britain, occasional i
southern England.
Note　*T. rufum*, which is quite variable in colour, external
resembles the above-described species, but is solid. There
a hint of hollowness at the base of *T. nitidum*.

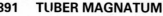

391 TUBER MAGNATUM

Common name White truffle.

Etymology From Latin, 'lordly'.

Description Carpophore variable, normally 2–8 cm, globose, regular or irregularly lobate, peridium ochreous, pale ochreous-yellow, tinged greenish, smooth or faintly papillate, thin and adherent. Gleba white, yellowish, then yellowish-grey, reddish-brown, reddish-grey, soft, tender, marbled with thin white veins, ramified and anastomosed. Penetrating odour of garlic, flavour complex, strong and pleasant. Spores brownish, globose or broadly elliptical, with large reticulum, 35–50 × 32–42 microns.

Edibility Excellent, cooked or raw.

Habitat Hypogeal in crumbly calcareous ground, beneath oak, poplar, willow and lime.

Season Summer to winter. Not known in Britain.

Note This highly prized hypogeal fungus has a very limited distribution: in central-northern Italy, in the Swiss canton of Ticino and in the Rhône Valley in France.

392 TERFEZIA ARENARIA

Synonym *Terfezia leonis*.

Etymology From Latin, 'pertaining to sand'.

Description Carpophore 6–12 cm in diameter, globose or pear-shaped, with a small short conical stipe; peridium smooth, whitish then yellowing, then darkening after turning reddish, quite spotted, often cracked. Gleba white, yellowish, rose-coloured or red, then greyish-brown, marbled with white. Odour faint, flavour pleasant, sweetish. Spores at first whitish, eventually ochreous, globose, very warty 19–26 microns.

Edibility Good, very popular in desert regions of North Africa and the Middle East.

Habitat In sandy ground, grassland or open places in oak woods, pinewoods and stands of eucalyptus, symbiotic with cistus and rockrose.

Season Winter and spring.

Note This is the famous truffle of classical antiquity (the Greek *hydnon* and the Roman *tuber*). It is still highly prized in Islamic countries, where it is called *terfaz*, which term embraces various other species of hypogeal fungi. The other principal truffles that grow in a sandy habitat are members of the genera *Lespiaultinia*, *Delastria* and *Tirmania*.

393 DALDINIA CONCENTRICA

Common name King Alfred's cakes.

Etymology From Latin, 'concentric'.

Description Stromata up to 5 cm in diameter, hemispherical, at first reddish-brown but soon turning black, smooth, shiny, dotted with the pores of the perithecia, which form in a zone beneath the crust. Flesh hard, fibrous, purple-brown, with darker concentric zones. Spores black, elliptical, fusiform, smooth, 12–17 × 6–9 microns.

Edibility Inedible because of woody texture.

Habitat On dead broadleaved wood, especially ash.

Season All year. Common.

Note In the first stage of growth reddish asexual spores called conidia are produced that initially colour the outer surface of the stromata; when mature the black ascospores are formed in asci within the perithecia. *D. vernicosa*, a small form sometimes recognized as a distinct species, occurs on burnt gorse bushes, often in great quantities.

394 HYPOXYLON FRAGIFORME

Etymology From Latin, 'strawberry-like', because of its appearance.

Description Stromata about 1 cm in diameter, hemispherical, salmon pink, when mature brick red, darkening with age, surface papillate corresponding to the upper part of the perithecia. Flesh hard, black, with a layer of small flask-shaped perithecia just beneath the outer surface. No odour or flavour. Spores dark brown, blackish, almost fusiform, smooth, 11–15 × 5–7 microns.

Edibility Of no value because of texture.

Habitat Normally gregarious on rotting beech.

Season All year, but grows in summer and autumn. Common.

Note All the species of this genus grow on wood; many form crust-like stromata; hemispherical stromata are formed by *H. fuscum* (on hazel or alder branches) and *H. multiforme* (on birch).

395 LYCOGALA EPIDENDRUM

Etymology From Greek, 'on trees', from its habitat.

Description Carpophores up to 2 cm in diameter, sessile, globose, at first orange-red, soft with a liquid interior, then brown with a peridium that becomes membranous, dry, with the inside becoming a brownish powdery mass. Spores greyish-brown, globose, reticulate, 4–6 microns.

Edibility Of no value because of texture.

Habitat On rotting coniferous and broadleaved wood and stumps.

Season All year but more common in summer and autumn. Common.

Note This fungus belongs to the class Myxomycetes, organisms difficult to place in the systematics of fungi. The life cycle includes a free, single-celled, creeping, amoeboid stage; then, because of the hormones produced by some of the 'amoebas', they join together and form a plasmodial stage that ultimately forms the fruit-bodies or sporangia. These contain tough-walled spores that are extremely resistant and long-lived (germination has been observed after 6 years of conservation). The characteristics of these organisms place them somewhere between animals (Protozoans) and the true fungi (Eumycetes).

396 SARCOSPHAERA CRASSA

Synonym *Sarcosphaera coronaria.*

Etymology From Latin, 'thick'.

Description Carpophore spheroidal, opening by a circular hole in the upper part, hypogeal, like an empty ball, then stellate, revealing its violet then violet-brown hymenium. The mature carpophores, when completely expanded, are up to 20 cm wide. Outer surface develops from a viscous stratum that starts splitting from the orifice where it appears like a cobweb veil that is detachable while moist, then adheres closely to outer part of carpophore, which is dirty white, finely downy, sometimes marked with yellow especially towards base, normally with earth residue. Flesh white, fragile, wax-like. No particular odour or flavour. Spores white, broadly elliptical, smooth, 13–14 × 7–8 microns.

Edibility Edible cooked, but indigestible for some; **poisonous raw.**

Habitat Common on calcareous ground, also beneath various broadleaved species such as beech.

Season Spring. Occasional.

Note *Peziza ammophila* forms carpophores half-immersed in sand. They open out like stars and reveal a brown hymenium.

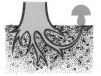

Caution Poisonous when raw.

397 BULGARIA INQUINANS

Common name Bachelor's buttons.

Etymology From Latin, 'dirtying', because if one touches the mature carpophores, the spores will stain the fingers blackish.

Description Carpophore 1–5 cm wide, up to 3 cm high, initially almost ovoid, discoid when mature with upper fertile part gradually expanding. The hymenium is at first concave then flat, smooth, shiny and black; outer surface violet-brown. Flesh thick, gelatinous, rubbery, marbled ochreous-brown. No particular smell or flavour. Spores soot brown, kidney-shaped, smooth, 10–13 × 6–7.5 microns.

Edibility Rather mediocre.

Habitat On rotting broadleaved wood, mainly oak and beech.

Season Late summer and autumn. Common.

Note This is an Ascomycete, and in each ascus half the spores remain colourless while the others become very dark brown.

---

398 PHAEOHELOTIUM SUBCARNEUM

Etymology From Latin, 'almost flesh-coloured'.

Description Carpophores 0.1–0.2 cm, cup-shaped or flat, with a small stipe, smooth, soft, entirely pale purple-pink. Spores pale brown, elliptical, smooth, 10–12 × 2.5–4 microns.

Edibility Of no value because of size.

Habitat In groups on wood stripped of bark.

Season Late summer and autumn. Occasional.

Note Wood or vegetable detritus offers an important substratum for a great many Ascomycetes with small cup-shaped carpophores, supported by a stalk or sessile. A related spcies, *P. flavum*, is yellow and its white-spored look-alike is the ubiquitous *Bisporella citrina* (**399**). Numerous other small cup-shaped Ascomycetes occur on wood; they are classified in various genera and their identification requires microscopic analysis. An equally large grouping occurs on leaves and stems, especially on fallen, rotting herbaceous material.

399 BISPORELLA CITRINA

Synonyms *Calycella citrina; Helotium citrinum.*
Etymology From Latin, 'lemon-like', because of the colour.
Description Carpophore up to 3 mm in diameter, deep yellow, slightly paler on the outside, tending to orange-yellow in dry weather, completely glabrous, with a fairly long peduncle; surface fertile, initially barely concave, then almost flat. Spores colourless, elliptical, sometimes with a single septum, smooth, 9–14 × 3–5 microns.
Edibility Of no value because of size.
Habitat Gregarious on dead broadleaved wood, often growing in vast quantities.
Season Autumn. Common.
Note This fungus is similar in appearance to species belonging to the genus *Hymenoscyphus*, which grow on herbaceous substrata, not on wood.

400 DASYSCYPHUS SULFUREUS

Synonym *Lachnella sulfurea.*
Etymology From Latin, 'sulphur-coloured'.
Description Carpophore 1–3 mm, sessile, hemispherical then flat, sometimes slightly undulate, hymenial surface white or whitish, outside covered with lemon or sulphur yellow hairs, tending to darken all over with age. Spores colourless, rod-like or very fusiform, often slightly curved, smooth, 23–35 × 2–3 microns.
Edibility Of no value because of size.
Habitat On rotting branches or the dead stems of herbaceous plants (not the Gramineae).
Season Spring and summer.
Note Among the many species that form small cup-shaped carpophores covered with hairs, the most easily identifiable are *D. virgineus*, with stalk, completely white and very common on vegetable fragments, and *D. bicolor*, with a very short stipe yellow inside and white outside.

401 HYMENOSCYPHUS FRUCTIGENUS

Synonym   *Helotium fructigenum*.
Etymology   From Latin, 'growing on fruit'.
Description   Carpophore up to 4 mm in diameter, entirely light yellow, fertile surface flat, peduncle and outer surface glabrous or finely pubescent with adpressed filaments. Spores colourless, often septate in the middle, elliptical, smooth, 13–25 × 3–5 microns.
Edibility   Of no value because of size.
Habitat   On the husks of rotting fruit of beech, hazel, hickory and oak; also reported on chestnuts and cherry stones.
Season   All year, but generally found in late summer and autumn. Common.
Note   There are many similar species and many of them are easily identifiable by their habitat. *H. scutula* grows on the stems of composites and mints; *H. repandus*, on the dead stems of thistle and iris, and on the husks of horse chestnuts; *H. caudatus*, typically on the rotting leaves of various broadleaved trees; *H. egenulus*, on dead stems of sheep sorrel; and *H. robustior*, on the dead stalks of marsh plants.

402 CHLOROSPLENIUM AERUGINOSUM

Common name   Greenstain.
Etymology   From Latin, 'copper green', from its colour.
Description   Carpophore up to 6 mm in diameter, bluish-green, hymenium becoming paler with age, often yellowish as well, edge irregularly undulate; stipe fairly short and glabrous. Spores colourless or faintly pale green, elliptical, smooth, 9–15 × 3.5–4.5 microns.
Edibility   Of no value because of size.
Habitat   In broadleaved woods on dead wood.
Season   Spring to autumn. Common.
Note   Wood attacked by this fungus turns blue-green. The stained wood is used in cabinet-making and carving in the production of Tunbridge Ware. *C. aeruginascens* is another similar species with the same distinctive action on wood, but differs by having smaller spores (6–10 × 1.5–2 microns). Other species that do not colour the host substratum include *C. versiforme*, on broadleaved trees; *C. elatinum*, on coniferous sticks; and *C. aeruginellum*, on the roots of *Filipendula*. All are green.

403 ASCOCORYNE SARCOIDES

Synonym *Coryne sarcoides*.
Etymology From Greek, 'fleshy'.
Description Carpophore 1–1.5 cm high, sessile or with short stipe, violet, pale lilac, or pale purple, cup-shape slightly concave at first, then open, undulate, lower p clearly venose and sometimes pruinose. Flesh soft a gelatinous, violet. No particular odour or flavour. Spo white, fusiform, slightly curved, smooth, septate when ve mature, 10–20 × 4–6 microns.
Edibility Of no value because of size.
Habitat On dead broadleaved wood.
Season All year. Common.

Note Because of its appearance this species may be tak for a jelly fungus, but it is in fact an Ascomycete because spores are produced inside sac-like structures (asci) rath than on the outside of clubs (basidia). *A. cylichnium* is ve similar but has longer ascospores, 18–30 × 4–6 micro which become multi-septate and bud off tiny round sec dary spores while still in the ascus.

---

404 DISCIOTIS VENOSA

Etymology From Latin, 'veined', from its appearance.
Description Carpophore 4–20 cm in diameter, initially su globose with the margin incurved, then open and undula flat, fairly dark brown, venously folded; whitish and tome tose below. Stipe short, thick and sulcate. Flesh very britt readily breaking. Slight odour of chlorine, virtually no f vour, although slightly bitter and astringent. Spores whitis elliptical, smooth with caducous granules at the tips, 21– × 12–15 microns.
Edibility Good when thoroughly cooked; **poisonous raw**
Habitat On the edge of woodland and in open places.
Season Spring. Occasional.

Note Other cup fungi, such as *Discina perlata* and *Pez repanda*, may resemble this fungus when mature with t carpophore completely expanded.
Caution Like many cup fungi, this mushroom is poisono if eaten raw or undercooked.

405 HUMARIA HEMISPHAERICA

Etymology From Latin, 'hemispherical'.

Description Carpophore up to 10–20 mm wide, at fir[st] subglobose, then cup-shaped and hemispherical, hymeni[al] surface smooth, greyish-white, ochreous and covered wi[th] brown hairs, fasciculate, pointed externally, edge with hai[r] up to 1 mm long. Flesh thin, wax-like. No odour or flavou[r]. Spores whitish, elliptical, warty when mature, 21–25 [×] 11–13 microns.

Edibility Of no value because of size.

Habitat In damp, humus-rich ground, in woodland, som[e] times also on fairly decomposed wood.

Season Autumn. Common.

Note Two similar species that are saucer-shaped instead [of] cup-shaped are *Trichophaea woolhopeia*, which grows [in] burnt places, and *T. hemispheroides*, which has the sam[e] habitat but seems to be associated with mosses of the gen[us] *Funaria*.

---

406 PAXINA ACETABULUM

Synonyms *Acetabula vulgaris; Helvella acetabulum.*

Description Carpophore up to 12 cm high and 6 cm wid[e], cup-shaped. Hymenium violet-brown, outer surface light[er], edge undulate and turned inwards, outer surface fine[ly] furfuraceous, pustular towards edge, becoming dark[er] brown with age. Stipe up to 6 cm high, with ramified ri[bs] that envelop the whitish base of the cup, darkening fro[m] bottom to top where it is the same colour as the cup. Fle[sh] wax-like, quite elastic in the stipe, white. No particular odo[ur] or flavour. Spores whitish, elliptical, smooth 18–22 × 12– microns.

Edibility Fair when cooked, especially after being boile[d]. **poisonous raw**.

Habitat In open places, on the edge of woodland, in san[dy] soils; solitary or gregarious, world-wide.

Season Spring. Occasional.

Note Mushrooms variously called *Acetabula* and *Paxi[na]* are indistinguishable microscopically from *Helvella*; th[e] fruit-bodies differ by being cup-shaped rather than sadd[le] shaped.

Caution Poisonous when raw.

407 PAXINA BARLAE

Synonym *Acetabula barlae.*
Etymology After the French mycologist Barla.
Description Carpophore 3–5 × 3–5 cm, cup-shaped, hymenial surface slate grey or blackish-violet, externally soot coloured, dark grey, blackish, sometimes olivaceous, finely furfuraceous. Stipe short, quite stout, white, sulcate with longitudinal ribs that become concolorous with the cups and ramify half-way up. Flesh whitish, wax-like. No odour or flavour. Spores white, elliptical, smooth, 20–22 × 11–? microns.
Edibility Good.
Habitat Isolated or in groups beneath or near pines on calcareous ground.
Season Spring. Not known in Britain.
Note *P. leucomelas*, which is British, is whitish on the exterior but has a dark greyish-brown hymenium. It grows under conifers during the winter months and occurs only occasionally.

408 TARZETTA CATINUS

Synonyms *Geopyxis catinus; Pustularia catinus.*
Etymology From Latin, 'small bowl', from its shape.
Description Carpophore 1–5 cm wide, cupulate, permanently goblet-shaped, often with short, slightly wrinkled and spongy stipe, cream-coloured internally; exterior yellowish-ochre and finely granular, with dentate, serrate margin. Flesh thin, fragile. No particular odour or flavour. Spores white, elliptical, smooth, 20–26 × 11–15 microns.
Edibility Mediocre.
Habitat Solitary or in groups more or less embedded in the humus under deciduous trees.
Season Autumn. Common.
Note In the early stages of development the cup orifice is covered by a web-like cortina. A similar species but greyish tan and typically not over 2 cm wide is *T. cupularis*; it is also found in deciduous woods in autumn.

409 ALEURIA AURANTIA

Synonym *Peziza aurantia.*
Common name Orange peel fungus.
Etymology From Latin, 'orange-like', from its colour.
Description Carpophore up to 10 cm in diameter, sessile, cup-shaped, margin undulate, when mature flat, irregular, often deformed by the mutual compression of adjacent carpophores. Hymenial surface bright orange-red above, finely pubescent and whitish below. Flesh thin, white, fragile. No clear odour or flavour. Spores white, elliptical, reticulate, 17–24 × 9–11 microns.
Edibility Good when cooked.
Habitat Gregarious, on bare ground in woodland, on paths, on the side of roads, in grassy places.
Season Autumn. Occasional.
Note The red pigment that colours this best-known of the cup fungi is quite common among the Discomycetes and is produced by pigments similar to the carotenoids found in the plant kingdom. Sunlight is necessary to produce these pigments.

410 OTIDEA ONOTICA

Etymology From Greek, 'like an ass's ear'.
Description Carpophores up to 10 cm high and 6 cm wide, tufted, shaped like a hare's ear, with a short stipe; inner fertile part ochreous tinged with pink, becoming deeper in colour as it dries out; outer sterile surface finely furfuraceous, at first almost the same colour as inner part, then clearly ochreous. Stipe white at the base. Flesh thin, white. No particular odour or flavour. Spores white, broadly elliptical, smooth, 10–13 × 5–6 microns.
Edibility Fair.
Habitat On the ground, often in tight groups, especially in broadleaved woods, particularly oak.
Season Autumn. Occasional.
Note Other ear-shaped cup fungi include yellow-brown *O. leporina* and the typically clustered *O. alutacea*, with a yellow-brown exterior and greyish-brown interior. None of these has a pink-to-rosy inner ear like *O. onotica*.

411 SCUTELLINIA SCUTELLATA

Common name Eyelash cup fungus.
Etymology From Latin, 'bowl-shaped' or 'flat'.
Description Carpophore 2–10 mm, sessile, first slight concave then flat, vermilion on the fertile upper surface, paler on lower surface, margin with long stiff, dark hair. Spores white, elliptical, slightly granulose, warty, 18–19 10–12 microns.
Edibility Of no value because of size.

Habitat Gregarious on decomposed wood or damp ground.
Season Spring to late autumn. Common.
Note Although small, this is a fairly conspicuous fungus both because of its bright colour and because it grows in groups. A very similar fungus called *S. trechispora*, with globose, warty spores, also grows on damp ground, often in moss. Other small Discomycetes with an outer ciliate surface belong to the genera *Sphaerosporella*, with a brown fertile surface; and *Cheilymenia* and *Neottiella*, with pale yellow or transparent hairs and the hymenium respectively yellow and red. The sterile surface of the terrestrial genus *Melastiza* is covered with short downy, brown, obtuse hairs; the same feature applies to the various species of *Anthracobia*, found in burnt places.

412 PEZIZA VESICULOSA

Etymology From Latin, 'with vesicles', because of the blistered appearance of the surface of the cap.
Description Carpophore 3–8 cm, initially subglobose, barely open at the top, then hemispherical with incurved margin, clearly crenulate and furfuraceous, then distended and cracked; light yellowish-ochre inside, whitish and at times tinged with reddish-brown; furfuraceous and downy outside, sessile or with a short stipe. Flesh light ochreous-brown, juicy, thick, fragile. No odour or flavour. Spores white, elliptical, smooth, 20–25 × 12–14 microns.
Edibility Fair.

Habitat Solitary or tufted, on old straw bales, garden mulch and manure heaps.
Season All year, especially in late winter and spring. Common.

413 RHIZINA UNDULATA

Etymology From Latin, 'wavy', from the form of the carpophore.

Description Carpophore up to 10 cm wide, flat or convex, irregularly lobate, fertile surface undulate, dark brown, sometimes blackish, with the margin paler; lower surface ochreous, with numerous cylindrical and ramified structures like small roots, 1–2 mm thick, which attach the carpophore to the ground. Flesh reddish-brown, slightly fibrous, then rather leathery. Spores whitish, fusiform, pointed at the tips, minutely verrucose, 22–40 × 8–11 microns.

Edibility Of no value because of texture.

Habitat Gregarious on the litter in sunny coniferous woods, in burnt areas; the cause of group dying of conifers with consequent loss to forestry.

Season Summer and autumn. Occasional.

414 RUTSTROEMIA ECHINOPHILA

Etymology From Greek, 'spine-loving', because of its habitat (on chestnut husks).

Description Carpophore 2–12 mm in diameter, cup-shaped, flat or slightly convex, reddish-brown, sometimes tinged pale purple, initially with the edge finely furfuraceous and denticulate, then entirely smooth. Stipe slender, 2–12 mm long, when young covered with fibrils, slightly paler than the hymenial surface, base blackish-brown, emerging from blackened areas inside the rotting husk. Spores whitish, elliptical, slightly curved, smooth, 18–20 × 5–6 microns, with one or two septi and sometimes a secondary spore.

Edibility Of no value because of size.

Habitat Emerging from the inside of the husks of sweet chestnut.

Season Autumn. Occasional.

Note Other brown species of *Rutstroemia* have different habitats. *R. sydowiana* is found on the stalks of oak leaves; *R. conformata*, on alder leaves; *R. fruticeti*, on blackberry bushes and brambles; *R. firma*, on oak branches; and *R. rhenana*, on apple and pear branches. The greenish *R. luteovirescens* grows on sycamore leaves.

415 SARCOSCYPHA COCCINEA

Common names Scarlet cup; pixie or elf cup.
Etymology From Latin, 'vermilion', because of the colour.
Description Carpophore 1–5 cm in diameter, cup-shaped, fairly open, scarlet or orange inside, pinkish and downy ouside, margin slightly incurved. Stipe absent or up to 2 cm high, villose at the base. Flesh wax-like and elastic. No particular odour or flavour. Spores whitish, elliptical, smooth, 24–40 × 10–12 microns.
Edibility Mediocre.
Habitat On rotting branches. In Britain, common in the west of England, rarer eastwards. Widespread in Europe.
Season Winter or early spring.

416 SEPULTARIA SUMNERIANA

Etymology After the mycologist Sumner.
Description Carpophores 3–7 cm in diameter, at first subspheroidal, barely open uppermost, hypogeal, then emerging, opening on the surface of the ground in irregular lobes, whitish and slightly ochreous inside, covered on the outside with down consisting of very long, septate filaments that incorporate loam. Flesh compact, two-layered, the hymenial one translucent, the outer one (beneath the hairy covering) white. No odour or flavour. Spores white, fusiform, smooth, 30–35 × 14–15 microns.
Edibility Edible after removing outer layer.
Habitat Hypogeal in lawns under cedar.
Season Late winter and spring. Occasional.
Note This fungus is common in Europe, specifically associated with cedars. There are other, somewhat rare, species of *Sepultaria*: *S. foliacea*, with the hymenial surface light greenish-yellow, growing in moss; *S. tenuis*, greyish-white inside, opening out in roundish laminae; *S. arenosa*, in sandy soil, splitting in a stellate manner; and *S. arenicola*, which occurs in the same habitat but has larger cups and spores measuring 23–28 × 14–16 microns. The genus *Sepultaria* represents a transitional form of the Discomycetes from the epigeal to the hypogeal environment.

417 MACROSCYPHUS MACROPUS

Synonym *Helvella macropus.*
Etymology From Greek, 'large-footed'.
Description Carpophore 3–4 cm in diameter, cup-shaped ash grey, granular-floccose outside. Stipe long, tapering slightly towards top, solid, sometimes sulcate at base, completely covered with grey woolly hairs that join to form tiny tufts. Flesh white, thin, wax-like. No odour or flavour. Spores white, elliptical, smooth, 20–30 × 10–12 microns.
Edibility Fair.
Habitat On the ground beneath broadleaved trees.
Season Autumn. Occasional.
Note Other cup-shaped species also have a well developed stipe. They belong to genera *Cyathipodia*; *Helvella* (in the broad sense such as *H. queletii* or *H. cupuliformis* with a light brown hymenium, greyish and hairy on the outside); and *Sowerbyella*, such as *S. radiculata*, which is autumnal, growing beneath conifers and broadleaved trees hymenium lemon yellow, sterile surface woolly and cream coloured, with a long irregular, rooting stipe covered with dense white hairs. The latter is rare in Britain.

418 RHYTISMA ACERINUM

Common name Tar spot of sycamore.
Etymology From Latin, 'pertaining to sycamore', because of its habitat.
Description Stromata up to 2 cm in diameter, fairly circular, distinct, shiny black, in the form of barely raised plaques or spots on the leaf surface, containing numerous very small fruit-bodies that open outwards cracking the crust of the stroma, fertile surface grey. Spores colourless, filiform, smooth, 60–80 × 1.5–2.5 microns.
Edibility Not suitable.
Habitat On the leaves of sycamore.
Season Summer, on living leaves; late winter to spring, on fallen leaves. Common.
Note In the asexual state this fungus is called *Melasmia acerina*, and is parasitic on the living leaves of various maples. The sexual state with fruit-bodies develops inside the stromata on fallen leaves in winter and spring. *R. salicinum* is a similar fungus that grows on willow leaves.

419 SPHAEROTHECA PANNOSA

Common name Rose mildew.

Etymology From Latin, 'tattered', because of its appearance on the host plant.

Description A very common mildew in the northern hemisphere, it attacks roses and, in a similar form, peaches and apricots. The damage caused by this disease consists of a deformation of the leaf laminae, which are covered by the white, powdery spores, then turn yellow and wither. The buds and young shoots as well as the flowers are affected. When the petals are affected these become marked and dry out quickly, withering at the same time. When mature the perithecia look like small black dots with a diameter of about 0.1 mm. Their surface is mosaic-like and they contain a single ascus. The fungus spends the winter in mycelial form (white).

Edibility Not suitable.

Habitat Roses, peaches, apricots.

Season Spring and summer, but overwinters on silky patches on the host plant.

420 USTILAGO MAYDIS

Common name Corn smut.

Etymology After its host plant, *Zea mays*.

Description An uncommon parasitic fungus, living on maize (originally an American plant), now found in every country where this crop is grown. It attacks the aerial parts of the plant and occasionally the root apparatus, producing irregular swellings or tumours that can reach a diameter of 15–20 cm. Those that form on the female inflorescence (the corn cob) are particularly large. Initially the tumour-like formation has a whitish coloration that gradually turns wine red and then black. When mature the surface is papery and fragile while the completely black inside is formed by a powdery spore mass.

Edibility If the spores come into contact with food they are reported to cause disorders similar to ergotism (see **Note** at *Claviceps purpurea*, **346**). The young tumours, on the other hand, which have a sugary and aromatic white pulp, are fairly sought after by some, and canned and sold commercially in Mexico, where they are considered a delicacy.

Habitat On maize.

Season Summer. As yet uncommon in Britain.

Caution See **Edibility**.

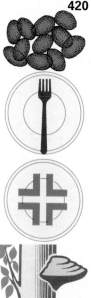

GLOSSARY

adnate (of gills) broadly attached to stipe (1).

adnexed (of gills) narrowly attached to stipe.

alveolate pitted like a honeycomb.

amyloid (of spores) when spores turn blue to blue-black in iodine-based reagent (Melzer's reagent).

anastomosed (of gills and ridges) an angular network formed by cross-veins.

annulus ring-like structure on stipe, derived from partial veil.

apical positioned at apex or top.

apiculus (of basidiospores) short projection at or near base of spore where it was attached to sterigma of basidium.

apothecium cup shaped fruit-body, typical of certain Ascomycetes (4).

appendiculate (of cap margin) adorned with fragments of velar material.

aerolate (of cap surface) cracked in mosiac pattern.

ascus sac-like microscopic structure which contains the spores of the Ascomycetes (5).

Ascomycetes fungi characterized by having asci, plural of ascus.

ball and socket (of cap and stipe attachment) where they are clearly separable from one another (18) (see *free*).

basidium club-shaped microscopic structure that bears the spores of the Basidiomycetes (6).

Basidiomycetes fungi characterized by having basidia, plural of basidium.

bulbous referring to an enlarged, bulb-shaped structure (7).

campanulate bell-shaped (8).

carpophore the fruit-body or conspicuous and familiar part of the higher fungi, which bears the reproductive structures (asci and basidia).

cespitose tufted.

ciliate fringed with hairs, like eyelashes (10).

claviform   club-shaped (11).
collarium   the ring-like collar at the apex of the stipe that separates gills from stipe in certain fungi (12).
concrescent   growing together (13).
connate   grown together.
coprophilous   growing on dung or droppings.
cortina   cobweb-like partial veil between cap margin and stipe of certain gilled fungi (14).
cuticle   outermost layer of cap or stipe.
cystidia   large sterile cells on cap, gill or stipe surface.
decurrent   gills that descend stipe to some degree (15).
deliquescent   tissue that liquefies, like *Coprinus* gills.
dextrinoid   (of spores) when spores turn reddish brown with starch-like, iodine-based reagent (Melzer's reagent).
disc   central part of the cap (16).
Discomycetes   cup fungi, with asci lining the cup or apothecium.
eccentric   (of stipe) not centrally attached to cap, off-centre.
echinulate   covered with small spines or warts (17).
ectotrophic   a form of mycorrhizal association in which the mycelium of the fungus forms an external covering, or mantle, on the root, e.g., of pine trees.
endoperidium   inner wall of a Gasteromycete fruit-body.
endotrophic   a form of mycorrhizal association in which the mycelium of the fungus grows within or between the cells of the root cortex, e.g., in many herbaceous or woody plants.
entomophagus   growing and feeding on insects.
epigeal   growing above ground.
exoperidium   outer tissue of a Gasteromycete fruit-body, often represented by spines and warts.
fasciculate   fungi with stipes in a tuft (19).
fibril   thread.
fibrillose   covered in threads.
fistular   tubular, hollow (20).
floccons   fluffy, cottony warts.
floccose   cottony to downy-woolly.

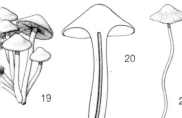

free (of gills) not attached to stipe (25).

fruit-body the carpophore or conspicuous and familiar part of the higher fungi that contains the reproductive structures (asci or basidia).

fugacious soon disappearing.

fusiform spindle-shaped (22).

gills radially arranged plate-like structures on the undersides of the caps of gilled fungi, which bear the basidia.

glabrous without any hairs or other ornamentation.

gleba the sporing tissue of Gasteromycetes.

glutinous sticky, glue-like in texture.

hymenium the spore-bearing surface of an Ascomycete or Basidiomycete.

hypha (pl. **hyphae**) a fungal filament that with others forms the hyphae of which the mycelium and flesh of the carpophores are composed.

hypogeal growing underground.

imbricate overlapping, like roof tiles.

infundibuliform (of cap) funnel-shaped (23).

involute (of cap margin) with the edge turned under, rolled in (24).

lamellae gills.

ligneous with a consistency like wood.

lignicolous growing on wood.

mamelon a breast-like protuberance at the centre of the cap of some gilled fungi (26).

mamelate nipple-shaped.

mycelium the vegetative part of the fungus, formed by hyphae; usually found in substrate (earth, wood, dung, etc.).

mycorrhiza the symbiotic relationship between fungi and green plants.

papilla (pl. **papillae**) a projection, such as the hairs on certain plants.

partial veil the tissue covering the young gills of certain fungi; as the cap expands this tissue breaks and may leave remnants along the cap margin or a ring or ring zone on the stipe.

503

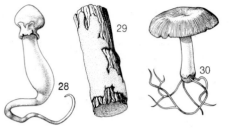

pellicle   the thin outer layer of the cap of certain mushrooms.

peridiole   a small, lens-shaped, spore-containing structure in certain Gasteromycetes.

peridium   the outer wall of fungal fruiting-bodies; it may be a single layer or, as in the Gasteromycetes, a complex, multilayered structure.

perithecium   one of the fruit-bodies of the Ascomycetes; a small, globose body with an apical hole, which contains the asci and the ascospores.

piriform   pear-shaped.

plicate   (of cap) furrowed, or folded like a fan (27).

pore   the orifice of the tubes that form the hymenium of the Boletaceae and the Polyporaceae.

pubescent   covered with very fine, thin, soft hairs.

punky   soft but tough.

radicant   of the stipe when it penetrates the ground like a root (28).

resupinate   of a carpophore when supine, lacking a free-standing cap, bracket, etc. (29).

reticulate   in the form of a net.

rhizomorph   mycelial formations resembling root-like structures (30).

ring   the remains of the partial veil on the stipe of certain gill and pore fungi (3).

rugose   wrinkled, rough.

scabrous   rough, with short, rigid projections.

scelerotium   a mass of tightly knotted hyphae forming very hard spheroidal or elongated structures. This enables certain fungi to survive adverse environmental conditions (31).

scrobiculate   having shallow botches or depressions (32).

septate   divided by cross-walls.

sessile   without a stipe.

setaceous   (of stipe) bristle-like (33).

squamose   having flat scales on the cap (35).

stipe the part of the carpophore that supports the cap or the hymenium in general; the stem or stalk of the fungus.

striate marked with thin lines that are radial on a cap surface and longitudinal on a spore or stem.

stroma (pl. **stromata**) compact mass of tissue on or in which perithecia are produced.

suberose corky, rubbery.

subgleba tissue beneath the gleba, eg., the stalk-like base of puff-balls.

sulcate grooved, furrowed (34).

teeth small pointed structures on the hymenium of the tooth fungi and certain polypores, on the surface of which the basidia are formed (2).

terrestrial growing on the ground.

tomentose (of cap or stipe) covered with wool or down.

tube tubular structures lined by the basidia in the boletes and polypores.

tufted growing in tight groups (9).

turbinate top-shaped

umbo a central broad swelling, as on the caps of many gilled fungi.

undulate wavy (21).

universal veil the tissue covering the immature carpophore of certain fungi; on expansion of the fungus this veil breaks and leaves patches or remnants on the cap or a sac-like cup or remnants about the base of the stipe.

velar pertaining to the veil (universal or partial).

verrucose having wart-like protuberances.

volva the remains of the universal veil which stay at the base of the skin of certain fungi (36).

INDEX

Numbers in Roman type refer to the entry number; those in *italics* refer to the page number of the Introduction.

Photographic References

Introduction

Ardea Photographics, London: 8–9; Lindau: 20. – Chaumeton, Paris: Chamalières: 50s, 50d; Lindau: 17, 34. – Coleman, London: 52, 53. – Jacana, Paris: 2. – Marka Graphic, Milan: 8, 9. – Natural History Photographic Agency, London: Preston-Mafham: 12; Bain: 372, 373; Hawkes: 27, 32; Janes: 26, 31. Giovanni Pacioni, l'Aquila: 15b, 23, 37, 39a, 40, 47a, 47b, 48, 49. – Luisa Ricciarini, Milan: Bertola: 19; P2: 39b.

Entries

Alauda, Milan: Galli: 171, 210, 211, 216; Sessi: 212; Soresina: 201; Ardea Photographics, London: 228, 264; Usidan: 8, 87, 103. – Carrese, Milan: Serafin: 36, 40, 141, 200. – Bruno Cetto, Trento: 13, 14, 98, 103, 109, 115, 129, 135, 138, 139, 161, 169, 174, 178, 195, 221, 238, 263, 299, 337, 339, 377, 390, 417. – Chaumeton, Paris: 19, 33, 34, 35, 43, 55, 56, 59, 62, 64, 67, 71, 74, 81, 99, 102, 111, 116, 117, 118, 133, 152, 160, 184, 185, 186, 208, 226, 233, 252, 256, 273, 279, 281, 284, 286, 290, 302, 316, 317, 320, 370, 398; Lanceau: 1, 4, 5, 6, 7, 10, 15, 18, 21. – Coleman, London: 2, 31, 67, 75, 82, 89, 90, 92, 106, 121, 140, 170, 180, 191, 204, 230, 267, 274, 293, 296, 305, 306, 318, 325, 328, 329, 340, 343, 344, 345, 346, 347, 353, 356, 362, 365, 384, 394, 402, 410, 411, 412, 416; Bisserani: 360, 383, 385. – Florestano Ferri, 260. – Gruppo Micologico DLF, Verona: 16, 37, 48, 49, 58, 65, 155, 193, 206, 207, 237, 262, 376, 396. – Marcello Intini, Florence: 312. – Jacana, Paris: 11, 20, 23, 28, 29, 30, 63, 68, 91, 94, 95, 100, 114, 119, 205, 214, 248, 253, 261, 277, 295, 297, 300, 308, 330, 342, 354, 355, 357, 361, 367, 368, 369, 371, 373, 389, 405, 415; – Champoroux: 167; Hawkes: 166: Konig: 406; Nardin: 96, 151; Pilloud: 321, 399; Ruffier-Lanche: 278. – Marka Graphic, Milan: 335. – Natural History Photographic Agency, London: Bain: 107; Allen: 225, 231; Hawkes: 79, 80, 190, 229, 235, 239, 240, 254, 275, 387; Hyde: 9, 32, 45, 147, 198, 202, 223, 307, 309, 341, 358, 419; IDA: 150; Janes: 326; Preston-Mafham: 24, 25, 27, 38, 39, 42, 70, 84, 108, 131, 142, 145, 188, 222, 285, 334, 386, 400, 403. – Giovanni Pacioni, l'Aquila: 47, 50, 54, 60, 69, 77, 86, 97, 120, 122, 123, 132, 134, 148, 153, 157, 163, 169, 172, 199, 209, 213, 215, 217, 219, 227, 232, 234, 255, 259, 276, 280, 287, 289, 315, 319, 322, 323, 324, 336, 338, 348, 351, 352, 366, 378, 380, 382, 388, 391, 392, 401, 404, 407, 408, 414. – Luisa Ricciarini, Milan; 17, 44, 149, 162, 247, 249, 251, 288, 310, 311; Bertola: 243; Leonardi: 72, 78, 83, 104, 110, 127, 137, 144, 173, 175, 177, 194, 241, 250, 270, 271, 294, 359; P2: 16, 22, 52, 85, 124, 130, 182, 265, 372, 379; Shaeff: 331; Unedi: 46. – SEF, Turin: 113, 242.

The illustrations at the beginning of each chapter are by Chaumeton, Paris (mushrooms with stems and gills, pp. 70–71); Chaumeton, Paris (mushrooms with pores, pp. 320–321); Natural History Photographic Agency, London: Bain: (bracket or crust mushrooms, pp. 372–373); Jacana, Paris (club mushrooms, pp. 410–411); Coleman, London (spheres, stars, pears, and cup-shaped mushrooms, pp. 440–441); Marka Graphic, Milan (Glossary, p. 500).